A Patch of Paradise

Visit www.patchofparadise.com for more details about
A Patch of Paradise and Gaia Grant.

ALSO BY GAIA GRANT

The Rhythm of Life

Living in Three Dimensions:
Building Positive Relationship Networks

A Patch of Paradise

a woman's search for a
real life in Bali

Gaia Grant

BANTAM BOOKS
SYDNEY • AUCKLAND • TORONTO • NEW YORK • LONDON

A PATCH OF PARADISE
A BANTAM BOOK

First published in Australia and New Zealand in 2002
by Bantam

National Library of Australia
Cataloguing-in-Publication Entry

  Grant, Gaia.
  A Patch of Paradise.

  ISBN: 1 86325 360 2.

  1. Grant, Gaia - Homes and haunts. 2. Bali Island (Indonesia) - Description and travel.
  3. Bali Island (Indonesia) - Social life and customs. I. Title.

915.986

Transworld Publishers,
a division of Random House Australia Pty Ltd
20 Alfred Street, Milsons Point, NSW 2061
http://www.randomhouse.com.au

Random House New Zealand Limited
18 Poland Road, Glenfield, Auckland

Transworld Publishers,
a division of The Random House Group Ltd
61-63 Uxbridge Road, London W5 5SA

Random House Inc
1540 Broadway, New York, New York 10036

Cover design by ignition
Internal photography (photographs 14, 15 and 16)
by Jason Childs
Epigraph from *Travels* © 1989 Michael Crichton,
Ballantine Books, courtesy of Pan Macmillan UK
Typeset by Midland Typesetters, Maryborough, Victoria
Printed and bound by Griffin Press, Netley, South Australia

10 9 8 7 6 5 4 3 2 1

Dedicated to my incredibly wonderful family—who've been with me all the way through this journey, and who have supported me through the process of recording and sharing our personal stories.

'Often I feel I need to go to some distant region of the world to be reminded of who I really am. There is no mystery about why this should be so. Stripped of your ordinary surroundings, your friends, your daily routines, your refrigerator full of your food, your closet full of your clothes—with all this taken away, you are forced into direct experience. Such direct experience inevitably makes you aware of who it is that is having the experience. That's not always comfortable, but it is always invigorating.'

Michael Crichton, *Travels*

Contents

Before I Begin . . .

I sit at a large, carved teak desk, furiously tapping away on an ergonomically designed computer keyboard. To my left are plastic in- and out-trays, forever awaiting their moment of liberation. To my right are bookshelves sagging under the weight of neatly labelled folders containing mountains of information about my business and clients, along with numerous writing and study projects. All the business basics are here, a laptop with internet connection, printer, fax, phones—nothing too hi-tech or elaborate, but this simple office connects me to the top level of the corporate world.

When I look straight ahead, however, taking a moment to rest my eyes from the mesmerising computer monitor and my mind from a busy work schedule, I am reminded that beyond the office lies a completely different world. Looking through large, wood-framed windows through lazy coconut palms, I can survey the patch of paradise that has become my home. The background to this scene is a panorama of glistening balmy sea with traditional *jukung* fishing boats drifting by; the foreground is a hive of bustling activity, a stretch of *warung* cafes planted firmly in the sand, part of a village famous for its barbequed seafood with unique stone-ground *bumbu* spice mix slathered generously over the top.

Stepping out the front door I find myself on an endless white sandy shore fringed by lush green tropical vegetation. From the back door I walk literally into a coconut grove, to be met by petite doe-eyed cows. I can pluck succulent fresh pawpaw from the trees on my doorstep, and the scent of frangipani and brilliant colours of bougainvillea fill the air. There is music in the soulful cries of the cows, the lilt of their wooden cowbells, and the rush of salty water being thrown on sandy shores.

I can feel as if I am worlds away from the 21st century, yet whenever I re-enter my thatched bamboo hut, the contemporary world comes to me. The strange interconnection of events and experiences that has brought me here still amuses and amazes me. I have found the best of both worlds, found the greener grass on the other side and been able to live there and enjoy it. I have a balanced life, and am deliriously content.

Here in my patch of paradise there is city and country, East and West, corporate access and community involvement. I can lounge around in a sarong all day, and then slip on a business suit for that important meeting or sit on the beach sipping fresh young coconut from the shell and watch my children play while writing a proposal for a client. I can be busy, yet feel completely calm.

Don't get me wrong; my paradise is not perfection—for I imagine perfection would be monotonous and uninteresting. No, paradise is not always idyllic—in fact it can be downright difficult; there are always new and unusual challenges coming our way. But to me paradise is a dynamic state of vital change, of vibrant living, of colour and contrast. And there is plenty of that here, in Bali.

Living and working here is like being inside a large impressionist painting; the joy is in the challenge of seeing the many different shades of contrast which lie within the overall beauty. Of finding the right light in which to appreciate the exciting drama and energy that is so much a part of the island.

My husband and I have lived in Bali for the last seven years, and our lives now revolve around the cosy home we have built up. Our two children have grown up here—one of whom was conceived here and initiated into the Indonesian way from birth. Our business is based here, and our way of life now has a distinctly Balinese flavour. We will always be foreigners, strangers in a strange land, but we have gradually come to feel that this island is a home for our spirits.

We did not land in paradise by accident. I searched far and wide for this patch, and it took a great deal of determination to get here. All sorts of fears and doubts accompanied me as I took each leap into the unknown. There were times when only faith in my dream kept me going. But in the end, that has all added to the adventure.

Let me share with you a little of my journey . . .

Chapter 1

Time for a Change

'I'll be home at six.'
Click.
That was it.

Andrew's simple statement had triggered off a number of anxieties. This was cutting it just too fine. I had so much to fit into the evening. How could I possibly get the shopping done, the dinner made, the baby ready for bed, and then be prepared to give my lecture by eight?

I swore a little too loudly to myself, hoping baby Zoe was far enough out of earshot. (No matter how carefully you plan those early educational speech experiences, kids always seem to prefer to repeat the most inappropriate of words, and usually at the most inappropriate of times.) The day had already been an exhausting marathon race. I'd sprinted to a health care appointment first thing in the morning, hurdled a few important business conversations in the crucial noise- and distraction-free zones when Zoe was napping, made a last-minute dash for the bank before it shut, leapt over a few study notes (not nearly enough), and generally organised the household—desperately trying to give my poor child the impression I was being an attentive and available mother in between.

Grabbing Andrew as he walked in the door, I clumsily swivelled him around on the spot. Left arm balancing baby on the left hip, right arm bent upwards hooking an assortment of bags and the car keys. (I'm sure women have developed an extraordinary range of skills and movements such as these through evolutionary necessity.) My husband was unwillingly swept forward with the unstoppable force of a determined woman on a mission, baby Zoe also being rushed along by the incredible power.

'What's going on?' Andrew asked.

Irritation.

'You're going to have to help me with the shopping. I can't get everything done and get back in time for work,' I responded emphatically.

Frustration.

'Are you kidding? I'm exhausted. I started really early and I've had a very tough day.'

Incredulity.

'We're all exhausted, and it's just got to be done. We can't eat until we've been shopping. Now just get in the car and open all the doors up, will you?'

Determination. More of a threat than a request.

'You've been home all day. What have you done? Why couldn't you do this before?'

'You have no idea what I have to cope with in a day . . . It's all right for you, being able to get out of the house and not worry about all the household duties . . .'

Irritation becomes indignation on both sides. Defence turns into attack.

The battle was on. It raged just below the surface right through the evening, becoming a devious guerrilla war, in which we sought to wound each other with subtly hurtful comments, and as the attacks continued we brought out the ammunition of years of carefully collected and stored disappointments and frustrations. We did get everything done. Just. And we did end up doing it together. But we both lay on our own sides of the bed at the end of the night, exhausted from the mental and physical effort of cramming too many things into the day, into our lives. We were both privately simmering, each feeling justified in our anger.

If it had been a one-off experience, we may have let it pass more easily, but it was becoming indicative of the loss of control we were starting to feel. Simple incidents were getting blown out of proportion. Our communication was being reduced to either straight facts or over-emotionalism. We were operating more and more in survival mode.

'Never let the sun go down on your anger,' the adage says, and this simple philosophy had kept our relationship going for fifteen years. Now, for the first time, it was all too much. We woke up the next morning hanging on to remnants of anger from the previous evening, neither wanting to be the first to initiate any form of reconciliation, both moving into automatic mode as a form of self-protection.

Eventually Andrew grabbed hold of me as our paths crossed, after we had eaten breakfast at opposite ends of the house. The silent tension hanging over us finally became too unbearable. We just clung on to each other, wondering where to go next. Two capable, coping people who had reached their limits.

We had been teenage sweethearts. Andrew and I had met while we were both still in high school, at an inter-school windsurfing and sailing competition miles from home. He was the archetypal sun-streaked blond, with long curly locks almost reaching to his shoulders. I was an idealistic teenager, ready for romance.

The day I first saw him, he was swaggering around with his surfing vest open, hanging back from the crowd, doing his best to convey a cool nonchalance. He leaned against a Torana with P-plates on it, shaking the keys, sending out the not-so-subtle message that he was independent and available. At fifteen, I was easily drawn in by the act. I was much more interested in him than in the ten or so other boys who eagerly offered to help me carry my boat up the beach. (At that age, there were some definite advantages to being involved in a male-dominated sport!)

Andrew eventually asked me if I would like to learn how to windsurf, and I jumped at the offer. A private lesson, on his windsurfer. Me hanging on to the boom for dear life. Him with one hand on my shoulder and the other around my waist, to help steady me, so he said. We soon fell into the lake together and thrashed around playfully for a while, invigorated by the shock of cold water and sheer teenage attraction.

That night I was serenaded with love songs on the guitar, and we stole our first kiss by the water, under the bright stars of an open country sky. It was the beginning of our future together. We went on through those grotty, pimply teenage years as boyfriend and girlfriend. Struggling through the issues teenagers struggle through, but also living the kind of life that you can only live when you're young and carefree. Free of any real responsibilities, the world at our feet. Nights at the movies; days on the beach surfing and windsurfing (Andrew the teacher, me the hesitant student); playing music together in a band.

As we got older we started holidaying together, loading up the old Corolla station wagon (which came a year or so after the Torana) with a few changes of clothes, some packets of dried food, and a couple of surfboards on top. We drove for hours and hours, searching the gorgeous Australian coast for the best waves in the most remote locations. Our goal was to try to find a dramatic headland where we could stay overnight, backing the car up to the very edge of the cliff so that in the early morning we could lift our heads from the mattress in the back and take in the broad view. We showered at the surf club toilets on alternate days. We ate cold food from tin cans. We rarely washed our clothes.

Living on the small earnings we made from odd jobs—working in shops, house-cleaning, tutoring, babysitting—life was simple but full. There was always an exciting air of anticipation about the future and what we could achieve together. We dreamed and made elaborate plans for the next stages in our lives. We felt we could take on the world together.

Though we had once enjoyed great freedom, quite a few years had passed since then. Things had changed. On the morning after our all-night conflict, we finally released ourselves from the despairing embrace and returned to our daily commitments. Andrew went off to work and I tried to get through the household chores. As the morning wore on, the clouds began to clear and the day started to feel a bit brighter so that by midday I was hanging out the washing under a cobalt blue sky while our baby slept. The heavens were now so vast and clear, saturated with intense colour. The sun was warming, the air crisp and light— seasoned with just a touch of salt.

Spontaneously, I lay down on the grass, feeling absolutely wicked for daring to take time out from the relentless schedule. The long-fringed lawn brushed against my skin, and I shut my eyes to savour the luxury of the moment. This was heaven. It felt like such a long time since I had really sunk into and enjoyed a single space in time. It had been a long time since I had given myself per- mission to let go.

While I was lying there, lost in the moment, a bright vision filled the dark corners of my mind. I was a young child in this vision, no more than six or seven, standing at the top of a grassy hill with my elder sister. The hill was built to hide a seventies-style concrete monstrosity, an office block in the university where our dad worked. Because it was man-made, the hill was perfectly graded, and the grass carefully manicured. To a young child, it was terrify- ingly steep and delightfully challenging.

My sister would always go first, throwing herself down in wild abandon, screaming as she rolled, increasing in speed till she finally reached the bottom. I would hesitate long enough to almost give up on the idea, but then would always eventually work up the courage and commit. As I rolled, the fear buried itself deep in my gut. I had the feeling I would never stop. The rolling became faster and faster until the real world became a blur, rushing by in strangely blended watercolour images with undefined edges. I only screamed when I reached the end, when I felt safe again and could truly enjoy the moment.

The journey always ended in hysterics—hair stuck out at all angles and sprinkled with cut grass, dress crumpled, skin prickling and itching. We usually bumped into each other and lay together for a long time, unable to control the laughing, red-faced and breathless. Inevitably, I would climb that hill again, and once more stand at the top, just as terrified as the first time. While waiting for

Dad to come out from the office, we continued to fill in the time with our reckless play. Whenever he finally did emerge, ready for us to take him home, we were often too absorbed in our games to notice.

I thought then of all the hills that Andrew and I had climbed. But things had gradually changed. The landscape was looking less challenging, and even when we did come across hills of opportunity, we were less inclined to throw ourselves down them. Becoming afraid, perhaps, of losing control, our circumstances were starting to control us.

When I finally opened my eyes again, I looked up at the bodiless clothes flapping around on the line, and then at the washing still in the basket, soggy and lifeless. I knew it was time for a change, before our crazy, city lifestyle completely changed us.

A human zoo. That is the metaphor Desmond Morris uses to describe modern cities in his book *The Human Animal*. You would have heard of the lions and tigers that, after being caged-in all their lives, will continue to pace the same sized area of ground long after being released. Of apes that continue to cling to trees made of concrete and plastic when the world is opened up to them. I wondered if I had become limited by my environment.

I had, for a long time, enjoyed city living. It can be exciting and invigorating. There are so many opportunities and options. But that same exciting busyness also becomes incredibly draining. While city living has its distinct advantages, it can also be overwhelming. You can start to find you can't keep up with the pace. You can start to feel disconnected, and the energy you have for making and maintaining fragile connections easily drains away.

Born and raised in the city, I was quite accustomed to its culture and conveniences. I was used to being able to go out any night of the week, to being able to choose exactly where I wanted to go and what I wanted to do. I had become a part of the cafe, cinema, and shopping-mall culture, with a dose of work and study projects and a commitment to social work thrown in for a supposedly healthy balance. But I now realised I just couldn't keep up.

Making appointments to meet with friends through voice-mail messages, not knowing my neighbours—not wanting to make the effort to get to know them in case they disappeared at the end of their lease—it was all wearing me down. As was having a part-time husband and a relationship that operated on shifts. I knew we could be getting more from our relationship, but we were often so focused on keeping up our work schedules that whatever time we had together was the leftover scraps in between deadlines, and even then we were sometimes too exhausted to make the most of them. I yearned for the carefree spirit and shared passions that had defined our early relationship.

I was also not getting the quality time with my baby that I so much desired. I treasured the opportunities we had to be alone together, learning about each other—the times we shared as a family, exploring the special bond that was ours alone—but these moments became rarer and rarer as I attempted to divide myself between the different compartments in our lives. Increasingly, I found myself trying to juggle the different roles I had taken on— wife, mother, teacher, friend, student . . . I ended up feeling frustrated both personally and professionally, not believing I was fulfilling any role to my best ability.

In the city, I began to realise, it was going to be difficult to get more than the most likely prospect of an over-stretched nine-to-five work day—day by day, year by year—in exchange for a handful of carefully protected escapist weeks of holiday. After being involved in different teaching and training jobs at different levels for eight years I was finding my work absolutely draining. Although I had loved the interaction, each session required so much creative and emotional energy, and it was not the sort of work that you could walk away from at the end of the day. I would often dream up new ideas in the middle of the night, or ponder how I was going to approach difficult problems over the weekend or through the holidays. The routine was getting me down, and I sometimes caught myself counting the minutes to the end of the teaching session, the hours to the end of the day, the days to the end of the week, the weeks to the end of semester.

I needed to give to others through my work—I could never have given this work up completely—and probably also felt I should continue to contribute to the family income. But rather than easing any pressures we may have experienced as a single-income family, I think it added a different type of pressure.

I had also started to find the constant onslaught of information from countless different sources each and every day too much to deal with. It just added to the pressure and stress. The TV, radio, newspapers, magazines, advertising . . . you can keep collecting information until your head feels like it can simply take no more. I've heard that in cities we're exposed to more than 3,000 advertisements a day. That sort of over-stimulation must take its toll after a while. I knew it was all taking its toll on me.

On that fateful day under the Hills Hoist, even though I eventually got up from the grass and got on with my regular responsibilities, the initial vision started to form into a clear dream that remained with me, day and night. I spent more and more time immersed in my dream; it kept me sane in an increasingly insane environment.

My dream was quite simple, really. The idea that consumed me was of giving it all up, of finding a hut on a beach on some tropical island and totally opting out of the rat race for a while. I dreamed of finding a simpler lifestyle, of getting back to the core values that made life meaningful for me. I wanted to find a traditional village somewhere and absorb myself in a different way of thinking and being.

The problem was that if I really wanted to make the dream come true, I was going to have to share it with Andrew, to draw him into my dream world, to let him experience it and appreciate it. I knew this was not going to be easy. In fact I was worried that it might be near impossible because as I became more and more of a dreamer, Andrew became more and more of a realist. Dreamers throw caution to the wind and enjoy the challenge of change. Realists hammer their stabilising pegs in deeper when the winds blow, to ensure they are not caught by the gusts and carried away unexpectedly.

Though Andrew and I had been carefree explorers in our early lives together, a secure home base became more important to him as our relationship progressed. I think he started to feel the responsibility of being a provider for the family, even though I had never placed that expectation on him. Many men must feel that same pressure. The more Andrew tried to establish this home base, the more I reacted against it. I craved travel and wanted to get out and take risks. At this stage I would have to convince him that life could go on without heading down the road of a steady income, a regular routine and a growing superannuation package. It was going to be a challenge.

Initially drawn to Andrew by his strong vision and passion for giving to others, as well as his ability to communicate openly and honestly, over the years I found we had developed a dedicated partnership that had taken us through many challenges successfully. The success of the partnership had depended not only on what we had in common, but also on our complementary skills and approaches to life. Of course, neither is right or wrong; they are simply different. By this time, though, our differences were turning into divisions, and we were each fighting to hold our own ground.

Earlier in our relationship we were able to compromise, experimenting with alternative, communal-style living arrangements, even going on extended working holidays to remote regions of the world. Andrew was incredibly understanding and giving, considering his growing desire for stability, but it was never enough for me. In the end we always returned to our regular jobs and routines, and I would feel that I was back to square one.

By this stage in my life I should really have felt quite settled and been able to sit back and enjoy the comforts we had built up around us—a large house near the beach with a reasonable mortgage, good steady work, a happy and healthy toddler, and a decent measure of good fortune. But I knew within myself that I would never be satisfied unless I really had a go at trying a different lifestyle. This time I needed more, our family relationships needed more. I wanted a real change. I wanted to reclaim the pleasures of love that were rightfully ours.

When I started pestering Andrew about my need to move

beyond the proverbial picket fence, I probably annoyed him more than inspired him. I only really confronted the subject head-on, however, one immaculate summer's day as we soaked up the afternoon sun. We were dawdling along a pristine beach on the New South Wales coast, miles away from the cares of the city. In my mind I was rolling in the grass again. The vision was clear. I had to take the plunge and commit. It was now or never.

'Wouldn't it be nice to be able to live like this every day?' I kicked the bubbly shore break for emphasis, scooping up the dripping sand and white foam. There was a gentle summer breeze blowing through our hair, the sun was moving towards the mountains and washing the sky with a deep reddish pink as it slid by. This had to be the right time. Life had never felt so good.

'It would be great.' I could tell he was feeling that irrepressible soft summer sensation, too.

'No, really—I think we should actually move away and do what we really want to do.' I was willing him to come with me.

'Uh-huh.' A slightly raised eyebrow. An ever so slight look of concern. This was the general pattern. Whenever we'd relaxed and settled into one phase in our life, I had immediately started to hurry him on to the next. He was obviously hoping it was just going to be a passing whim, but one look at me confirmed his fears.

'I'm serious. I want to look into our options. I really think we need some time out.'

'We've always taken time out when we've needed it. We've travelled a lot, we've explored a lot of places—the way you've always wanted. What's the problem?'

I explained how scared I was of becoming stuck in a rut. As I spoke I could see he was trying to take in what I was saying, trying to understand me, but it obviously wasn't easy. He could not comprehend my need for change. I wondered, fleetingly, whether I was being selfish, whether it was unfair of me to try to uproot the family, but then immediately came back to my hopes. I really did believe that if only we could change our circumstances for a while, we could all get closer to what I believed we should be able to be.

'Anyway, how do you think all this would happen?' Andrew

responded. 'You can't just pack up and leave, you know. You have to have some sort of income, something to do, somewhere to go . . .'

I tried to casually dismiss the practical details with a nonchalant flick of the fingers and a winning smile. 'No problem at all,' I said.

Then I moved in as fast as I could with the pre-prepared practicality arguments—having anticipated the questions—hoping to get through as many answers as I could before I lost him completely. I explained how it only needed to be a short time—a mere year or two. How we could always just take leave from our jobs and return to them afterwards if necessary. We could easily survive on the rent from our house, I told him, and the continued sale of some successful educational resources we'd published. I explained how we could live really simply, inexpensively, in a hut on a beach somewhere, how I'd done the figures and was sure we could manage.

But it all came out a little too quickly. I was over-enthusiastic in my arguments. Andrew was not convinced.

With an unmistakeable hint of skepticism in his voice, he asked me where exactly this hut on the beach might be. Unperturbed, I rushed through a list of possibilities. Africa . . . South America . . . the Pacific . . . Asia . . . anywhere was possible . . . The slight smirk remained firmly planted on his face. I could see I was digging a grave for my ideals.

We continued walking in silence for a while, both thinking of how we could progress from this point.

'Do you think things are really that bad?' Andrew finally asked.

'I'm sorry. We do have a good life. I just feel that it's not the best it could be, and we should at least try something different. I feel like we're pushing ourselves too hard. Our relationship is suffering. Our family life is suffering . . . I would love to have the time and space to be able to get back to what we believe is really important. To have more time together, to find a different way of living that makes more sense . . . I think we can do it.'

I became aware that I was gripping his hand tightly in hope of an affirmation. My dear husband has always had an incredible patience and commitment that has helped us get through thick and thin together. But this was obviously the ultimate test. He looked like he had just been asked to sit for the final school exams all over again. Then it suddenly hit me: I had been talking about *my* frustrations and *my* dreams. I hadn't thought enough about addressing his needs. He probably needed to hear that he wasn't simply being asked to follow me and my wild ideas around. That there was a deeper value in the experience.

'I think you need to take time off for yourself,' I continued, 'to really relax and unwind for a while. Why don't we find a good surfing beach, where you can sit in a hammock and play with Zoe until the waves come up?' I was barely stopping for breath, but I was determined to say everything I needed to say . . . 'I'll work on that writing project I've always wanted to finish, and you can be a surfing househusband, dividing your time between our child and the sea. We can work all the details out as we go. I know we can. And by giving back to ourselves for a while, I believe we'll renew our strength to give to others.'

Eventually, Andrew's expression softened, became less anguished and more open, more pensive. At last, I thought to myself, I had found a way to connect with him. I realised he had been missing out on many of those special 'baby first' moments while he was out working. He had often been too exhausted to put a lot of emotional energy into our relationship. He had craved the flexibility that I had been able to take advantage of by working from home since having Zoe. He also had a career that demanded so much of his energy. He needed replenishment as much as I did.

Ever since I had known him Andrew had needed to get out into the ocean as often as he could, to really unwind and get away from it all. Gliding over the open waters freed his mind and opened him up to creative new ideas, gave him the energy to continue to cope with stress. But I had not understood his need for escape. I had instead tried to limit this time and demand more from him at home, and this had been a source of tension between us.

Andrew took a slow, deep breath and looked out to the ocean, thinking long and hard. His need for an ongoing connection with the sea came through to me stronger than ever, perhaps really hitting me for the first time.

'Hmm . . . If we were going to give it a try, you'd have to prove to me that you can work out all the details . . .' he finally said.

I knew that was as good as a yes, that it was the closest to a green light I was going to get.

'*Yeehah*!' I cried. 'It can't hurt just to give it a go, can it? It's going to change our lives. I know it will!'

I skipped around on the sand and attempted a clumsy cart-wheel, knocking myself over and landing with a sloshy thump in the breaking water. I started laughing, at first embarrassed, then with an uncontrollable release of energy.

'Well,' Andrew mused, the mature onlooker. 'I haven't seen that free spirit for quite some time.'

Spontaneously, I grabbed hold of him and pulled him into the watery depths with me. He looked shocked at first, but then started to crack up, obviously beginning to feel something of that same sense of liberation. We thrashed around in the froth for a while, laughing and fooling around until the salty water blurred our eyesight and we were too exhausted to continue. I had a sudden flashback to the wet exhilaration of that first windsurfing lesson he gave me. It was a great feeling.

We eventually pulled ourselves back up to standing, and then resumed our walk. Soggy and sobered, but energised. There was time to let the significance of the moment sink in as we headed back to the place where we were staying, back to where Zoe was waiting with a neighbouring camping family. When a wave suddenly rushed on shore and swirled around our ankles, it drew us back out towards the ocean as it receded, and we became silently lost in possibilities. I was overcome with relief and gratitude. I knew he was a saint of a husband, prepared to consider giving up our secure lifestyle in exchange for a dream. My dream. A crazy dream. But I now believed it could become his dream, too.

That night we played and laughed with Zoe; good, deep belly laughs. After she drifted off to sleep, exhausted from the excessive mirth, we fell into each other's arms like young lovers. For the first time in a long time, longer than we cared to remember, we were not simply behaving like cohabiting marriage partners, strangers in the hallway. It probably sealed the deal.

Chapter 2

Following a Dream

I dragged Andrew into a travel agent not more than a day or two later, as soon as we were once again back in civilisation. If there were going to be any second thoughts on Andrew's part, they weren't going to get the slightest look in.

'Just for ideas,' I told him.

While we waited to see the agent, we examined the world map on the wall. It was so vast. The opportunities were endless. I imagined us on safari through Africa, roaming the open plains, passing numerous herds of wild animals before arriving at a mud-brick hut that would be our simple home. I looked to the east of the map, and the next mental image that came to mind was of us slashing our way through thick jungle somewhere in South America, finally breaking through to a crystal clear bay where our hut was waiting.

My daydream was interrupted when I overheard the couple ahead of us discussing their travel plans. I shifted my attention to them, and made a quick visual assessment: young, probably mid-twenties. Most likely not married. No wedding rings. Beautiful people. Trendily dressed. Making plenty of money. They could only spare five days because of work commitments, they told the agent. They didn't want to travel too far. They wanted to go somewhere they could just sit and relax. Do nothing. The agent happily pulled out the best and glossiest package brochures of the most exotic destinations. He wore a smart outfit and his best and most enthusiastic sales smile.

As the couple walked away loaded with a pile of brochures, I felt very smug. Hah. That wasn't travel! We were about to plan the ultimate travel experience. We had decided we could explore a few different destinations—both new locations and places we had been to before—to see if we could discover where this perfect beach hut with surf scene might actually be found. Once we had found our hut, according to my plan, we would then settle down for the year.

The sales smile welcomed us into the chairs, and we enthusiastically joined him.

'So, how can I help you? Where are you planning to go?' The smile was even more dazzling up close. I would have bought anything from this guy.

'We don't know yet, just getting some ideas at this stage. Possibly Africa for starters.'

He started pulling the big glossy brochures off the shelf.

'Maybe South America, too.'

He reached up for more brochures. 'Now we have some great packages to both continents . . .'

'Oh no, we're probably looking at airfares only. We'll be on a tight budget. And we want at least a year-long ticket.'

The smile dimmed just a touch. 'Okay, how about an around-the-world fare then? Where in Africa and South America would you like to have stopovers?'

That question kept us going for the next twenty minutes or so. We ended up with a spectacular world tour, including six stopovers that pretty well covered the map. By this stage the agent was showing signs of fatigue, and eagerness to move on to the next prospective sale. He did manage, however, a final stretch of the mouth as we departed, promising to ring through the quote when he had put it together.

The call came the next day.

'Just $15,000 each!' he proudly announced. 'How's that for a world tour? Not bad, eh?'

I thanked him, told him we'd get back to him about it, and hung up the phone—mortified. I was angry with him and his sales smile for having led us right up the garden path. And I kicked myself for being so stupid in thinking we could plan such a trip on a shoe-string. I had travelled extensively before, and knew what sorts of costs were involved. My over-enthusiasm and desire to cram in as many experiences and opportunities as possible had brought out a kind of naiveté in me. How could I possibly tell Andrew our inex-pensive, self-sufficient year overseas could cost us $30,000 before we'd even left the country?

Poor Andrew paled significantly when he heard the price, and immediately opened up a computer spreadsheet to try to make some sort of sense of the horror. He was buried in the spreadsheets for the next two days, solidly, before finally emerging. No, this was just not possible, he confirmed.

It was back to the drawing board. I was going to have to come up with other ways to go about this. Fast.

The world extravaganza tour plan was soon reduced to something a little more manageable: Asia. On our doorstep, fairly familiar. And only $600 one way! I think this revived the dream for Andrew just in time, before I lost him completely to the suburban abyss.

Asia. Still so much scope. Apparently there are more than 3,781,169,000 people living in Asia, with 1,433 languages, and twenty-eight religions (according to the ABC Asia-Pacific ad—I'm sure they would have done their homework!). So it's not really fair to treat the Asian region as a whole. It's difficult to compress the region into one simple term. That one small word encompasses so many different images. There is a huge amount of variation in cultures and customs from country to country, even province to province.

You can start with the discreet, prayerful manner of the Buddhist Thais, or the simple, colourful lives of the hill tribes that often cross freely between Thailand, Myanmar and China. The bustling pristine efficiency of major cities such as Singapore and Hong Kong, contrasted with the rural village vistas that have remained unchanged for generations in Malaysia, the Philippines and Indonesia. And within countries such as India, religions and rituals change from region to region as quickly as the scenery.

So many areas are so fascinating, and so attractive. But we had one major criterion that was going to have to be fulfilled above all others: I had promised a hut on a surfing beach. It was part of my sales spiel to Andrew. There would have to be surf.

Now, any unsuspecting non-surfer might assume that finding surf would be easy. After all, two-thirds of the earth is covered in ocean. Someone uninitiated into the intricacies of the science of surfing might expect that you would simply look at a map and randomly poke a finger at anywhere surrounded by ocean. There are plenty of countries in Asia that would fulfil this simple requirement. There are islands galore. The Philippines boast 3,000 islands (the actual number at any one time depends on the tides!), and Indonesia consists of more than 13,700 in total—and that's just for starters.

But the whole concept of finding a suitable surf location is actually much more complicated than that. To understand the great difficulties involved, you really need to appreciate the complex science of finding good waves, not just a basic stretch of salty water. You learn all these things when you live with a surfer!

Swell movements around the earth can be traced from windstorms that push surges of water northwards from Antarctica, and the currents that result tend to move in north-easterly patterns. The significant swells that reach the eastern, southern and western coasts of Australia are well known, and New Zealand, South Africa and some South American countries also have the advantage of first impact. But these swells can also travel for tens of thousands of kilometres as well—so long as there is an open enough expanse of water for them to move over. Strong currents cross the Pacific Ocean to reach Hawaii, which is infamous for the sheer size and power of its waves. Huge swells also cross the Atlantic Ocean, getting as far north as France and Scotland, gathering strength and power as they go. A bizarre island off the Scottish coast is surrounded by warm waters brought from the equatorial region, and hosts a variety of tropical plant species swept up from there. So, good swell can be found around the world. However, much of Asia is protected from these currents by neighbouring landmasses.

And the complications don't stop there. It is not enough for a surfer just to have swell. The reefs on a beach need to be lined up in such a way that the current wraps around them and is forced into perfect peeling waves that consistently roll into the shore, one after the other. Rocks and sand bars perform the same function, but they can be dangerous and changeable, respectively. Then the wind conditions also have to be just right, blowing off-shore so that the wave takes on a smooth 'glassy' shape.

Hard-core surfers will do anything to follow and ride the best waves. They will either live on next to nothing in order to be ready and available for that 'big Wednesday', or will find themselves well-paid work that gives great flexibility and plenty of time off. The intense thrill of the ride, the great adrenaline rush lasting usually no more than a few seconds at a time—these are enough to keep the die-hard surfer hoping and waiting. No withdrawal from any heavy mind-altering substance could be stronger than the deep emotional trough the surfer falls into after a period of wave deprivation.

Considering the general lack of surf in Asia, the obvious choice became Indonesia. It was in an ideal position, having exposure to the southern swells. With the world-class surfing conditions, a great environment, a welcoming local village culture and tasty food, Indonesia fast became the top contender in the great beach-hut search. We were already familiar with Indonesia, too, and felt that it could have exactly what we were after.

The search had finally narrowed down. Indonesia . . . waves . . . We came up with two possible locations within the country: Pelabuhan Ratu on the Javanese coast south of Jakarta, and Bali.

We had it all sorted out. A mission, a place, and even a time. We had decided that we would leave at the end of the year, after fulfilling our current work commitments. Now we just needed to work out the details . . .

I had an idea.

I thought about it for a while, and then when I felt I had covered some of the possible arguments against it in my head, I announced it to Andrew. Why don't we approach one of the aid agencies that send people overseas on aid assignments? I suggested. If we were working through an agency, I told him, at least we'd have a basic income to rely on. And it would also give us the opportunity to really learn from the people we'd be living with. To immerse ourselves in their way of life, rather than just plonking ourselves alongside them.

Andrew had joined me on short-term aid-work projects earlier in our relationship, and although very committed to the belief that we need to be able to give to those who are needy, he knew the realities of these situations. Aid work can be really tough. But perhaps the possibility of having the security of an organisation behind us and a steady income—no matter how minimal—would sway him.

This kind of work would also add another, deeper dimension to the experience, I reflected. Andrew and I had always shared a strong sense of faith and values which we believed made life worthwhile, and one of those core values was giving to others. I couldn't simply walk away from that. I wanted to be able to find a new spiritual connection, a new sense of purpose that wouldn't leave us feeling physically and emotionally drained. I wanted to have the chance to rethink and rework the faith that was fast becoming simply a part of the regular routine.

Andrew hesitated before responding. That was a good sign. Being a very alert thinker, capable of covering all possibilities in a matter of a few seconds, I knew he would have responded with sensible objections by this stage, if he had come up with any. Instead, he told me that if we were to pursue the idea I would, again, need to put all the legwork in, to really look seriously at the viability.

That was all the encouragement I needed. I was on to it the next day. I was good at procrastinating while dreaming, but quick to take action when worried my dreams might be threatened. We were down in the government aid agency office within the week.

We arrived at our first agency interview with a shopping list of placement requirements, the exact locations pinpointed down to latitudes and longitudes. We soon discovered, however, that the system worked in reverse. You had to be interviewed extensively, and then would be carefully offered a two year placement based on their assessment of you. Because our previous involvement in aid projects had always been on a short-term basis, this more complicated process for long-term placements was a little daunting. I became concerned that rather than giving us the freedom I was hoping for, it might actually limit our freedom.

The lovely lady assigned to our case went through all the official procedures meticulously, ignoring our straight-to-the-point-let's-not-beat-around-the-bush approach. I'm sure she was convinced that the system worked so well that she could ascertain our needs and desires better than we could. We had been through much of this lengthy process, when she suggested we attend a 'familiarisation evening' in which applicants could ask questions of a real-life placement survivor. I'm still not sure if this evening was intended to reassure us or scare us off. I do think a good dose of hardship toughens up the soul, but this survivor seemed to have endured pure torture.

There had been an air of excitement among us eager applicants on the night of the familiarisation. We had been sitting nibbling on the crudités and sipping the apple juice that had been provided, when in walked a poor, washed-out lady, grey before she should have been, looking like her best years had passed her by. She was dressed in a simple cotton print dress. Exhibit A had spent years in Samoa, apparently doing penance for goodness knows what personal transgressions.

She sat as the guest of honour at the front of the room, and question time began.

'So what was the highlight of your time in Samoa?'

'When I reached the end and could look back and see that I had achieved something, I had survived a very tough time.'

A great, inspiring start.

'What was the hardest part, then?'

'Although I had my own house, I had no privacy. The whole village followed the creed, 'What's yours is mine', except that they apparently forgot the reciprocal part of the saying: 'What's mine is yours'. One day I'd wake up to find that a dress had gone, the next, my car. Eventually, the objects would return, but not always—and often in a state of disrepair. That's kind of hard to live with when you're not used to it. But that wasn't really the hardest part . . .'

After a long sigh and an excessive raising of the eyebrows, she continued. 'The work itself was a nightmare. The bureaucratic red tape was overwhelming, I was never really sure what I was meant to be doing and why I was there at all. Apparently it looked good for them to have foreign assistance, but then they didn't want you showing them up and doing the actual work. It was frustrating not being able to do anything really useful, and feeling you are wasting your time away.'

'What else . . .?' We were not sure that we really wanted to know. It wasn't easy having the prospect that we had been pursuing neatly dissected and brutally discarded, piece by piece.

The woman went on to describe the cross-cultural communication problems, the religious restrictions, the monotony of a simple existence. We knew that aid work could be difficult, but this sounded like too much. It would be incredibly hard to maintain a commitment under these circumstances over the long term. My heart sank deep into my chest as I realised this was not going to be a way to replenish ourselves, to rebuild our own lives.

'Life was very mundane, with nothing much to brighten up the day. Your meals are limited to tinned corned beef, sweet potatoes and yams—very few fresh fruits and green vegetables, and no fresh meats and dairy products. Certainly no luxury food items. You'd often get cravings for the strangest things—jellybeans, cinnamon or mayonnaise.'

'Was there anything at all to brighten up the day?' Please, we implored in our minds, give us something positive to help salvage at least a small scrap of hope.

'Oh yes, I enjoyed getting together with the few other foreigners on the island on the odd occasion we were in contact. We could all commiserate together.'

Fantastic. A really positive statement to finish off her description. Was there no joy in this woman's exotic island existence? Was her experience really so desperate? We'd well and truly heard enough by this stage, but soon discovered that it wasn't actually the end of the story. Even though she had apparently officially finished her prison-like term on the island, she was unofficially only on temporary good behaviour leave. She had married a local man, realising the implications of her choice only on returning to her home country, and now had a child stuck between two countries and cultures.

We hesitated for quite some time before venturing to ask the final risky question: 'Was it really worth it?'

'Oh yes,' she reassured us, 'it really was worth it—in the end. I have grown so much from the experience.'

I could have sworn that in actual fact she was shrinking by the minute.

By the end we felt quite depressed and deflated. As we walked towards our car, both clutching on to a shared umbrella in the autumn rain, we talked about how disappointing the experience had been.

'It's not going to be much of a year off if we end up feeling like her,' Andrew said.

What could I say? He was right. That was not really what I'd had in mind for us when I started exploring the possibilities. But I did feel, too, that perhaps with a more positive attitude our experience could be different from hers.

'Let's agree now,' I said, 'that wherever we end up and whatever we end up doing we will keep our eyes firmly fixed on what we set out to do, and on the need for our own renewal. We must ensure we maintain a positive outlook, no matter what.'

Andrew opened the car door for me, and I jumped the kerbside puddle and slid in. We drove home with sheets of water flicking from side to side on the windscreen, our thoughts following the erratic movements of raindrops.

When the first offer for a job placement finally came through from the agency, it was way off the mark. It was for school teaching positions in a remote area of a Pacific island. It wasn't an area of work we were interested in exploring—we had most recently been involved in curriculum development and had moved on to adult education by this stage—and it was nowhere near the surf! We knew immediately that the idea just wasn't going to work out.

The experience was a significant setback for our quest. Enough to cause Andrew to begin to question whether it was all worth 'it. I was going to have to work extra hard to keep the momentum and enthusiasm going. It had, however, been an important lesson in being realistic about dreams. As much as we had invested considerable time and effort into pursuing this option, we had to walk away from it. I had learnt, more than ever, that we needed to find a niche that was right for us.

We could do it on our own, I figured. Easy. I thought we could make our own significant contribution to the planet while rediscovering ourselves in the village location of our choice—without the strings attached.

I have never had a reason to escape, and have had nothing to escape from. No deep-seated childhood traumas. Not even any dissatisfaction about the way I'd been brought up. A very warm, caring mother, an open and trusting father, and two wonderful sisters I still consider my best friends. I had a very normal, very happy childhood. I have, however, developed a very strong determined streak. I've always known what I've wanted and I don't easily give up—perhaps precisely because I have been given so much and suffered so little.

Growing up, I probably came across as straight. Quite bright, but not outstandingly brilliant, I survived my teenage years by carving out my own path. I never got into smoking, drugs or drinking—not because I didn't have the opportunity, but because I had absolutely no desire to. No need to. I had nothing to prove. Nothing to rebel against. I just didn't care what other people thought.

But although I have always had an inward strength, it took me quite a while to develop outward confidence. What I did to overcome my inhibitions was take on challenges to test my limits— pushing my mind and body beyond what I naturally felt comfortable with. I accompanied some more adventurous friends and went caving into the bowels of the earth, hiking up mountains, abseiling down them again, canoeing along wild river rapids. I was not athletic and these skills did not come easily, so each challenge became a real test of my determination. Spending a few years in drama class helped too, transforming me from a blushing young introvert, into a reasonably confident speaker—so much so that speaking to groups of people became a major part of my career.

But as strong and determined as I had become, this idea of living overseas was turning out to be a much tougher battle than I had predicted. Certainly much tougher than many of the challenges I had faced before. This time the stakes were much higher, and much more emotionally deep seated. Though the dream had begun with a small grain of an idea, it had now grown into an overwhelming obsession. I had become determined to see it through, and my passion was bringing Andrew and me to a point of no return. My heart was now set on a course that I did not want to change, and which I could not willingly have changed without experiencing utter despair. But I had taken on the responsibility of also setting a course for the destiny of my family, for my husband and child.

Andrew was aware of how much this opportunity had come to mean to me. He knew that he had to give me the chance to explore my vision, that it might be the way to satiate the deeper need underlying my ongoing desire for change, a need that was continually welling up inside me. He realised that I needed a sense of balance and contentment, but it was still not a path he would have chosen on his own. Perhaps he was only able to keep going by reminding himself that in a year or so we could return to our old jobs and a sense of normality, hopefully no worse for wear.

Yet every outwardly confident step I took towards that point of no return triggered anxiety attacks about whether I was really doing the right thing. For every deliberate change, countless obstacles happily presented themselves, forcing me to continually assess and reassess.

While packing everything up into a garage and throwing darts at the world map to find some strange new destination was definitely appealing, it was never going to be that simple. Of course not! Negotiating time off work, working out where you're actually going and how you're going to get there, calculating the costs and finding the necessary funds, cleaning up and renting out the house, redirecting the mail, getting visas and passports . . . you can't just walk away. And time was now getting tight. We had eight months in all from the day I brought up the idea on that coastal beach to the day we left. It might sound like plenty of time to develop a course of action and rearrange your life. It's not. It goes so fast.

But where there's a will there's a way—and with two wills like ours, I knew we'd get there. As I continued giving definition to the sandcastle in the air we had started building, more clearly outlining our soon-to-be idyllic existence, my better half was running around after me, grounding everything down to the finest details—just as he had expected he would end up doing. He had been busy working out the real figures, anxiously playing devil's advocate. By the time we were ready to leave he'd calculated the actual dimensions of that sandcastle and had spreadsheets with detailed costs and all the necessary paperwork prepared. What a team!

The whole journey preparation phase had tested our endurance, but was ultimately part of the process of bringing us closer. By the time of our departure, we had already achieved so much together, and the thrill of adventure was finally close enough to taste. We started to enjoy the prospects. To imagine the possibilities. It was terrifying, but exhilarating. A roller coaster, heart-in-your-mouth experience that sent the adrenaline pulsing through our bodies. We found ourselves sitting on top of the world.

It's funny, but if you stop to consider just how difficult the practical obstacles can be in attempting to climb a mountain, it's easy to want to give up and walk away. You can feel you just don't have the strength to climb it. But once you do persevere with that uphill trek, little by little, you find that each step along the way has its rewards. Each small step brings you closer to where you want to be and higher than you have been before. You gain new vantage points, and discover new sources of strength within yourself.

After that eight-month stretch, we finally reached the point where we were ready to leave all our Australian responsibilities behind, and to venture out into the great unknown. With a few weeks to go and only the last few details to be tied up, we were ready to start rolling down that hill. We had an open ticket to Indonesia and nothing too specific planned beyond that. There would be no turning back.

Chapter 3

Travellers' Tales

The explorer's tenacity is in my blood, inherited, no doubt, from my father. I grew up travelling to fascinating and exotic places, following his unusual impulses. Ever since, I have enjoyed exploring, searching, pursuing interesting paths.

When I was six my father had an overseas placement in a Philippines university, and from then on the journeying theme became a defining quality of my early life—as it became for my adult life. We were not gypsies, we always had a home to return to, but we enjoyed discovering new people and places. Some snapshot images of my early travel days will always remain firmly fixed in my mind. I have strong memories of Asia: the invasion of personal space when dark strangers in the street wanted to touch my hair; the excitement of having climbed to the top of an active volcano, being able to view the awesome beauty of a crater within a crater; the isolation of being the only Australian in an international school class, being terrified to speak in case I wasn't understood; adjusting to the sight of men in army fatigues carrying shotguns in the street. There are clear imprints from Europe, too: a cosy Christmas with snow and plum puddings and a real baked dinner; walking through royal palaces with fairytale gardens; humorous moments when living out of a campervan, five of us crammed into the small space for weeks on end; the great confusion as we moved rapidly from country to country and language to language.

These emotionally charged memories came from living in the Philippines and England, and from travelling through at least ten countries in Europe as well as Thailand, Malaysia and Indonesia. They must have been instrumental in helping to toughen me up. They certainly opened up the world of possibilities for me. I think that sort of travel at such a young, impressionable age can have one of two effects: you can either crave a regular, settled life, or you can become a free, wandering spirit, with an insatiable appetite for different experiences. It had the latter effect on me. I launched into the world of independent singles travel as soon as I left school, when I went to Fiji with a uni project team. But the adventures had only just begun.

We married six years after that first windsurfing lesson, barely out of our teens, continuing the adventurous water theme that had defined our relationship by being wed on a harbour cruise and honeymooning on a house boat. The honeymoon was a little wild—motoring around on a vast lake with no-one else in sight, braving a wild storm, reliving a scene from *Attack of the Killer Mosquitoes*—but once home again our lives settled into a more regular daily routine.

A few years into our marriage I started to get itchy feet again, and came up with an ambitious plan—to travel throughout South-East Asia. We, or more accurately, I, planned a trip starting in relatively tourist-friendly Bali (to settle Andrew, and two friends who would join us, in to the idea), travelling overland by bus and train through Java to the northernmost tip of Sumatra, by boat to Malaysia, then overland by train again to the north of Thailand. We were all excited by the adventure of it all, although looking back I can now see how this sort of journey was really throwing the others in the deep end—with no life-saving devices in sight.

Andrew and I were the first to depart. We were to be the trail-blazers. As this was Andrew's first foray out of Australia, I wanted to start him off on the right foot by taking him along the less trodden path. This would also be his first real experience of my rather fearless attitude to travelling abroad.

'It's all right. I know what to do,' I assured him when we arrived in Bali, our first stop. This was somewhere I had been before, with my family. I could handle this, no problems. 'If we just walk a couple of hundred metres out the gate we'll find the *bemos* (local minivan transport).'

'Hang on—there's a taxi stand. We've got so much gear. Why don't we just get in a taxi?' Andrew asked, not unreasonably.

'Oh, no no no. The taxis are much more expensive. It's not far, really.'

I convinced him to lug the gear out of the airport, both of us sweltering under the steamy sun. There would be no inflated tourist taxi prices for us. No way. We saved a good fifty cents.

We squashed into the *bemo* with a few Indonesian families and their ducks and chickens. We then lugged all our gear, including the security blanket surfboard, down every *gang* or alley in Kuta looking for accommodation, with me determined to get the best position and price possible.

'No need to pre-book accommodation,' I had told him before we left. 'There's plenty around, and it's much cheaper if you find it yourself.'

'*It's cheaper if you find it yourself*,' Andrew mimicked as we trudged along wearily. 'Yeah, and much more painful. I don't know why I bother listening to you!'

We ended up in what we thought was the ideal location—a short walk to the beach, of course—at a place that offered several different standards of accommodation. I automatically moved us into the cheapest room option, a dark little number with a holey mosquito net and creaky fan. But hey, it was only the price of a cup of coffee back home! What more could you want!

Our friends, when they arrived, opted for the next step up, with white-painted walls and air-conditioning—still only the price of a cup of coffee and a slice of cake. This was to be the pattern for accommodation throughout the journey. They opted for comfort, while I insisted Andrew and I take the cheapest possible option. Naturally, we actually hung out in our friends' air-conditioned room and swam in the pool attached to their accommodation, only sleeping and changing in our own room. We must have really annoyed them.

Freaking at the sight of cockroaches, craving McDonald's and

Mars Bars, and generally gritting their teeth with each new challenge, our companions no doubt secretly wished they could be anywhere else but where we were. They valiantly kept going, though, and proved themselves to be much tougher than us in the end.

A planned trek through the mountains in the north of Thailand was to be the highlight of the trip for me, but must have been a looming horror for our female companion. Used to a fairly sedentary lifestyle, the prospect of walking uphill for hours terrified her. She had to be coaxed up the first hill ever so gently, and she struggled with her immediate desire to give up. She picked up the pace admirably, though—so much so that when our male companion got amoebic dysentery a few days into the journey, she was the one who offered to carry his pack for him and coaxed him on. We were exhausted ourselves by the journey, and were astounded at their courage and determination.

It's amazing how our problems and attitudes are put in perspective when we consider the experiences of others. Overseas backpacker travel is certainly a constant experience of new perspectives, even if it can be a tough learning process. During our travels we had been with many people who appeared to be materially impoverished, but who had a wealth of insight. We had eaten meals with communities living in garbage dumps, had stayed with villagers who had to walk miles each day for fresh water, had visited victims of war. It's difficult not to get reverse culture shock when you return home to your petty concerns and problems, only to be rudely confronted by fresh memories of how most of the world lives.

These travels had sparked an interest in finding out more about the people we met along the way and how they lived. They triggered a desire to become more involved in these people's lives through development work. Andrew must have forgiven me for his abrupt initiation into backpacker travel, because over the next few years I was able to talk him into some extensive travel and work on development projects. After our initial journey together, we lived and worked in a university in the Philippines, and worked with the border tribes in Thailand and Nagaland, as well as with orphans in

El Salvador. We travelled through North and Central America—overland through the States, Mexico, Costa Rica, Guatemala, and Panama, and then on to England, France and the Netherlands.

Yes, we had travelled extensively through the first few years of our marriage. But then we'd spent five years in Sydney where the pressures of city living and the responsibilities of work, marriage and then parenting had begun to overwhelm us. This time we needed to reclaim more than a sense of adventure—we needed to reclaim ourselves.

But not before one last-minute change of plans . . .

The telephone rang, jangling my nerves and taking a chunk out of my concentration. With only the last few weeks to go until D-day (the set departure date for our year-long trip), we were making lists upon lists and desperately trying to cross off as many items as possible before they overtook our lives completely. I found the phone, picked it up and the familiar voice of a friend on the other end delivered a startling proposition: 'My father's off to India on a health education project, but his main assistant has just had to pull out. Can you help?'

Luckily I had answered the phone (perhaps unluckily from Andrew's perspective), and I had our names signed up before there could be any hesitation.

This wasn't exactly what I had in mind—I didn't imagine that our hut would be found in India—but I knew this project would give us a focus for the first part of the year, a chance to really leave behind our city life and switch into something positive right away, before going it alone. It was only going to be a two-month commitment, rather than the two-year contract the other aid agency had required, which was also appealing. On that basis I managed to sell it to Andrew, who must have been quite numb to the idea of wild abandon by this stage. He must have been happy that we had somewhere definite to go and something to do, as he didn't even bring up the fact that there is no surf in India. Or perhaps he had his own version of optimistic enthusiasm, as the surfboard ended up going with us anyway.

We added a few more items to the lists we had been writing then and there, and in the days following got down to the serious and exciting business of preparing for a new destination and new direction. Before we knew it we had tickets to India, we were sampling curries, and I'd had lessons in the art of tying saris.

After sharing a few teary goodbyes at the departure gate, and grabbing a few koala key rings from the concourse souvenir shop, we were on our way. There'd been eight months of dreaming and scheming. Nothing was going to stop us now.

I must admit the hours spent in a silver tube time capsule are always pure bliss to me. No interruptions, no schedule to keep to. Nothing to do but to drink more free wine and try to decipher the miniscule in-flight movie. Time to think, time to switch off, time to talk. The process of travel is, I find, extremely cathartic. Call me strange, but I even enjoy hanging around at airports, just watching planes come and go, wondering what exciting adventures other people might be having. Wondering how their lives are connecting with others around the world. I have to confess, too, that I enjoy pulling open that little tinfoil tray cover to check if I made the right 'chicken or fish' choice. I like using the freezing cold cutlery and breaking open the dry bread rolls. I like adding the French dressing to the two limp lettuce leaves and one-sixteenth of a tomato that is supposed to pass as an entrée. I'll even eat the brightly coloured, strongly sweetened, indeterminate dessert.

As long as I'm not stuck on a plane for countless hours on end and making dramatic time zone crossings—as long as I'm not the one left gagging a screaming child—I really enjoy plane travel. (These incidents have happened, of course, but they must end up being quickly assigned to some dark storage file in the back of my mind.) Perhaps that's why I can never get enough of it. I'm obviously an addict.

This time, though, travel was only the means to a much more exciting end. We hoped it was going to lead us to the place where we could settle down and enjoy a different way of life.

With our heads in the clouds, we savoured our time together on the flight to India before emerging into a different time and place. We came back down to earth literally, though, as soon as we stepped off the aeroplane. The reality of what we were getting ourselves into hit us like a smack in the face.

The heat was really dense and all-consuming. That was my first experience of the country. The second was the revealing trip from the airport to the 'wealthy man's' house we were to stay in.

There was a nicely treed highway running from the airport to Madras city, but on either side of it was filth and poverty. People wrapped in dirty, flimsy cloths and lying in the streets, animals defecating, bits of plywood and tin thrown together in an attempt to keep the masses slightly protected from the elements. Although I had seen much poverty and suffering, the sense of hopelessness I now felt was so overwhelming. I kept expecting that eventually we'd break out of the poorer areas and emerge into wealthier suburbs, but it never happened.

The rich man lived in a street slightly wider than the others and a little less populated, but otherwise there was not much else to distinguish it from the rest. We finally turned into a grimy driveway and entered a worn-out old house, with paint peeling and extensive mouldy growth inside and out. The man who owned it was a contact from a friend of a friend, but he wasn't there to greet us when we arrived. He was, apparently, overseas in his rich man's London apartment. In his absence, his servants were told to look after us. They included a grotty shoeless houseboy of no more than ten or twelve years with absolutely no idea of what to do, and a huge Tarzan with overdeveloped muscles and long flowing hair. Apparently Tarzan was an ex Mr India. It was surreal.

We were already feeling very uncomfortable in this situation, but we knew it was time to move on the day after we arrived, when Tarzan offered us massages. He insisted on showing us how strongly he could massage, but then proceeded to prod and poke the private parts. That was it. We were out of there in no time. We had hoped that by staying in a 'real' Indian household we might gain a deeper insight into the way of life there, but we were now relieved to meet up with the project team and move into the modest but clean and uncomplicated hotel assigned to us.

Bollywood films must be India's way of dealing with reality. Hollywood's Indian counterpart produces scores of movies each year, and they are far more successful than Hollywood in terms of numbers of movies produced and numbers of viewers. These movies stick to a very basic but, apparently, effective formula. Beautiful young men and women are tormented by love, but break into dramatic song and dance routines whenever the heat is on. As it was forbidden to show kissing on screen in India—let alone anything even slightly more sordid—a director somewhere along the line must have decided that this is the best way to show ecstasy. The locations may change, the costumes may vary slightly, but the formula is always exactly the same. Never any sign of the real urban India in the background. Never any clue to the ordinary daily challenges the ordinary person faces. Pure escapism.

After just a short time in the country, we began to understand why. It didn't take long to discover that while India does have an incredibly fascinating culture and a rich and colourful history, it can be a tough place to live in. These movies identify the elements that make life worthwhile, and embellish them.

While the reality of life in India threatened to wear us down fast—the oppressive heat, the overwhelming poverty, the crazy driving—we were committed to making the most of the opportunity. By giving, we would receive. I came to firmly trust, too, that this would be an important first step in the journey to wherever we might end up. That once we had opened ourselves up to possibilities, the right path ahead would become obvious.

The project in which we were to participate was aimed at writing and implementing a health curriculum that would cover all areas of health development—physical, social and emotional—and would completely span a child's schooling years. This was revolutionary, and if properly implemented, could educate new generations of children about important health principles. If children were encouraged to pass on what they had learned to their parents and other community members, it could transform the whole nation.

We were inspired, and we worked day and night to help see our part of the project through. Each day we'd travel from our temporary home to the workshop site, making the perilous journey in a rickety old van. After dodging an assortment of cars, bikes, pedestrians and animals, we were always glad to reach our destination and begin work.

Zoe, who was two years old by the time we reached India, would sometimes play with the children living on the campus, and sometimes sit in with us—helping with the training by writing on the whiteboard below where we were writing, or playing her own quiet games down the back of the room. It was an interesting experience for us to have her welcomed into the work rather than feeling we needed to shift her off to childcare.

I was so relieved and excited that in this situation, at last, we were able to enjoy being together as a whole family—even while working! I had seen the way Asian families lived and worked together before, and had craved that sort of ongoing contact for ourselves. I began to feel confident that this was a foretaste of what our lifestyle could become, that we would be able to continue to enjoy living and working as a whole family when we'd found our hut by the beach.

The whole teaching process in India was fascinating, too, and energy and enthusiasm filled the weeks ahead. It was difficult, however, not to feel frustrated at the enormity of the task: we were challenging a whole system, a whole approach to education, one that says that the elders hold the knowledge and power and are not to be questioned.

This country had a dismal failure in a sex education campaign just a few years before. Seventy-five percent of males who had been to sex education classes were found to have been putting a condom on a carrot before having sex, just as they had seen in the demonstration. Over ninety percent of male participants also started taking the female hormone pill themselves after the classes. It was going to be a real challenge to convert people to

forms of education that involved real appreciation and understanding, not just imitation and repetition on call. Nonetheless it
was exciting to be involved in the genesis of such an ambitious
project, and to be in the privileged position of seeing it developing, slowly but surely. It was exciting, too, to feel our own dream
taking shape.

India's subtle charms had been steadily at work. While busily
focusing on the project, we had unwittingly been growing more
and more fond of the country and her people. When we were
finally free to leave, we discovered we were not ready to go. We
wanted to experience more.

We had grown accustomed to Indian food. To *talis*—huge trays
which hold an array of spicy Indian delicacies—and to the wonderful *pappadams* and *naan* bread. We had become attached to the
people, a people with a great passion for life. I could even almost
wear a *sari* with some semblance of grace and ease. Curious to get
outside of the city and discover a little more of the original India,
we were gradually enticed to spread our wings a little further, to
unearth a little more of the country's vibrant beauty.

Well, we thought, why not? There was no rush, no time
schedule to keep to. We were free to take up any opportunities
that came our way. There had initially been some concern about
bringing our young child to a place where she could be exposed
to all sorts of weird and wonderful tropical diseases, but having
survived the first phase of our stay disease free, we were confident that all would be well if we did a little travelling.

Shiva, one of the workshop participants, invited us to visit
his home in the south of India—only a few thousand miles away—
and we accepted with little hesitation. This was to be a real
adventure.

The journey involved taking a few buses and an overnight
train. When we arrived at our destination we were greeted with
enthusiasm by the whole extended family, who met us at the train
station. They engaged in some serious cheek pinching of the
white-haired, white-skinned, blue-eyed child, then piled into the

1930s-style sedan, taking us and our luggage with them. I think I counted ten people in all, along with our backpacks and, of course, the surfboard.

Once we had settled in at Shiva's house, we were offered an excursion to the southernmost tip of India, not more than a half-hour away. The journey, however, took quite some time getting started. I'm sure we had more people crammed in the car this time, although I couldn't actually see around all the bodies to make an accurate head count once we were stuffed inside. Embarrassingly, even though our family of three was definitely in the minority, we demanded the most attention.

We were slotted into specific jigsaw positions in the car and the engine had started when our demands began.

'Do you mind if we just duck back into the house to get a nappy?' We were suddenly not too confident about Zoe's toilet training.

One by one we disconnected ourselves from the jumble. A few minutes later, we were back in the car in similarly complicated positions. The car pulled out onto the street.

'Mummy, I'm hungry.'

'Okay, darling, we can buy something when we get to where we're going.'

'No Mummy, I'm hungry now. I have to eat now.'

I'd been here before. I could either give in at that point and save the pain, or subject us all to the whining. It only took another whinge or two before I decided the first option may be the best. 'Ever so sorry. Would you mind terribly if we just grab a snack from the house?'

The car pulled over to the side of the road, reversed back to the house, and I was once again running inside at top speed.

'Okay. That should be all now. Thanks very much.'

Wishful thinking. We did actually depart from the house, but it wasn't long before it all started up again—a litany of complaints from Zoe about thirst, tiredness, discomfort, etc etc etc. Of course, during this charade there was not a sound from the other children present, none of them had urgent nappy requirements or death-threatening hunger spasms. They all sat quietly and calmly, considering the strange foreign family and their excessive needs.

We were all relieved to finally be able to extricate ourselves from the car when we reached our destination. Then we enjoyed an interesting boat ride out to an historic island temple, a fun splash at the beach, and being in the noteworthy position of standing on the most southern tip of the country. From our vantage point we could confirm the rumour—definitely no surfing in India. There was not the slightest ripple to break up the ocean.

At the end of our day-trip, the foreign family entertainment resumed and continued all the way back to the house, as we tried to deal with toilet stops, drink stops and the general difficulties of looking after a sodden child for whom we'd brought no change of clothes.

It wasn't hard to be blown away by our host family's unfettered, uncomplicated approach to life. These people, who have so little, are able to give so much. They'll vacate rooms for you to sleep in, provide you with the best foods, and go out of their way to show you the best of what their part of the world has to offer.

In the end, our trip to India had not been a small side trip; it had put everything back into perspective for us. The incredible complexity of our lives had been placed in stark contrast against this minimalist backdrop. I realised, at this point, that learning to let go would have to be one of the important stages in our de-stressing process. The trip had reminded us of what could be achieved with a clear vision and some commitment, and of how simple life could be. I hoped that we could carry this important realisation with us to our eventual destination. That we could learn to live more simply ourselves.

'8 Suicide Bombers Found in Colombo'.

The newspaper headlines jumped off the front page and into our imaginations. We turned to each other in a sudden state of panic.

At the time we had been standing in an airport queue in the south of India, only three people away from making a journey to a death trap. Lured by the promise of warm beaches, good surf and the chance to meet up with some Sri Lankan friends. It had been a spur-of-the-moment decision, one that had come to us quickly when we were considering what exciting travel option we might take on the way to our ultimate paradise.

We looked at Zoe. She looked intently back at us with her gorgeous big blue eyes, the ultimate picture of trust. We had already brought her much further than we had anticipated. She sank her head into my chest, needing to be protected. Andrew and I looked at each other, dejected but decided. There was no way we could go ahead with this plan and feel comfortable with the decision. Dodging suicide bombers was just not sensible.

There had been a time when we'd taken risks more freely—when we'd had more of a gung ho approach to travel. In our earlier travels I had dragged Andrew to El Salvador in the height of civil war (surfboard firmly in his grasp). Hearing bombs go off. Seeing soldiers lining the streets, crouched behind sandbags with their fingers on triggers, ready for any emergency. Being stopped by soldiers on the bus or while walking down the street for security checks. We had worked in an orphanage with homeless kids, victims of the war. We had seen a darker side of life.

In the Philippines we had been on a hijacked bus when a guerrilla soldier carrying a machine gun had decided he needed transport, and had journeyed through a disaster zone, crossing the massive mud flows and wading through the ash after the eruption of Mt Pinatubo. We had been near tribal disputes in the golden triangle at a time when people were suddenly disappearing in the jungle, and had escaped violent theft and potentially lethal scorpion attacks in Mexico.

No, this time around we didn't need to take any more risks. Andrew wouldn't have stood for it. We needed a break. We needed some time out after working long and hard on the project. We needed to find somewhere safe to bring our child.

After pulling out of the queue and collapsing into a nearby lounge, we once again considered our options. I noticed the departures information sign was flashing—the plane to the Maldives was boarding.

'It's a sign!' I enthused. 'The Maldives are beckoning us!' Still the promise of warm beaches and good surf. A great place to unwind. A brilliant idea, I decided.

'Yes, great idea,' Andrew responded, decidedly unenthusiastically. 'If we could only justify the price.'

Through his extensive travel research, Andrew had heard that the Maldives had great waves, but had then discovered that it's almost impossible to find accommodation there for under $400 a night. So that idea was quickly quashed.

There we were, sitting in an airport, money in our pockets ready to spend on plane tickets. In a position of absolute freedom of choice. We had told our Indonesian friend Tiani that we would arrive in Jakarta in the middle of the month, so we still had a few weeks to spare. But although the options seemed limitless at the time, they were being quickly narrowed down for us by circumstance.

'How about Nepal?' Andrew ventured. No planes direct from the south of India, no beach huts there. But we were fast running out of neighbouring countries with surf, so I guess he figured we might as well try something completely different.

'Sounds good to me.' We were totally unprepared for snowy winter conditions, but what the heck. It certainly fulfilled the exciting adventure criteria!

The dreaded Indian travel diarrhoea finally caught up with us in the form of giardia. It was on the train ride north, on our way up to Nepal. It was a reminder of the flip side of the coin we had chosen to toss, that where things are exotic and different they can also be risky.

No doubt the illness had come from a pre-prepared cold curry mash brought on to the train at each station by local vendors. Luckily the toilets were close and we had decided to splurge on sleeper cabins. We constantly moved between the toilets and the sleeper beds for the thirty-six or more hours.

Although we had started in third class at the beginning of the trip, we had not anticipated wooden bench seats and oven-like air gushing through the windows. It had been a great experience at first (the people were decidedly friendlier and more relaxed in third class—they all had open picnics—and you got to spend time well inside each other's personal space), but it was going to be tough to sustain for long-distance travel. Besides, when you're feeling sick, you need all the creature comforts you can find.

The only stopover we made en route to Nepal was Calcutta, which came and went in a grimy blur. We had arranged to fly from Calcutta to Nepal, and spent the night in the only inexpensive hotel that had rooms free. Zoe had developed a nasty chest infection by this stage, but was fortunately taken care of by a travelling healer (who drew all the negative energy out of her and whisked it away with a dramatic flourish) and a French doctor (who prescribed a good dose of antibiotics).

When we finally arrived in Kathmandu, we were world-weary travellers needing to recuperate. A few pills, a few days of rest, and some disgusting traditional ayurvedic tonic got us back on track, and eager to get back to the adventuring.

'A day-trip would be nice,' Andrew announced almost cheerily one day, when we'd finally begun to absorb and enjoy our surroundings. 'Up into the hills for a few hours and then back down again. It wouldn't be too hard.'

'We'll have to take it easy,' I reminded him. 'We're in no state for anything that requires too much exertion.'

Hah! Famous last words. We ventured out that afternoon to buy a jacket each, and returned to the hotel loaded up with sleeping bags, hiking shoes and extra backpacks as well. We just couldn't help ourselves. The opportunity was there, we had to take it. We were now equipped and ready for some serious hiking!

We had climbed quite a height and trekked quite a distance before facing the ultimate challenge—negotiating a steep crevasse. I slipped and fell. There I was, on my butt, sliding out of control through snowy slush down a chasm. It was the ultimate *Romancing the Stone* scenario. Unfortunately, Zoe was trapped in the backpack on my back, screaming in utter terror.

When we finally came to a stop, I examined myself for broken bones. I found that most body parts were moveable, if somewhat bruised and battered. Zoe was a little damp and mud splattered, but had thankfully been well protected by the padded backpack. The screaming continued.

'I want to go home, Mummy!'

I could relate. At that very moment, we were a long way from home. A very long way from home. We were way up in the Himalayas, covering a part of the Anapurna circuit. A good three hours' walk through hilly terrain from the last village, and the next village was a good three hours ahead. As we sat in the slush together, recovering, I pulled out a muesli bar—the last of the carefully rationed imported provisions—as some sort of peace offering. How do you explain geographical location to a two-year-old? When we eventually got going again, I focused on just getting one foot in front of the other, and she buried herself deep into the backpack, pulling a rain jacket tightly over her head as protection against the icy snow. We were both learning important survival skills.

It had been a journey of extremes—extreme pleasure and pain, extreme heat and cold, extreme fantasy and reality. The scenery was absolutely amazing, but it hurt. At one moment we were standing on top of the world, watching the sun come up over dramatic, glistening, iced peaks, at the next, trudging up hills with significant inclines, willing ourselves to get to the top. But, of course, the tougher the challenge, the greater the appreciation of the destination.

A crackling open fire and cups of hot chocolate greeted us at our next stopover. The trauma of the day soon evaporated with the chocolaty steam, and we joked about my giant slide. No sooner had we snuggled into our sleeping bags in our compartmentalised sleeping area (not unlike primitive versions of the Japanese sleeping capsules), than we sank into a deep sleep.

There was, however, one last challenge for the day: midnight toileting. Night-time toilet training is difficult enough in regular circumstances, but when the toilet is a long walk past several other sleeping compartments and at least ten metres from the main building, it's another thing altogether. And being held over a small hole in the ground and exposed to the icy midnight air is not anyone's idea of fun, least of all a toddler's. We had not packed nappies, knowing they would have to be carried around with us for the full two weeks, so we just had to suffer through the exercise together.

Snuggled back into our warm sleeping bags, at one-thirty in the morning, a small voice broke the stillness.

'I want to go walking.'

Aaah! At last! Zoe had finally recovered enough to enjoy the process of hiking and now, in the middle of the night, she was recharged and ready to go.

'Don't worry, sweetie, there'll be lots of walking to do in the morning,' I responded. We all chuckled sleepily, snuggled in tighter, and fell into dreams of adventures yet to come.

It had been a deep sleep that night, partly due to exhaustion and partly due to the satisfaction of having experienced—and survived—so much together. When we eventually came down from our mountain sojourn we were relaxed and invigorated, fuelled by an incredible sense of achievement. We had literally been to the top of the mountain and back, and had come that little bit closer to our dream. All our travelling had been like serious training for the main event. Had been edging us gradually closer to the dream, step by step. It was time to really focus on finding that hut in Indonesia. We felt like we could face anything now.

Chapter 4

The Search for Paradise

The taxi slowed down as we neared the address. I had another look at the grubby bit of paper clutched tightly in my hand, and then back at the street signs. Gang XI, Gang XII, Gang XIII. We passed street upon street on our way through the busy Jakarta urban landscape. They all looked the same. It would be impossible to give the sort of instructions we were used to back home—'on the left after the large old gum tree, turn right after the orange sign, wind down around the river and over the bridge . . .' There were few landmarks here.

Unlike the area I come from back in Sydney, this suburb of Jakarta had been meticulously planned and carefully laid out. Every street was measured to ensure they were each the same distance apart, and every house design came from the same architect's office and used materials from the same supplier. It felt like driving through an oversized Legoland village. We could only really tell we were at the right place when, after turning a few more nondescript corners, we spotted our friend Tiani out in the street madly waving us down, grinning from ear to ear. There was hardly time to get out of the taxi before she was upon us, smothering us in kisses and hugs and exclamations of how much Zoe had grown. Oh, she cried, she had missed us so much.

Tiani had introduced us to the concept of living Indonesian-style when she and another lady, Justina, had stayed with us in Australia while they were English-language students. In a way, the time we shared together in Sydney had influenced the path our lives were taking now, and it struck me how so many individual incidents had pointed the way here to Indonesia, fitting together like the pieces of a puzzle.

Tiani, no doubt, was eager to have the opportunity to return our hospitality in her own home country. As soon as we arrived at her place we were whisked inside, taken on a detailed tour of the compact house, and positioned like living statues on display in the lounge room. Out came the best cut crystal glasses with the best tinned pineapple juice, freshly prepared salty fried savouries and brightly coloured coconut sweets. We had already overeaten on the flight and were exhausted from the travelling, but she wanted to keep talking and eating for hours, keen to cover every detail of our time apart.

A brand-new three-quarter mattress for the three of us to sleep on had been squeezed into her cupboard-sized spare room. Additional decorative touches—such as a wall clock, a calendar and a few pot plants—gave us the impression she was hoping we'd settle in on a semi-permanent basis. It was difficult to break the news to her that our stay was to be but a fleeting visit.

Unfortunately, our introduction to the city had not been too flattering, and we were not keen to stay longer than we had to. We had flown in through the winter-weight smog blanket covering Jakarta, battled the heavy traffic, and generally observed the burden of dense Asian city living en route to Tiani's house. As we were lying in bed that night—in the small space in the small house in a street of many others in a large sprawling city—we knew we would have to move on. After attempting to escape city life, here we were in an urban setting, already feeling claustrophobic. Although we were in the country we hoped would provide us with an alternative approach to life, we were still obviously a long way from that.

When we awoke the next morning, though, and peered out the window, we glimpsed quite a different perspective. Busy, lively calling and cackling coming from outdoors had awoken us and alerted us to the fact that the rest of the neighbourhood was awake and active. It appeared that everyone in the street had gathered outside. Was there something special going on, we asked Tiani as we ambled downstairs for breakfast? On no, she told us, just a normal Sunday.

After eating and dressing, she took us outside to meet the neighbours, and we discovered that her brother and his wife lived nearby—as did an assortment of other relatives. Children were playing on the street, and peddlers were selling chicken soup in large boiling pots on small wheelbarrow-style stands, or thin sticks of *sate* sizzling over hot coals. Friends were calling out to each other down the road, or sitting in the gutters watching and commenting on the rest of the neighbourhood in action.

It was fascinating to discover how Indonesian village living persisted in the city. Even westernised designs and structures could not change the shape of traditional culture. These people had moulded their living environment to fit their natural inclinations, maintaining the community model they knew best. It was an encouraging reminder of the significance of this way of life. Of how it would endure.

Anxious to find the place we would finally settle into, we prepared to move on again, thanking Tiani for her warm welcome into the country and for giving us an insight into what life could become for us. We hoped this move would be the deciding one. There were still two destinations in our travel plans: Pelabuhan Ratu, the sleepy village on the south Java coast renowned for its surfing, and Bali. We had researched both possibilities but were leaning towards Java because we knew it was more remote and untouched. I was originally quite sure my hut was not going to be found in Bali, having been to the island and knowing that it was fast becoming overrun with tourists. Though we knew that Bali was no longer the quaint and quiet haven it once was, we decided, in the end, that we should at least visit and trial Bali first, figuring that there might be more opportunities and more choices there.

Most of our baggage was stored at Tiani's place, as we expected to pass through again on the way to Pelabuhan Ratu. We had told her we would be back soon, to spend some more time with her and pick up our luggage. But fate had another plan in mind. We never did return.

We awoke to the sensation of a wild swerve and the sound of a frightful screech. In the next split second came the ear-piercing shriek of glass shattering and a dull thud as our bus came to rest against a tree. They say that the road to heaven is narrow, and we discovered that it is also very dangerous and scary when negotiated at high speeds.

The super-deluxe ultra-luxury coach would be, we imagined, a comfortable way to view the beautiful Javanese countryside en route. We had been looking forward to some relaxed, easy travel. As the brochures had promised, the bus did indeed have a pretty fab setup—with super-deluxe ultra-luxury reclining seats sporting plush velveteen covers and an almost 180-degree recline. Moving at close to the speed of light, however, the country views had flashed by in a blur, and when not suffering from tennis viewer's cricked neck from trying to catch just exactly what had been momentarily sighted out the window, we had our eyes glued shut in total fear of what might loom up over the horizon. Playing dodgem cars at high speed on a thin winding road was just not our thing. We had begun to feel like pinballs being tossed around various obstacles, likely to shoot out through the glass top of the machine at any time.

And there was to be thirty-six hours of this.

Our worst fears were confirmed when the bus crashed soon after midnight, just when we had more or less relaxed into semi-consciousness. Apparently, according to the rumour ripple that soon spread to every corner of the bus, the driver had fallen asleep at the wheel and gone off the road. Almost simultaneously on impact heads popped up all over the place, like a whole field of bleary-eyed startled rabbits. The only person who appeared to be hurt, though, was Andrew, who had been sprinkled with the shattered glass and was frantically trying to pull small slivers out of his hair and off his skin and clothing. It was quite an operation to clean him up. Fortunately, Zoe and I had been sleeping on a different seat away from Andrew's, and had managed to escape the fallout.

The driver's damage control operation for the bus was, in contrast to de-glassing Andrew, relatively straightforward. The shattered window was completely knocked out, and we drove open-air for a good few hours before some plastic sheeting was acquired and taped on to the empty window space to seal it up. We had imagined that the accident would be a lesson to the driver to teach him to slow down and take it easy. We were wrong. Completely wrong. He simply drove faster and with more of a sense of urgency, as we were now well behind schedule. It was such a relief to finally step off the death trap and find our land legs again.

Suddenly, Bali seemed like an incredibly beautiful place—the ideal place to make real our fantasy. There was no way I was going back on one of those buses again to return to Java, anyway. It was yet another example of how we were being slowly but surely nudged towards our ideal. Often in unpredictable ways! We had committed ourselves to making a difference in our lives, and destiny was helping us along. In the same way that we were searching for paradise, paradise was—it seems—reaching out to us.

Our journey across Java was symbolic. We had no idea at the time, but we had unwittingly traced a well-worn historic path. The travel option we had taken would have been significantly faster, and probably much more comfortable (high-speed accidents aside), but we must have felt something of what earlier arrivals had felt after travelling for thousands of miles and coming across a luxuriant island. It was easy to imagine our predecessors also happily stopping here, in Bali, and wanting to go no further.

I must confess that my knowledge of the culture and history of Indonesia was still pretty limited when we arrived. We both had some basic Indonesian lessons to give us a head start, and I had picked up and studied carefully any snippets of information I had come across before we left. I had also a tourist's level of understanding from travelling to the country before. But I had never really delved into the deeper intricacies of the culture.

Apparently, so I later discovered, we were but the most recent in an established history of paradise seekers. Bronze-bearing animistic Malays had come down to Bali from the north-west by land and boat more than 3,000 years ago. They were joined by another wave of Malays some time later. This second group ended up being responsible for the rice terracing system, with its complex irrigation channels, such an icon of the Balinese physical and cultural landscape today. It's now impossible to imagine Bali without the fluorescent green steps that wind their way down many of the central mountain slopes towards the plains.

The Indians were the next to arrive, also sweeping down from the north-west. Hinduism made an epic journey through time and cultural space from India, through Java, before finally resting in the island of Bali itself in the first century. It came via Brahmin priests, who had accompanied Indian traders searching for the renowned wealth of the south. They added another defining quality to the island culture, shaping its religious landscape. The Hindu religion was not firmly established, however, until the fifteenth century, when the Hindu Majapahit Empire stretched across Java before eventually finding a resting place in Bali. This empire had been very powerful in Java for a long time, but the faithful followers were forced out when the Muslim religion moved in, passing through from west to east.

A 'pig-headed' king of Bali at the time was strongly resistant to the arrival of these religious refugees. His heroic obstinacy made him a legendary figure, and you can still see the man with the pig's head being revered today. (Sometimes the comparison of animal and man really does seem apt!) The average Balinese person, however, openly welcomed this significant step towards 'civilisation'.

It was easy for me to see that Bali had now become a deeply religious place. It is a unique Hindu state—the only one of its kind in all of Indonesia—but it has developed a distinctive form of Hinduism, a blend of all the other faiths that have touched the island in some way or other. The strange mix of traditional Indian Siwa Hinduism and Mahayana Buddhism that had arrived from India adopted some Javanese shamanism en route, and then absorbed Bali's own form of animism on arrival at its new home.

The result is an earthy, primitive religion that is also incredibly rich in colour and mythological detail.

Eclectic spirituality has always fascinated me. It represents, I feel, an openness to the positive that can be found everywhere, in different faiths and traditions. As someone who has needed to feel comfortable with my faith in different situations, as someone who has learned to appreciate the importance of sharing beliefs and ideas, Bali's spirituality was an inspiration for me.

When we first arrived we found ourselves immediately swept into the Balinese way simply through our hopes of discovering for ourselves something of the natural wealth of the island. We were not at all sure, in the beginning, if this was where we were meant to be, but little by little we began to feel welcomed and somehow at home in the quirky land of contrasts.

It would be some time before we began to meld somewhat into the Balinese backdrop, some time before our souls rested comfortably alongside the others already here, but, at this point in time, we were certainly quite happy to stop and go no further.

'Want to buy a watch?'

Bali's best sales people covered the streets, on the lookout for any potential customer. They were our first contact with the 'locals' in Kuta, where we spent our first night.

'I give you cheap price.'

There they were, ready to greet us at every turn.

'Morning price. Just for you.'

They were persistent. From our previous experience of Kuta we knew to keep our heads down, to shoot out a quick greeting, then keep walking.

'You remember me, Ketut?'

From when we had visited five years before? Somehow, I didn't think they would have remembered us. The seller's trick was obviously to ensure you develop a personal relationship, to build a sense of obligation, a clever technique that had been honed after many years of tourism development on the island.

We had been concerned about Bali not being a suitable place to move to, about feeling like tourists rather than being able to settle in on a longer term basis. Our previous visit had revealed the shallower tourist side of the island, and these early experiences only confirmed our fears. But looking back, what could we have expected? Kuta was the most infamous tourist hangout—the sleazy bargain and flesh-hunter's Mecca of Bali. The tourists in this area appeared to outnumber the locals. And shops and stalls appeared to significantly outnumber domestic residences.

Bali has, for quite some time, had a reputation worldwide for its great shopping bargains, its numerous beaches, and its unique culture—but as I have now learnt, it was actually already established as a tourist haven by the 1930s, when the exotic island of the gods was drawing in curious visitors from far and wide. Shiploads of tourists started arriving, and the island was rapidly developed to accommodate them. New roads were built, automobiles were imported and rented out, homes were transformed into homestays, works of art became souvenirs.

There was a setback period in tourism from 1946 to the late 1960s, when the island was completely closed to foreigners after President Sukarno declared independence. Towards the latter part of the sixties, a series of disasters struck the island. Plagues, famine, and a volcanic eruption on an unprecedented scale brought a great deal of suffering and despair. The island was, however, opened up to tourism once more in the late 1960s, when Soeharto came into power and decided he wanted to capitalise on the island's economic potential. The current tourist paradise has grown from there. Apparently, there are now up to 5,000,000 tourist arrivals per year, with jet-loads of tourists arriving every five to ten minutes. Literally hundreds of hotels cater for these tourists, offering every standard of accommodation from the quaint homestays through to exclusive boutique hotels and luxury private villas.

Through those first few months we were stuck in Kuta, we couldn't relax and enjoy the holiday atmosphere as a tourist might, but we hadn't yet settled in as long termers, either. After the first night in a *losmen*, a single room designed for travelling backpackers, we moved on to a bungalow in a family compound, which helped with the transition. It was a more suitable place to base our-selves for our early explorations of the island and our potential opportunities there, as travellers cum hopeful settlers. We started to explore the deeper layers that exist below the surface and to discover things that we would grow to really love on the island—and which eventually led us to want to stay. But it all took time. It was frustrating to feel so near to paradise and yet so far.

To get around, we rented an aging VW Safari with a leaking canopy, but weaving our way through the cramped and often flooded one-way streets surrounding our bungalow soon lost its novelty. Because we were in the centre of Kuta, which had already become a concrete jungle, we were constantly feeling hot and bothered, unable to escape the oppressive humidity and depressing tourist traps. We were enjoying the warm welcome of the Balinese people we were getting to know, and the positive cultural glimpses that slipped through the Kuta façade—the deeper colour and passion of this exotic island—but we needed to be able to get much closer to all that.

When I had been in Kuta with my family a good ten years before, only a few bamboo stalls had lined thin dirt paths occupied by bicycles and motorbikes, and the beaches were but a casual stroll through peaceful coconut groves. By my next visit with Andrew and friends, just five years later, the roads were already paved and congested with a variety of larger vehicles, and many of the bamboo stalls had become smart, glass-fronted shops. Now, we could see all around us, development was continuing to increase at a frightening rate. We had to come up with a solution before we felt totally trapped. By this stage we knew our hut was to be found in Bali somewhere, but if we didn't find it soon we were going to have to give up on the dream and return home with our tails between our legs, feeling disillusioned and dissatisfied. I didn't know quite how to move ahead, but I wasn't yet prepared to go back, either. My pride would have been hurt and my hopes for real change defeated.

We had pursued the ideal this far. I knew that we could be happy if we found the right place. But that final small step felt like it was going to be the biggest hurdle yet.

Chapter 5

Home, Sweet Adopted Home

We did find our hut. It was perfect, just as I had imagined in my dreams. But as is often the case with making dreams come true, it didn't come at all easily.

At the time we were looking there were no real estate agents with large glossy photos on display behind glass. You couldn't open up a yellow pages telephone book and let your fingers do the walking, or search the internet for the most suitable property pictures and descriptions. You either had to have the right contacts or put in the hard work yourself. We had arrived with no contacts whatsoever, so we just had to do the legwork. We were searching for the ideal location: peaceful and quiet, on the beach, near Kuta for convenience, but well and truly out of the more developed tourist areas. We were looking for somewhere to call home. Fulfilling that sort of high expectation took time.

It took patience and perseverance, a lot of time and running around in the stinking heat, but eventually we found exactly what we had been looking for. After literally walking through the more traditional village areas on the coast for hour upon sweaty hour, week after week, we eventually stumbled across the hut. As soon as we found it, I knew. What we had found was the perfect patch of paradise.

The discovery came after we had been exploring a fishing village, walking down its narrow winding streets past peaceful clusters of buildings positioned in family compounds, each with tall bamboo poles and long bright flags marking the entrances, and often with the open smiling faces of the inhabitants greeting us at the gates. The villagers seemed especially amused at the sight of Zoe in her special backpack on Andrew's back. I could tell we were attracting extra smiles and comments, perhaps even tacit approval, and we didn't feel out of place or uncomfortable. We were not hassled to buy things. We were not propositioned or harassed. It was so wonderful to feel more like welcome visitors than vulnerable tourists.

Curious to get more of a feel for this area, we diverted out of the main part of the village and followed a small dirt track that traced along the edge of the ocean, enjoying the shady coolness of the lush vegetation. It was a small but significant patch of natural beauty. So tucked away. So quiet.

An old man carrying a machete suddenly emerged from the undergrowth. We were caught by surprise, having momentarily believed that we were somehow completely cut off from civilisation. We all stared at each other for a moment, unsure of the most appropriate greeting. Then I snapped out of the 'lost civilisations' moment and did what had become natural during those weeks. I introduced myself and asked about possible rental opportunities in what I thought was perfect Indonesian.

'*Permisi.* (Excuse me.) *Nama saya Jaya.* (My name is Jaya—the Indonesianised version of my name.) *Tolong, ada rumah dikontrakkan disini?*' (Are there any houses to rent around here?) Perfect accent for a virtual beginner, I thought.

The man continued staring at me. I might as well have asked him if he wanted to go to the moon.

I suddenly wondered whether he spoke Indonesian at all. Although it is the national language, it is actually adapted from a Javanese dialect—which is vastly different from the local Balinese dialect. Many elderly people have not been schooled, and still only speak Balinese. I had learnt that much in our language preparations.

We had opted not to try to learn Balinese because it is such a complex language. In Bali there is a four-level caste system according to Hindu traditions, and you need to know the appropriate way to address people at all levels—it's actually like learning four completely different languages. But I now wondered if we might be limited in our communication if we couldn't speak the local dialect.

Andrew and I looked at each other and considered the next most appropriate step. Andrew had found the language much more difficult than I, so he shrugged his shoulders as if to indicate we might as well give up and move on. But I didn't want to give up too quickly. I thought it might be worth trying my basic Indonesian one more time, this time a little slower and more clearly, before I started thinking of alternative strategies:

'Permisi, ada rumah dikontrakkan?'

He stared a little longer, and then it obviously registered. He simply nodded and indicated for us to follow him, shuffling down the narrow laneway, deeper into the foliage. I was relieved that what I had said had made some sort of sense, but was surprised that we were heading further into the vegetation rather than out of it. I wondered if we were going to get ourselves into some sort of trouble.

When we stopped at a place almost fifty metres from where we had met the man, though, I almost jumped out of my skin. There in front of us was the hut I had been searching for. It was gorgeous. This hut had all the elements of the image I had been carrying around in my dream: simplicity, seclusion . . . an exotic other-worldliness.

I simply stood and looked in awe at a tall majestic traditional-style bungalow with bamboo and grass thatched roofing draped down the sides and forming the walls. As soon as the old man could arouse me from my elated trance, we were led through an enticing Balinese gate formed from sandstone and with intricately carved wooden double doors. I immediately felt drawn into the heart of the place.

Inside the compound was an amazing template of Balinese communal-style living. There were a number of individual buildings nestled inside the walls, and the whole property was obviously designed for sharing. A large thatched building stood behind the first one we had seen from the outside, with a wild and embracing tropical garden reaching into its open-air construction. It had been designed to be built without walls, but it was also clearly unfinished. Two other buildings that were even more basic—barely skeletons—stood to the far left side.

I immediately started to plan for the future. There was no stopping my imagination. One day, I thought to myself, all these buildings would make the ideal community-living setting. So intimate, and yet each could be private. With a little bit of work and enough creativity, it could become the cosy living environment I had been searching for. I knew I had the optimism to make it happen—I'm sure Andrew would say I had an oversupply of that particular quality—but wondered if I could will the other factors to come together in such unknown circumstances.

The one finished property—the hut we had first seen from the outside—was locked, but by climbing the compound walls I could view the whole area. There were extraordinary views through the coconut fronds to the ocean at the front, and over extensive cow paddocks and fields to the back. There was one other solitary house just to the south, and a stone wall to the north delineating the beginning of sprawling hotel gardens. A small overgrown temple compound also bordered the property at the front and joined with the hotel wall. But those few buildings were so tucked away that all I could see around me was bright green, with occasional flashes of glinting blue and silver from the sparkling ocean water.

The garden may have been overgrown, the paint peeling, the concrete crumbling—but to me this place was heaven. Nothing could have been more perfect.

Using my pretty basic Indonesian, and sometimes the handy little phrase book, I tried to find out what I could about the owner and the property.

'*Apa ini?*' (What's this?) I was pointing at the large building.

'*Rumah besar,*' (Big house) the man replied.

A good start!

'*Apa ini?*' I asked again, pointing to the two unfinished buildings.

'*Rumah tamu.*'

I flicked through the dictionary to check the 'tamu'. Guest. Guest houses!

'*Apa ini?*' I asked, now pointing to the front building, the one with the steep thatched roof. This was easy. We were making real progress now.

'*Garasi.*'

Hmm. A few flicks later—garage. We were looking at living in a garage! Novel!

We had a good look around. The property had, apparently, been left untouched for quite some time. It looked like it was someone else's unfinished dream. According to this extravagant plan, the large house was going to be the grand residence, the hut was to be the garage with servants' quarters above, and the other two buildings had been designated as guest rooms. While waiting to be finished off, the main building had been used as a factory floor and the front building as makeshift offices, but I could see that this place had much more potential. There was even a large fully concreted hole in the ground that was destined to become a swimming pool, though at this stage it was not much more than a huge mosquito breeding ground. The garage was the most finished of the four buildings, but it was still going to take a bit of work to make it liveable.

When I had gathered as much information as possible, I pulled Andrew aside to gauge his reaction. 'Well, what do you think,' I asked keenly.

'It needs a lot of work,' was his careful response.

'Yes, but can't you see the potential? Can't you feel how magical this place is? It's got everything we've been looking for. It's simple, it has a traditional Indonesian style, it's so quiet and peaceful here . . . and it's right on the beach!'

'Let's try for the front hut—that's the most complete and would probably be the least expensive. If we can get it for a good price, and if the owner can fix it up before we pay, then I'll be willing to consider it.'

Yes! A virtual agreement! Andrew looked calm—probably considering all the possibilities—but that was it for me. I was doing cartwheels inside. At last the dream was almost a reality.

I asked the old man if we could meet with the owner as soon as possible. I'm not sure how I made such a complicated request in Indonesian. Perhaps another example of how resourceful you can be when you are determined enough.

'*Terimah kasih banyak, pak*,' I thanked the old man after the arrangement had been made. We were effusive in our appreciation. This man had brought us to the most idyllic location we could ever have found. '*Tolong, siapa nama anda?*' (What is your name?) I asked as we began walking together back towards the village.

'Pak Gendeg.' He pronounced the words slowly and clearly, especially for the uninitiated foreigners.

That name was to feature heavily in our new Balinese lives. Pak Gendeg ended up being our link to the local village. Tired of the distraction of conversation, Pak eventually shuffled off, disappearing through the break in the foliage from which he had first appeared, heading back to the fields.

All in a day's work for him. A significant change in destiny for us.

It felt strange to be on the verge of establishing a home again at this stage in our lives, but it was exciting, too. We had the chance to build our new home from scratch, to start over again; this time in a new country, a different setting, with a unique type of property. As adults we had experienced many different living situations before, but I had never really settled into a feeling of 'home'. I had yet to discover the contentment of what I hoped a home could be.

When I had first moved out of my parents' home, I shared a small fibro garden granny flat with a friend; it was positioned among the geese, sheep and rabbits of a semi-rural dwelling. It was a fun communal environment, I guess a taste of village living in the city, but it was not going to be a long-term prospect. As soon as we married, Andrew and I shared a tiny one-bedroom unit in a highrise. Although that time was special for us as young newlyweds, I soon felt that living there would have to be a stepping stone to finding a more meaningful living context.

I was never going to be a dedicated homemaker—I was always off on too many different projects to have time for that—but I did have a sense that a home should be a place where people would feel welcomed, where ideas and experiences could be shared. Not only within the immediate family, but also with the wider community. I soon discovered, though, that attempting communal living in the urban city context is not easy.

My first communal living experiment after we were married was in a semi-style unit in a block of four. We shared this unit with friends, but the limited living space made it difficult—and we had to put up with the whale rescue and crystal gazing stories of the woman next door, as well as the constant knocks under the floor from the elderly couple downstairs, whenever we made a little too much noise.

Next, we moved into a larger house which still provided communal living opportunities, but where we could also divide up the living spaces to provide more privacy. Unfortunately there were still tensions over who was going to do the washing up and how the bills were going to be paid. We discovered what usually happens in these situations. The more responsible married couple ends up having to clean up after everyone else. Unperturbed, I came up with the grand idea of turning the house into a bed and breakfast guest house. But that was hard work, too. We still ended up constantly cooking and cleaning for others, and found the contact too forced and super-ficial. Back to the drawing board. The house was transformed into a spiritual retreat. This would give us, I had hoped, the satisfaction of being able to relate to others in a more meaningful way as well as giving to others. But we soon found the responsibility was too intense. Perhaps we needed our own space and time to develop as a young married couple, as we felt like we were giving more than we were gaining. I switched to hosting international language students, which was easier on our relationship, but it still felt a bit like extra parenting responsibilities were being thrust upon us.

Andrew became incredibly frustrated with all my community living experiments and it had begun to put pressure on our relationship. Couldn't we just live like a normal husband and wife? Couldn't we just settle down to our own chops and three veggies at the end of the day in our own space and live with our own mess? Was I never going to be satisfied?

It was around this time that Tiani and another Indonesian student—Justina—came to live with us. Through them I found the closest link to what I hoped a real home could be. They shared house care with us, whipping up exotic spicy dishes and following through with practical household assistance. They played enthusiastically with Zoe. They sat around and chatted regularly, watched the world go by—not always in a mad panic, but simply enjoying the value of relationships in the here and now. We were drawn in by the warm extended family feeling. We had no idea at the time that we were going to end up in Indonesia ourselves, and could not have anticipated that the Indonesian community that had been created in our house in Australia was later going to be the basis for our new lifestyle. When we moved back to nuclear family living, when we were buried in our own personal stresses and irritations, we forgot about what we had learnt from our Indonesian friends. Even when we started to plan the year away, we hadn't made the connection.

The arrival at Tiani's house in Jakarta had been an important trigger and highlighted the significance of her stay in Australia. As we started to become involved in Balinese village living, it struck an even deeper chord. I could tell the Indonesian way of life was going to play a significant role in shaping ours.

The hut that we found in Bali would become the starting point for this new way of living. A beautiful, basic structure with a curved thatched roof, nestled in a coconut grove by the sea. A peaceful position, a sense of simple retreat.

It would be our first real family home.

'You must try this delicate fruit, brought down from the mountains of Singaraja by my own hands just today.'

The smooth opaque flesh of the *salak* was encased in a leathery snakeskin shell, which had to be cracked open little by little like an egg shell. It had a subtle but sweet flavour, something like a cross between a lychee and an apple, with a firm and crunchy texture. I soon discovered several in a row can be easily consumed before it sinks in just how more-ish they are.

We should have shown more restraint right from the beginning, as difficult as it was to resist Pak Kadek's enthusiastic hospitality. The *salak*, it turned out, was but a light appetiser for the range of courses yet to come, in the same way that this hospitality was the starting point for an ongoing friendship.

Pak was the father of Justina, the other English language student we had taken into our house and looked after while she was staying in Australia. By sheer fluke we only found out once we had arrived on the island that her father had moved from Kalimantan and set up a house in Bali. Another significant piece in the puzzle had fallen into place.

Justina was but one of many children of Pak Kadek's two wives (as is the custom with many men here)—one of whom was still living in Kalimantan and one who was now living in Bali—but as Justina was his eldest, and the first to have flown the nest, she was the one he was currently most protective of, and Kadek obviously felt like he wanted to look after us in gratitude for our care of his daughter.

The first time we were invited to his house, on the occasion of his Balinese son's birthday, he greeted us at the front gate as if we were his long lost children. Wealthy by Indonesian standards, his large house in the centre of the main city, Denpasar, was surrounded by a high wall with shattered glass embedded threateningly along the top. Pak ushered us past his not inexpensive collection of cars and into the main foyer, where we left our shoes according to the Balinese custom. When we rounded the corner into the expansive lounge room we were met by a sea of eager faces. Every friend and family member had been invited to share in the occasion, and, to ensure no-one would go hungry, a huge mound of food sat waiting on a vast sideboard.

'I made these deep-fried prawn bites myself, from a special recipe. Oh no, you cannot just have one—you must have several to truly appreciate the unique flavour.'

The small wanton-wrapped parcels were delicious, and we were only too obliging at this stage to enjoy the treats and give the necessary compliments. But food continued to be served to us from the sideboard on platter after platter, and the more we ate the more we realised we were going to have to eat.

Then, when we were sure there was going to be no more, the birthday cake arrived: a huge torte with layer upon layer of bright blue icing, artificial cream, and sugary sponge.

'Please have some of the cake. It was made in a shop owned by my friends.'

Pak Kadek's idea of hospitality was to fill you up with a feast of delicious delicacies, and he had treated us like kings and queens from the time of our arrival. His most loved and most often repeated joke was that his favourite pastime was eating, and sharing his love of good food with others was obviously his next favourite pastime.

When we had finished working our way through the multitude of courses and could take in no more, we crashed on one of the many lounges and spent some time chatting with and getting to know our host. We were astounded to discover, by some strange stroke of luck, that Pak Kadek was in fact a friend of the owner of the house we were looking at. He was eager to assist by acting as a go-between in negotiations. This was an amazing discovery for us. We had found the house on our own, but now we had the all-important contact to help with the next step, to act as a mediator. We were set!

The evening finished with a rousing Indonesian version of 'Happy Birthday', complete with enthusiastic clapping, and we were then rolled out of the house, with a balloon and a large takeaway package of food in hand to ensure we didn't starve on the way home.

A couple of important lessons also accompanied us as we left that night. We realised we were going to have to learn to accept the overwhelming hospitality of the Indonesian people, as well as the importance of the need to make good social contacts in Bali. We were quickly absorbing the fact that because Bali is so relationship oriented, so much of what is achieved on the island is not due to what you know, but rather whom you know. This was a new insight for us—at times making us feel quite uncomfortable—but we had come to Bali to learn the Balinese way. We were grateful to Pak Kadek for his hospitality—and his introduction to the Balinese approach to business. Discovering a new perspective is certainly always interesting.

After some to-ing and fro-ing through Pak Kadek, the house rental contract was settled with the owner on a handshake. When the negotiations had begun we had discovered that there are tourist prices and local prices, and we were hoping to get somewhere in between. Settling on forty dollars a week, we thought we had a good deal. It was more than our Indonesian neighbours would have paid, but certainly wouldn't break our bank.

Work began almost immediately. Impatient to finish our Kuta prison sentence, we turned up regularly to check on the progress. It was to be an interesting time and motion study of local building strategies, as we watched the project proceed slowly but surely, roughly according to the following (apparently standard) schedule:

STEP 1: Workers (*tukang*) arrive. Many bring their own tools—a shovel or hammer. You often see casual construction workers in lines by the side of the road. They get picked up by the dozen in trucks, and have to have their own tools to get a look in.

STEP 2: Work begins. Workers seem to be divided into two categories—semi-skilled workers and assistants. The assistants collect the materials—sand, concrete, bricks, etc—while the more skilled workers sit down and wait. Then the work roles are reversed. The more skilled workers do their thing while their assistants wait. So, for example, there may be only one person who is the 'official' cement renderer; one of his assistants will carry the cement from the truck, then stand and watch; another assistant will mix the cement, then stand and watch; and another will hold the cement on a tray for the renderer and stand and watch. Women are often the ones who do the heavy carrying, but they are also employed to do more of the finishing work.

STEP 3: Everyone takes a break. All men have a smoko and pee against the back wall.

STEP 2 is repeated until lunchtime, until the supervisor leaves the premises, or until the materials run out (which happens on a regular basis—the workers often don't have transport of their own and must wait until the supervisor organises a delivery of materials).

STEP 3 then kicks in again.

STEPS 2 and 3 will then continue to be repeated throughout the day.

I refer to one of the types of workers as 'semi-skilled' because in reality I have learnt these people are not necessarily specifically trained or officially apprenticed in their field. They are more likely to be people who have observed and copied a process, often inaccurately, and often without understanding exactly what they are doing and why they are doing it.

As a result, the quality of work does not always appear to be the best. It seems that money needs to be saved in any possible way. It might mean that more sand is put in the concrete mix, so that the resultant concoction is very easily eroded by the weather. It might mean that the paint is watered down so much that the concrete still shows through in grey streaks. It will most certainly mean that the bricks will be slapped on quickly rather than carefully, so that no wall line is quite straight and the bricks crack and fall apart under the pressure. Building is quite a happy social occasion for the workers, as you can imagine, but it did take some time for the task to be completed. And we did wonder about the safety of the final product.

The owner had agreed that he would make a few basic additions and alterations to adapt the hut to meet our needs and to turn it into more of a house than a garage, promising the building would take no more than four weeks. After coming and going and observing the building process on several different occasions, we were pleased when it was nearing completion after eight weeks. The year was ticking away—five months had now passed since we had left Australia—and we were desperate to move in. Although we continually exclaimed to each other and tut-tutted over the quality and efficiency of the house-building process, in the end we were just happy to have something reasonably sensible and safe to live in. We were thrilled that we would be able to stay in our new patch of paradise on the shoestring budget we had set aside for the year, and in the very hut I had dreamed of.

The building actually had three levels—the ground-floor garage, and two rooms the same size stacked on top of each other forming the next two levels up. A simple tiled bench with a sink was installed along one wall of the garage level and the floor was tiled and the walls painted, turning the small space into a compact living-cooking-dining room. An open-roofed bathroom with toilet and shower was attached to the back of the building, and stair rails added to the narrow, steep stairs leading to the two upper levels. The main remaining feature was the original garage roller-door. We planned to open it up completely during the day and look out through the coconut grove to the beach. Because of the usually mild weather conditions in Bali, open-plan living can be very open.

With the few simple additions and alterations, the building was finally ready for habitation. *Voila!* The converted garage-hut was going to become our home at last!

Moving-in day started off as a much simpler and less stressful procedure than any other in our house-moving history. We merely threw our backpacks onto the back seat of the Safari with some very basic kitchen utensils and essential linen items (three towels, a teatowel, and a set of sheets), and strapped a foam mattress to the roof, along with two bamboo stools and the surfboards. Zoe was positioned somewhere in the middle of it all, looking a little peeved by the fact that no sooner had we settled down for a decent stretch of time than we were uprooting her again, and in such undesirable circumstances.

Of course it started raining after we left Kuta, so by the time we arrived the mattress was soggy and the linen damp from the leaking canopy in the car. Zoe was letting us know how unhappy she was about the whole kerfuffle, in typical two-year-old style. Unperturbed, we thrust open the garage door, ready to celebrate our arrival. Instantaneously we were hit by a strong smell of drying paint and festering mildew, and a rat immediately scuttled along the edge of the bamboo roofing, startled by the clang of rattling aluminium. We peered into the half light, checking out just how bad the situation might be, uncertain if we were really ready to make a grand entry.

As soon as I sensed our mutual disappointment, I switched gears and did my best to keep the cheery adventurous spirit going.

'Well, here we are! Let's open this place right up and get some fresh sea air running through it. I can tell it's been waiting for some decent inhabitants for so long. It's just so exciting to be here, isn't it!'

'Do you really think we're doing the right thing?' Andrew ventured. 'I mean, this isn't quite what we were expecting—is it?'

'Oh, don't worry about it. We'll get it cleared up in no time at all.'

'Are you sure? Is it really going to be healthy for Zoe?'

'We've stayed in worse places than this before. It'll be just fine. You'll see . . .' I hoped I sounded more confident than I felt . . .

Our first night was less than comfortable. All three of us sharing a small mattress that had been wrung out as much as possible, but that was still damp and uninviting. It was so quiet that at times it was creepy. We awoke with every little sound. The occasional frog belching, the intermittent sound of thundering waves crashing, sometimes a distant dog howling. I spent the night anxiously praying that we had made the right decision. It had to work. This was it. This was the dream. It was my last chance.

Thankfully, with the fresh, new sunny day, our outlook began to look brighter. Our belongings were put out to dry, and we jumped in the car for a mad shopping frenzy to buy all those items that would have made that first night much more pleasant. By the time we settled back in on the second evening, our spirits had lifted. There was enough time to duck down to the beach for sunset—a wild spread of reds and oranges—all three of us splashing and whooping at the water's edge, and then we were ready to enjoy some *sate* from a local cart for dinner, before returning to the hut and the promise of a more restful night's sleep.

This time around, we consciously focused on the sounds of tranquillity, on nature's little conversations. We slept much more heavily, and the only time I awoke, I was drawn to look out the window at the full silver moon, partially obscured from view by dark coconut-leaf stripes swaying in the light wind. I was so thankful for where we were right at that moment. For the tranquillity. It's amazing how the mindset you have often makes all the difference to your perspective.

It didn't take long to get to know the local faces, the local characters of the villagers from nearby, and although we were initially treated as a bit of a novelty, curiosity soon gave way to familiarity. This village was not cut off from foreigners, it was still well within the tourist belt, but there will probably always be a fascination about the different world we come from, just as we continue to have a fascination with their world.

For quite a while, every time we walked down the street we would be bombarded with questions and comments:

'Where are you going?'

'What is your baby's name?'

'Where are you from?'

'How many children will you have?'

'How long have you been married?'

'What is your work?' . . . and so on.

Initially, it was hard not to take these sorts of interrogations as a bit of a personal affront, but we learnt that this was simply the friendly conversational style of local Indonesians. The way they live, in close-knit communities, I guess nothing can be kept secret for too long!

Slowly but surely, we became part of the neighbourhood fabric, though always somewhat isolated and separated—not only by our more remote location, but also by our completely different background and approach to life. We had to realise that we were never going to be simply absorbed into the local Balinese community, but that we would at times be able to participate in that village life, at others simply live and move alongside it.

There were already many different layers of social strata in the community, and our presence was merely one part of one of those layers. At the base were the original fishing families, who had once been considered the poorest of the poor by the other Balinese. The land in our village had at one time been judged as useless because it could not be converted into rice fields. Landowners in the area would often literally give the land away rather than being stuck with apparently worthless property.

The original village inhabitants were, we soon discovered, still quite tribal in many ways. I imagine they would originally have been resistant to the changes that were slowly but surely sweeping through the area. But, being made up mostly of lower-caste people with a limited education, they probably wouldn't have had much of a say. Anyway, by the time tourism became established in Bali, most Balinese communities were recognising the benefits: increased access to good resources, better services, and—most importantly—more money.

Suddenly, the untouched natural coastal area to the south, which had once been considered to be worth nothing, came into high demand by foreigners, who valued green open spaces, white sandy beaches and loads of coconut trees. To support the growth in the tourism industry, people started coming in from other parts of Bali and from other parts of Indonesia. The out-of-towners mostly consisted of those who had superior training and skills in these areas, such as the upper-class Jakartans, and those who could provide cheap labour, such as the people from the islands to the east. It meant the local villagers now had another source of income—renting out houses and rooms within their compounds.

So we discovered we had neighbours from all over the archipelago, and from all over the world. Here, a large extended family from Ambon, living in an overcrowded compound. There, a wealthy Jakartan family, living in a large house and driving luxury cars. Around the corner some entrepreneurial westerners, making money from exporting handicrafts. But mostly we had daily contact with our local Balinese neighbours: the people who sold sarongs and wind chimes on the beach, the people who worked as gardeners and waitresses in the hotels, the people who came from fishing families of way back.

We made the transition to a somewhat Balinese lifestyle, taking on board something of the locals' simple way of life, and adapting it and enjoying it for ourselves. Now that we had the chance to start over—to build a house that could become more of a home—we became determined to set up a simple house this time around. The idea was to focus on making space and time for our relationships, and to limit the distractions of time-consuming appliances and objects.

Before long there were opportunities to take on some part-time work contracts, and we also pursued our own dreams. I tucked myself away in the small attic room with vast ocean views and wrote articles for local and international magazines, while Andrew went surfing for hours on end—both of us still having plenty of time for our daughter and each other in between. We talked a lot, ate out a lot—sometimes a greasy local dish from a roadside stall, sometimes a meal at a cheap, western-style restaurant—and we generally relaxed. It was bliss.

Our early days in Bali could be clearly characterised by what we did without, rather than what we had, and they will always be remembered as a particularly special time for us as a family. Five-star camping. That was how we began. We initially fitted out the house with only the basics: a two-burner benchtop gas stove for cooking, a bench seat for the living room, the mattress on the floor in the bedroom, a few simple crockery items, and some baskets from the local markets for storage. Enough to live with, but not so much that we were no longer as in touch with our natural environment and with ourselves. Mind you, we never gave up those little western luxuries that it's hard to let go of: like a western-style toilet bowl and toilet paper. There was only so far we were prepared to go in this simple living experiment!

Each day we'd open our garage door wide, enjoy some fresh fruits, and look out through the paddocks to the ocean. Who could have wanted more?

Chapter 6

Into the Village

Our Bali housewarming party was a very low-key affair. After all, there is only so much you can do with a thatched garage in a coconut patch.

We were now six months into the year, three months into our time in Bali, and we had been living in the house for one month. We had accumulated just a few acquaintances by this stage, and as it was we were spilling out onto the dirt path in front of the garage, halfway into the cow paddocks beyond the path. It was a dark night and we were overshadowed by the coconut trees from the field, so we defined the space with some bamboo flare torches, giving the area a haunting, tribal feel.

Pak Gendeg and his family were invited, as were contacts we had made through some of the odd jobs we had picked up—Amelia and her husband Chris, whose children we had started tutoring, for example—and acquaintances we had made through playmates Zoe had started to meet. Andrew's new tennis partner, Greg, a professional from an exclusive resort, and his actor friend Sarah were present, as well as some surfing mates—Cam and Francois. It was a pretty strange mish mash of the contemporary social scene in Bali. However, we learnt straightaway—the hard way—that there are distinct social groups that happily coexist side by side in Bali, but that ne'er the twain should meet!

Just as within our own village there was a mix of cultures and social strata, we soon discovered there was also a huge range of people living all over Bali. As far as the Indonesians go, there seemed to be pockets of different cultural groups living in different parts of the island. The wealthier people of Jakartan origin tended to live in the capital city Denpasar, in large extravagant properties. At the other extreme, the slum areas (as limited as these are) were likely to be occupied by the poorer Javanese and migrants from islands to the north and east. There were also communities of Muslims living in the mountains in the centre of the island and to the west.

Similarly, I discovered, you could almost stereotype the expat scene. At one end of the social strata would be those working on a contract basis for large companies. At another level were people working in the embassies and in development work. Both of these groups of people would mostly live in a defined area between the city and the coast, or on the properties where they were employed.

In general, expat families lived in quiet, safe Sanur, and singles on the other side of the island, in Kuta, Legian or Seminyak. Backpackers who came for a short holiday and had opted to stay on, continued to live in Kuta in small single rooms; they appeared to be content to party at night and laze away the day, and exported suitcase-loads of sarongs or cheap jewellery when they needed the money to leave the country in order to get a new visa.

The more serious importers and exporters set up on a longer-term basis lived further north of Kuta, in Legian and Seminyak—in the trendy shopping and nightclub sprawl. These areas also seemed to attract the summer migrations from Europe, gorgeous French, Italian and Spanish people who managed to maintain a year-round full body tan and who enjoyed the wild full-moon parties of the tropics. The arts community lived in Ubud, an area that had traditionally attracted creatives, along with new-age, new-generation hippies with the urge to get back to nature and to seek out authentic cultural experiences. The long-term surfing community lived in the southern Bukit peninsula, in easy reach of the surf—obviously.

And people like us? We tried to fit in somewhere in between.

Attempting to maintain contact with and enjoy the range of outlooks of different people from different backgrounds was not at all easy, but was definitely enriching. In fact I think it was a wonderful cross-cultural and international experience. We joined in with local banter when we could, and then switched to the outsider's viewpoint when we needed to. It didn't take long to discover that survival and ultimate contentment in this context really hinge on the ability to see situations from all perspectives and adapt as necessary. Trying to bridge cultural gaps was a great challenge—and it didn't always work successfully!

At the housewarming, the Gendeg family felt most comfortable in a quiet spot off to the side, handling the barbequing of the fish and the grinding of the special Balinese *bumbu* spice mix. They chatted noisily, smoking and laughing as they worked, content to have something to focus on in this unfamiliar environment. Every so often, one of them hacked up a huge mouthful of slag, which was subsequently loudly discharged somewhere onto the ground near the other guests. I immediately discerned looks of semi-controlled alarm on the faces of these people, who were ever so slowly distancing themselves further and further away from this corner. The trouble was, there just wasn't a whole lot more space to move into. And the others were having trouble finding points of common contact anyway. Conversations were slow and strained—particularly against such an uncouth backdrop.

Those who worked were happy to talk work. Those who had kids were happy to talk to the few others with kids. The surfers stuck together and talked surf. But otherwise there wasn't much mixing going on. I made a desperate attempt to salvage the situation by flitting around and chatting to as many people as I could—which is not at all my forte.

'So, how long have you been living in Bali?' My question was directed to an impeccably dressed European lady, Caroline, married to a man who had been relocated to Bali by his company.

'Two years too long. Dirty, filthy place, really—not the paradise everyone says it is—and the people can be so difficult. I can't wait till my husband gets a transfer.'

I was immediately squirming. 'Oh yes, I see.' I had no idea how to respond. For me, being on the island had become like being on a neverending honeymoon. I loved the place and the people. I was glad, at least, that the Gendeg family couldn't understand much English. Luckily, Caroline made the next move.

'So, what work was your husband transferred here with?'

'Um, there was no transfer . . . we actually chose to come and live here.' This is going to be interesting, I thought.

'How are you coping with living here? Its just so . . . so . . . primitive.' She surveyed the scene with an air of disdain, and turned back to me with her nose turned up, a classic sour lemon look on her face.

I hesitated over whether I should just nod and agree—after all, we couldn't afford to lose friends this early in the piece—but I was really not comfortable going down that path. 'Well, we really love it so far,' I said simply.

'Just you wait until you've been here long enough. It drives you insane.'

'Hmm . . . Oh—would you excuse me a minute—I just want to check if anyone else needs drinks . . .'

I moved on to a more casually dressed couple with open, relaxed faces. Ricky and Paula were expats from the neighbourhood, and Zoe had become friends with their child.

'So, what brought you two to Bali?'

'We're doing some studies for a cultural program, learning the language, trying to get a feel for the contemporary Balinese way of life.'

Good! This sounded like a more positive start to a conversation. They shared a little more about their interesting experiences researching the Balinese culture and customs before I ventured an introduction.

'Have you met Amy yet? She writes magazine articles about Bali, I believe.'

'Oh yes,' Paula hurried to answer. 'We know Amy, but she really comes from a different place. She writes for tourist magazines, and her material is very strongly influenced by marketing constraints. We don't really have much in common. We don't like to compromise our position . . . or that of the beautiful Balinese people.'

Uh oh, I'd hit a brick wall again. All right, I was not yet defeated. I decided to make one more attempt at facilitating conversation before giving up, and approached Marg and Budiman, who looked uncomfortable enough to be ready to leave.

'Tell me, how did you go with getting Sam into the new school?' I asked.

Budiman looked down and shifted from one foot to the other, just like an energetic little boy waiting for a church service to end. Clearly Marg, who was Australian, usually took control of these situations, and she did so now, answering in her blunt, matter-of-fact way, 'Oh, my god! It's just too bloody expensive! I don't know where they think they're going to get bloody kids from. The money doesn't grow on trees around here. Don't know if I want a stuck-up little kid anyway. I know *she's* got her little one in,' she gestured with a raised thumb towards Miss Two-years-in-Bali-and-can't-wait-to-get-out, 'and she's a right little snob. No, I don't think it's the right place for our Sam. Is it, Budiman?' shove, shove.

Stuck between the local Balinese and the expat scene, poor Budiman, a quiet, gentle Javanese, just wasn't sure how to behave, other than to nod readily in agreement. He shifted a few more times while there was an awkward lull in the conversation, and then Marg announced their departure.

'Anyway, we'll be out of here, won't we Budi.' An imperative instruction rather than a question. Not open to discussion. A shy smile from Budi, and they were off into the dark night, leaving me wondering what on earth to do next.

At this point I desperately made a beeline for Andrew, who had pinned Greg to a corner for at least the last hour, obviously having given up on everyone else ages before I had.

'I can't deal with this!' I hissed as inconspicuously as I could out of the corner of my mouth.

'This party was your idea!' he replied with a definite smirk on his face.

Yes, he had me there. Great idea. Oh well, nothing like learning from experience.

Our housewarming party, not surprisingly, finished quite early. We were relieved when we were on our own again, left laughing at the fascinating absurdity of our new life between cultures and its many contradictions.

As soon as we were reasonably well settled in, Pak Gendeg invited us back to visit his family compound—a gesture of welcome for the new neighbours, no doubt.

It's amazing how you can visit this island so many times and yet still not have much of an idea of what it is really about until you actually step inside and spend time in a village compound. We were immediately struck by the way whole thriving communities are so ingeniously tucked away behind seemingly inconsequential compound walls.

The first person we met in Pak Gendeg's compound was a small lady with a wizened face and a black, almost toothless grin. She was slowly weaving her way around the assortment of people and animals gathered in the compound. Stooped with the weight of age, her lifeless breasts hung loose from her hollow chest. She may no longer have been the imposing figure she once was, but she still carried a matriarch's air of authority. By carefully following Pak's gestures, we worked out that this lady was in fact his wife, Ibu Gendeg. Ibu followed after a small child—one of her grand-children. She capably picked the child up when he cried, constantly chattering words of warning, advice and encouragement—I could tell by the tone. After a while, she sat the child down with her, ready to start the tedious process of grinding some spices for the evening meal. Pak Gendeg joined her, amusing the child to keep him out of his wife's way.

The nature of the activity we observed in the compound intrigued us. No-one was moving fast. No-one was looking anxious or stressed. But everyone seemed to have something important to do. We propped ourselves against the wall near the kitchen, and began fiddling with some coconut leaves alongside a group of women who were weaving them into ceremonial containers. Their hands moved quickly, and they were able to produce mounds of intricate works of art. We had a try ourselves, and ended up merely fumbling through, barely able to complete one dishevelled attempt.

The strong community orientation was obvious. We immediately felt, and over time learnt, that the Balinese are able to remain close to each other through their intimate living arrangements. Not in the warm sharing-all-your-secrets-with-best-friends way that westerners might associate with being 'close', but rather in a more relaxed atmosphere of companionship. They live in extended family groups, where the son's wife is required to move to the compound of her husband's parents (or grandparents) upon marriage. Three to four generations might share a large compound, with a high stone gate to mark the entrance and a rabbit warren of internal living quarters. Within this compound, each nuclear family occupies a single room that is essentially one of a row of rooms or small bungalows. The central cooking, eating and lounging areas are communal, and everyone is directly responsible for making sure the whole household runs smoothly.

We came to appreciate that these compounds are active communal centres where, at any given time, there will be a myriad of interesting goings-on. The women, who are responsible for the cooking and cleaning, are constantly bent over large pots, stick brooms, or the intricate coconut leaf offerings. The men enjoy whittling bamboo, tinkling on the gamelan instruments, and teasing the children. There are not usually specifically designated childcare roles, as different family members will share the responsibility as the need arises. Many individuals will be either glued to some bizarre family game show on the communal television or sitting around chatting in an animated fashion and laughing wildly at the slightest joke.

Balinese communities laugh and cry together, eat and sleep together, share and fight, celebrate and commiserate, work and play together—they live and die together.

There were no rocking chairs ready for Ibu Gendeg. She would not need to be moved on to a nursing home. In fact there are no nursing homes! She would remain a responsible and valuable member of her family community, like any other elderly person in Bali, until she became physically incapable or died. At all times she would be supported by the community. Because extended families live and work together so closely, the social structure easily caters for each family member's individual needs. It provides a network of personal care. The government has not needed to provide care for the elderly, disabled, ill, disadvantaged, or unemployed—there has been no need for them to set up nursing homes, childcare centres, hospices, or work projects—as all of these people can be taken care of to a great extent within the family.

Beyond the family, there is also the Banjar, a tightly structured organisation that ensures every family in the wider community is taken care of. The Banjar has the salubrious role of 'the sharing of joy and pain', and its dedicated members (you become totally socially isolated if you don't become a part of this community experience) work for each other and serve each other in many practical ways through special social work arrangements—or *ayahan*—that bind the community together. We saw the amazing way the Banjar works from the outside only. It somehow seemed to be a sacred space for the Balinese, a dedicated centre of religious and cultural activity, and we wanted to respect that.

Throughout all the tourist development that has gripped the island, the secret to the island's attraction has remained the same. There are still extensive rural areas that have stayed essentially untouched over time, and many of the Balinese themselves still pretty much live the lives they have led for centuries. Most importantly, they continue to live the committed, communal village lifestyle that has ensured social cohesion through times of dramatic change.

Not long after our visit to his home, Pak Gendeg turned up at our front door accompanied by an attractive, well-groomed young lady. He grinned broadly as he held on tightly to the girl, obviously proud to introduce her to us. We held out our hands to shake hers, which seemed to be the most appropriate thing to do. Surprisingly, she had a strong, confident grip.

'Excuse me, sir. My name is Made Sri. My uncle has brought me here because I am looking for work. Perhaps you have some work that I can do?'

Her English was quite good, she had a charming smile, and she presented well—but we had no work to offer her.

'We're so sorry,' I told her, 'We have no jobs going here. But I can ask around and can certainly let you know if I hear of anyone looking for staff.'

'Please, sir,' (she obviously thought that she was addressing the decision maker), 'I don't think you have anyone working in your house yet. I can cook, I can clean—and I love looking after children.'

Zoe picked up on that part of the conversation, and giggled profusely. The young lady noticed her interest, and played a quick game of hide and seek. She was doing well. She was winning us all over quickly. But we were unprepared for the idea of having someone work for us in our house.

Andrew and I looked at each other, both of us making quick mental assessments of the situation. I think we could both tell it would be difficult to say no. I raised my eyebrows, indicating that we should give the girl a chance, and Andrew picked up on it.

'We had not actually thought about having anyone work in our house,' Andrew said to her, 'but if you'd like, you can come by tomorrow and help us out a little while we consider whether we need anyone—or look for a suitable alternative.'

The charming smile broke into a delighted grin. 'Oh, thank you so much. Thank you so much, sir. I will be here ready to help at nine in the morning. You don't know what this means to me. Thank you so much!'

The old man and the young lady walked off together, arm in arm, both grinning from ear to ear. As soon as they had disappeared behind the bushes, Andrew and I turned to each other again, both stunned and bemused at how quickly we had employed someone for a position we had not even considered necessary only a few minutes before!

Andrew brought up the subject later that night, as he looked in dismay at the pot of burnt rice we were attempting to cook (we are both children of the technological age—the only rice we had ever made before was in a microwave!). The smell alone was an incentive to consider alternatives. Perhaps it could be part of our role as 'wealthier' foreigners, we reflected, to provide jobs for the community. Andrew pointed out that Made Sri obviously really needed a job, and it was a way we could contribute to the village in return for the warm hospitality we had received.

I wondered whether it might be strange having someone working for us like that. Whether I might feel uncomfortable. But then again, I realised, we often had ways of easing the domestic burden back in Australia. Commercial house cleaners had come through to give the place a good scrub down every other week, we had often relied on instant microwaveable meals and easily available takeaway food, and we had needed to make use of childcare services. While I was thinking about it, I doled out the almost identifiable coffee-coloured squelchy lumps of rice onto plastic plates. I considered the positives: that we would have someone we could get to know helping to look after Zoe in our own home while we worked, that we would have someone to assist with the more time-consuming household duties. Perhaps that would be nicer than having to outsource some of those duties to strangers. And perhaps Made Sri could teach us to cook some of the wonderful Indonesian foods—even rice!

There was time to ponder on the decision as we looked out to the ocean. In fact, we had plenty of time to chew it over. There was nothing much else going on in our little coconut field. A quiet night in, as always.

Made Sri arrived the next morning, promptly at nine. She whisked her way through the house, and kept Zoe happily entertained while we worked. It was amazing how she immediately knew what to do and did it so efficiently. By the end of the day there was no question about whether or not she would stay with us, and she became a valued part of our household in no time at all.

We had a strong déjà vu experience about a week later, though, when Pak Gendeg turned up to our front door again—this time clutching on to a young man. The grin was just as wide as when he'd left the week before, so he was obviously confident of similarly positive outcomes from this introduction. I just had time to catch Andrew's horrified expression before they came into full view. What other staff would we possibly be employing next? This time, Pak Gendeg's companion turned out to be his son, Nyoman. We recognised him from our visit to the family compound and from our housewarming—as one of the slag-on-the-ground culprits. He could not speak a word of English. Well, I thought to myself, at least Made could translate for us. What would we have done without her?!

Made Sri let us know that her cousin was also looking for work. We would need a gardener, driver, and security man, she informed us, and he could capably do one or more of these jobs. It was beginning to feel a bit ridiculous. We were living in a converted garage hut, not a palace, but we were already beginning to feel like privileged royalty.

Smiling our way through the conversation, Andrew and I tried to send telepathic messages to each other to come up with a suitable response. We didn't want to offend anyone, and were getting the idea that our future happiness in the village could well depend on our generosity in these situations. We ended up promising the young man a similar trial period, also letting him know that apart from some overnight security and a little gardening (which actually consisted of watering a few potplants on the edge of the field), there really wasn't too much work to do. We were certainly not going to feel comfortable being chauffeured around in our ancient car.

Thanking Pak Gendeg one more time for all his assistance, we tried to let him know that we really couldn't employ anyone else—that we now had all the staff we could possibly need. Fortunately, he didn't turn up with any other family members after that.

Nyoman started his first shift at nine o'clock that night, and was due to finish at seven the next morning. We didn't really know what someone in security should be doing, but we had an inkling that it should involve a little more than sleeping in the garden. Before long we were highly amused by our security guard, who looked as though he'd fall over if you blew on him too hard, and who was a very, very heavy sleeper.

When we went out one night a few weeks after he'd started,

returning home at around ten, we knocked on the compound door—expecting that Nyoman would be there, ready to open the door for us and greet us. We started to bang on the door in case he was patrolling out the back—way out the back—and couldn't hear us. We shouted and screamed over the wall, trying to get his attention somehow, but it was all to no avail. Eventually we had to climb over the high stone wall, scrambling inexpertly over the top ledge and scraping ourselves on the way down. Once inside, we traipsed around the property in search of Nyoman, and found him happily sleeping away in a dark cosy nook. Now shouting at him from point-blank range, we proceeded to pinch and prod him until he finally woke up. This time we were not very amused.

We talked to Made Sri about our concerns the following day.

'Oh,' she said, 'he's probably tired because he has to work all day and then only has an hour or two off before he arrives for his night job.'

Yes, well. That rather explained it. But what could we do about it? We couldn't sack the guy, or we would risk offending his father.

Andrew then came up with a clever new system, and Made Sri explained it to Nyoman in Indonesian when he arrived for duty that night. We placed a chart up on our back door with hourly slots scheduled onto it, and asked him to sign it every hour, on the hour. After a few nights of gamely trying to adapt to the system, poor Nyoman turned up to greet us one morning, looking exhausted and bleary-eyed.

'I am so sorry, sir,' translated Made Sri, 'but I am unable to work to your system. I am afraid I will be unable to continue working for you.'

Thank goodness. The situation had resolved itself.

It was a lesson, though, in how to manage circumstances like this. We soon understood that it was our responsibility to know and be explicitly clear in our expectations. That our instructions would need to be laid out from the beginning, and that it would not always be possible to assume independent responsibility. This knowledge helped us to take the time to identify our expectations in future business interactions and approach any new situations with sensible caution.

As it turned out, there was an interesting twist to the story of our first experience as employers. We found out a few months later that Made Sri had fallen pregnant—Nyoman was the father of the baby. They married a few months after that.

The wedding was an extraordinarily grand event. In the week leading up to it, the Gendeg household busily prepared the food and decorations for the two-day program of extensive feasting and celebrating.

When we entered the compound on the first day we thought we had come to the wrong place. It had been so completely transformed from the rather drab, rundown, motley gathering of buildings we had visited so regularly. Instead, the area resembled an ancient royal palace, with gold-stamped cloth swathing all the columns, elaborate coconut-leaf and flower decorations hanging from tall bamboo poles, and coconut-leaf streamers adorning the ceilings and reaching down from the skies in the courtyard spaces.

The people, too, were like exotic royalty straight off the pages of a history book. They were radiant in their glittering robes. The ladies' lace tops shone like polished pearls—mostly in pink, cream and apricot pastels. They had obviously spent a lot of money on these, and on delicate sarongs that shimmered in the morning sun. Most of them had swept their hair up in the large wave shape characteristic of ceremonies, fastened down by long, gold-leaf pins. The men wore cockatoo-like crests made of thick strips of cloth and wrapped proudly around their foreheads, as well as the distinctive white button-down shirts with Chinese collars and double-layered sarongs—a long traditional batik sarong underneath and shorter gold silk wrap over the top. Even the smallest of children wore these outfits—heavy makeup included. They were gorgeous miniature dolls, every bit as serious and sincere as the occasion demanded.

The married couple welcomed their guests, both looking quite uncomfortable in their tight, heavy clothing, and weighted by the sudden responsibilities of what we at first assumed was a shot-gun marriage. But Made Sri and Nyoman, so we found out, were typical of many Balinese young couples, who tend to get married after the girl falls pregnant. Sometimes the couple may have been simply fooling around, not necessarily considering anything more serious. If a boy does get a girl pregnant, though, then it's his responsibility to marry her. A man might also want to test out the childbearing capabilities of a woman before agreeing to marry her. Because children are considered to be so important, many men will want to check first—and there's only one way to check that!

At this wedding, both bride and groom were wrapped in long strips of gold painted cloth—the same type of cloth that had been used to drape the household pillars, except much thinner—with their shoulders left bare. Made Sri's growing baby bulge was cleverly concealed by the gold cloth, which was wrapped around the upper part of her body so many times that if the material had been the traditional western colour of white, she would have looked like a well-bound Egyptian mummy.

The bride and the groom had the same heavy makeup on: plastered foundation as a base, a bright pink rouge buffing the cheeks, strong red lipstick, and dark kohl defining the eyes and the eyebrows in thick black lines—as well as a mark on her forehead between her eyes like the Hindu bindi. They wore intricate gold accessories and jewellery: elaborate neck pieces and belts, and tiara-like headpieces.

I eventually got close enough to the bride to be able to give my personal best wishes.

'Congratulations, Made. You look beautiful.'

'Thank you, Gaia. I can't believe I'm getting married.'

'It's incredible, isn't it. Marriage always is a shock to the system,' I reassured her. 'But it's nice to be able to move into the next phase of life.'

'I just don't know if I'm ready,' Made Sri suddenly confided. 'I came to my uncle's house in this village to find work only a few months ago, and look at me now. Married and with a baby on the way. I'm only twenty-three years old, Gaia. I thought I would have a much fuller life. I thought I would travel the world. I don't know how to look after a family.' Her eyes were ever so slightly teary. I couldn't bear to see her special day marred—and that heavy makeup become a mixed palette.

84

'But you're very good with people. And you're great with children. You'll be fine.' I squeezed her arm as inconspicuously as I could, and tried to cheer her up with some of my own optimism. I realised that it must have been daunting for her, but hoped that she would be supported by her family.

Somebody turned up with a camera. 'Smile!'

At that point Made managed to blink away the moisture in the corners of her eyes, and pull together a decent smile. She was soon swept away by the crowd, called on to fulfil her social obligations, but I noticed later that she had started looking a little more comfortable with the prospect of marriage. We made eye contact at some stage, and I could see a slight twinkle in her eye—perhaps a sign of resignation or acceptance, perhaps a flame still burning from that independent spirit—I've never been sure.

By night everyone was looking more relaxed, full and satisfied from the day's feasting. A few specialties had been eagerly received: the spicy finely chopped meats wrapped in banana leaves smoked over a fire—often turtle meat—or *babi guling*, roasted whole pig, cooked over a spit, and devoured along with coconut milk and palm sugar sweets, rice wine . . .

Apparently these weddings cost a bomb. Parents must save up for years for their children's weddings, and often other members of the family will have to pitch in to meet the expectations. At the lower end of the scale, the average cost of a wedding—$2,000 to $3,000—would take the average Balinese person about two years to earn. It's a huge amount for these families, equivalent to us spending between $60,000 to $100,000.

The religious ceremonies, with all the intricate rites and rituals of Balinese Hinduism, took the better part of the next day, before the newly married couple finally retreated to their married quarters—which was simply a separate bedroom in the husband's family compound.

Returning to our corner of the village, we reflected on the privilege of gaining such an intimate insight into our neighbours' lives, and sensed that our own fate had started to become entwined in the community. We were still very much on the edge, but becoming more and more aware of and affected by what was going on around us.

We reflected on our own wedding and marriage, too, as you often do when you go to someone else's wedding. Everything had been done the 'right' way according to our society's traditional values. We had been together for a long time before marrying. Then saved up our money for a long time before starting a family. Everything had been reasonably planned and controlled. In comparison, Made's start to married life was tougher, in many respects, but I knew that no matter how difficult the shock of marriage and parenting might be she would most likely always have the support of her community. This support would act as a safety net that many western couples just don't have, simply because we tend to live so separately from each other.

Made Sri took some time off for the wedding and the birth of the baby. We kept visiting her during that time, watching her belly grow, being there soon after the baby was born, and then enjoying seeing the baby develop. She wasn't able to return to live with us after that, but she remained a close friend. Quite a bit later when she was finally ready to go out and work part-time again, she took a job at the local kindergarten Zoe attended, and continued to be an important influence in our lives.

After her wedding we didn't talk about the way she had felt on that day. I could see that she had resigned herself to the fact that this was her destiny in life, and had made the most of her circumstances. Made must have come to terms with the fact that she was marrying into a whole family and would need to start becoming responsible to them. She quickly became the good wife and mother that many Balinese women become, and was promptly accepted into her husband's family community. I know that it may not have been her preferred choice in life, but I never again saw her looking weighed down by the circumstances. She simply readjusted her expectations and moved on.

It may sound like a harsh reality to us westerners, but I think there is a certain strength of character in people like Made Sri. Simply 'getting on with life' is definitely a strong Balinese trait—a trait I have seen in many women all around Asia. Made had learned to take her destiny as it had been laid out for her and adapt to it. Many women are in arranged marriages, others have no choice once they're pregnant. But they accept their lot. The community helps them through.

Sometimes I wonder if we have too much choice in relationships in our own society. There is deliberation over who and when to marry. Over whether or not to have children. Over when to have them and how many. Over whether to divorce or stick out the hard times. I think having so many options—and possible escape routes—can lead to disappointment and dissatisfaction. Instead of adapting to the way things become, we are taught to continue to fight for what we personally desire—even if it is at the expense of others. No-one should have to put up with destructive relationships, of course, but I do wonder whether having more realistic expectations and more of a commitment to the choices we make might help us to learn to adapt and progress more positively.

It was a challenge for Andrew and me personally, anyway, to always try to make the most of our relationship, no matter what we were going through. Though we were still enjoying the second honeymoon our life in Bali had given us, we knew that if and when circumstances changed and there was once more stress on our relationship, we would have to find a way ahead. Together.

Chapter 7

Living in (Almost) Perfect Harmony

With Made Sri married and gone, it didn't take long to feel the loss. We were all pining for that bright and friendly face. And, I must admit, we had quickly adapted to being able to share the childcare and the domestic workload with her. It had made a huge difference in our personal productivity—and sanity. Another of those situations where you don't realise how beneficial something can be until it becomes a part of your life—in our case quite unexpectedly.

Things just weren't the same without Made Sri. It's true, you don't really appreciate what you've got till it's gone. We began to think about finding someone else to fill the gap that had been left in our household. Just as we were deliberating over where to go for help and what to do, the answer came to us. Yet again, providence stepped in. It came to us in two different ways, in two different stages.

The first answer came when our friend Amelia was visiting one day. All her four children, aged between three and eight, were with her—we had been helping to tutor the older two and Zoe was friends with the younger two. As we sat and talked, we watched the children playing in the dirt on the driveway in front of our hut, kicking up dust and generally getting themselves quite grimy. I felt a tinge of embarrassment as I thought about how smart and sterile her children's regular play environment probably was. She lived in a hotel, and would have been more used to hotel luxuries and conveniences.

Perhaps she was thinking something similar, because the scene before us triggered off an idea in her mind. She suddenly announced that she would like to start up a playgroup for younger children so they would have a safe and positive communal environment to play in. It sounded like a great idea to me. When Made had been with us, Zoe had gone out with her to play with the village children, and she was now missing that regular social interaction. A more structured playgroup, I thought, might help to meet that need. It would ensure Zoe was happily and constructively occupied in a supervised environment while we worked, and would help to ease those domestic responsibilities we were once again having to deal with.

Amelia's idea then inspired me further. Why not use the space in the large house out the back of ours, I thought to myself? I jumped up enthusiastically and started to usher her outside, sure that I had come up with the perfect solution.

Her eyes lit up at first with the mention of the idea, but then I couldn't help but notice a distinct shadow of disappointment pass over her face as we emerged out the back. As soon as the back building came into view, I could tell she wasn't seeing what I was seeing. I saw an open, idyllic niche—she obviously saw a rundown half-built building and an overgrown garden. But I was not going to give up that easily, of course. Now fuelled by the prospect, I tried to talk Amelia through the possibilities. By cutting back the garden and planting some fresh grass, by painting the walls and tiling the rough concrete sections of flooring—surely it would only take a little work and a small investment to improve the space? Some bright material inside here, some paving stones outside there—it wouldn't take much, I argued . . . Yes, she eventually agreed, the space itself was good, and such a beautiful peaceful environment for children to be playing in, but she was going to have to think about it.

It was only a few days later, however, that Amelia came back to me. She had decided that she wanted to go ahead and she had worked out how it would be possible—she even had a proposed budget and a development plan. Just what I wanted to hear! Someone who could help shape the next phase of my dream! After negotiating the details with the owner, with whom we had now developed a good relationship, and making the necessary changes to the garden and the building, we soon had a wonderful solution to our need.

The playgroup became a fantastic community project, where children and parents of all nationalities could gather. We would hear the happy chatter of people coming and going each morning, and could step outside our house to catch people as they passed on their way through the large carved wooden gates. From the second floor of our house, where our office was set up, we could simply look out the back window to see how Zoe was going at any time, enjoying the delightful sounds of laughter and creative play. We couldn't have planned it better if we'd thought of it ourselves!

Amelia renovated one small room at the back of the property for a playgroup assistant and her caretaker husband to live in. As soon as Heni and Santo moved in and started sharing our compound, they automatically became part of our new extended family. They had a child who happened to be only a few weeks older than Zoe, so there was always a playmate right on site at any time. When playgroup wasn't on, the two children had the run of the property, and all those wonderful toys to play with.

We now had a great little compound community of our own.

Our second answer came one day when playgroup had finished up for the morning and Andrew and I were rushing around out the back trying to get the clothes hung out before a meeting. The children were busily playing together, and Heni was sitting beside them, commenting loudly when some sort of intervention was required. Heni turned to see what we were fussing about. She only needed to watch us running about like headless chooks for a few moments to appreciate what was going on. Then and there she came up with a great solution. As she was only working half a day with the playgroup, she explained, she would be willing and available to take on more work. She could not go outside to work because of her child, so we could help her out by giving her part-time work in our house—which would obviously also greatly help us. A wonderful win-win prospect. We were so delighted to be able to maximise the resources of our new community compound.

It was a great idea and it worked really well for the first few weeks, but then things changed, as they often do. Perhaps we should have anticipated that it would not stop there. It was too nice a setup to last forever. Heni approached us only a few weeks after she started working with us, saying that she had a friend from her home town in Java who really needed work. This other lady could help look after the children, and help in the house also.

Two household staff! For a family of three living in a tiny three-roomed hut! It was beginning to feel pretty over the top once again. But we knew. This was the way it was done. You employ one extended family member, and you could potentially end up employing them all. We couldn't say no.

The young friend arrived three days later—just enough time to pack up her small bag of belongings, say her goodbyes, and take the long bus trip. We had paid her way from Java, and she rang us from the bus stop, her voice barely audible and her words unclear because of her nervousness and total lack of English. Although Heni had been working with foreigners for a while, her friend—Nancy—was just out of school and pretty much fresh off working in the rice paddies, so far as I could tell. She was young and inex-perienced, but she was incredibly tough, and a fast learner. So much so that she soon had the whole house under her control.

Before long Nancy had set some strict household rules and reg-ulations, and had us anxiously obeying her every command. She had an incredible drive for perfection in cleaning, and we were quickly admonished for any breaches of her rigid standards. We wondered what ever had happened to the quiet little local girl from the backwaters of Java! No dirt to be walked into the house. No clothes to be left on the floor. The fridge door must always be shut. Sheets were not to be used to make kids' cubby houses. We may have been limited by language barriers, but there was no misun-derstanding her instructions. The slightest infringements became punishable by thunderous glares. We came to refer to Nancy as the boss of the house. It didn't matter who was paying and who was receiving the monthly salary. She was definitely the boss.

There were times when she was so angry and moody about our occasional lapses into sloppiness that it became uncomfortable for us to be living in our own house. At those times we all tiptoed around the place, fearful of falling victim to her temper. But then we learnt a new technique. We learnt to laugh about the situation, and to make her laugh with us.

'Are you *uring-uringan* today?' I would ask (using the east Javanese dialect term for 'cranky'), and I would imitate her angry response to my misdemeanor. Or I would respond like a grovelling servant to her barking commands. 'Sorry, boss. So sorry, boss,' I would plead—laughing at the absurdity of it all and encouraging her to laugh with me. She would often be in fits of laughter with us by the end of the charade. Nancy really was a lovely, lively individual underneath that sharp exterior.

However, not only did she dominate in our household, but Nancy also started to create havoc in the neighbourhood. She got to know a fair few others in the area—mainly other young Javanese job seekers, and mainly male, so it seemed. Screeching off on the back of some young man's motorbike after finishing her work, she would sometimes return late at night and wake us with her raucous cackling at the gate, obviously revelling in her newfound freedom.

Heni was not at all impressed. She had provided this working opportunity for her shy friend from Java, and her friend had ended up running the show. Heni was the older and more settled of the two (by only a year or two)—with husband and child and all—so she became the surrogate mother, telling Nancy off for her wild and domineering behaviour. Obviously unfitting for a young Javanese girl. They started to argue about everything. They disagreed over appropriate dress, appropriate behaviour, appropriate company to keep, and appropriate household working arrangements and manners.

Although we had now learnt to cope with the moods—after all, she was incredibly thorough in her work and did keep the house at a high standard of cleanliness—the relationship between the two women continued to deteriorate. After a long period of them not talking to each other—only talking about each other to us, and slinging the occasional rude comment in hearing distance of the other—we knew the stormy household scenario would have to change. At that time the conflict shifted to an even more serious level. It became an either-she-goes-or-I-go stalemate, which put us in a difficult situation. As much as we never could have imagined we'd need two ladies, we had become reliant on them both—and they were both special to us in different ways. Even though they really had become a part of our growing extended family household, it just wasn't going to work out between them.

Nancy was the newcomer to the scene, so we explained to her that unless the rift could be mended, we would need to find another suitable position for her. Unfortunately the girls were never able to patch things up so we recommended her to some friends, giving her a last-minute pep talk on mood management, and wished her luck. Nancy lasted three weeks in her new job. Great housekeeper, our friends told us, but too moody. Such a shame.

Soon after that Nancy fell pregnant to one of the boys she had been seeing, married the father of the child, and moved back to Java. She had come and gone from our house so quickly, but not without showing us something important. Below the calm surface of any household, we realised, there can always be disagreements and differences of opinion, no matter how controlled the social circumstances. I think some Javanese may be a little more strong willed and fiery tempered than the Balinese, who tend to have a fairly relaxed and peaceful approach to life, but every so often we'd see similar conflict in the local communities. The dense social structures can help deal with conflict, but they can also create tension as well.

There are always two sides to a coin.

Of course it's not just people who make up the Indonesian village landscape. We didn't only need to learn to live with our extended

family household and human neighbours—there were numerous
varieties of local animals to contend with as well. No Indonesian
village household is complete, we discovered, without its fair share
of animal occupants, great and small.

The open-style housing of the Balinese literally invites in a large
range of animal friends, and animals living alongside people help
to create the wonderful communal village atmosphere. Our own
house quickly became a sort of free-range reserve for many.

Some of the surprise animal visitors we had in the beginning
ranged from geckos up to thirty centimetres long, to bats, rodents,
snakes and spiders . . . I could go on. The largest and most memorable of these visitors was the occasional village cow, that might
simply saunter up to our 'front door' to say hello, sometimes even
stick its nose inside our house and help itself to one of our indoor
plants—obviously a special delicacy.

The smaller of these animal intruders were often the most difficult to deal with, though. We had to learn to live with the mosquitoes, for starters. Luckily there was no malaria in Bali. (A friend
who lived for thirteen years in some of Indonesia's eastern islands
with her four children had to learn to predict the regular
onslaughts of malaria and try to combat it with a papaya leaf concoction in the same way that we try to combat regular colds with
vitamin C.) The mosquitoes themselves are a damned nuisance,
though, and another mosquito-borne disease—dengue fever—was
a problem.

Just as vicious in the insect department were the local ant varieties. There is a miniscule, barely visible, brown critter that can
easily creep up your legs unnoticed before the army general gives the
order to attack. You could be admiring the tropical flowers in the
garden one minute and cursing the tropical bugs the next, jumping
up and down and scratching yourself furiously. At the other extreme
is a huge red ant variety—just as vicious, but these little buggers
seem to prefer to drop down from the trees in surprise attacks.

Other drop attacks came from the geckos, the local lizards with
suctioned footpads that specialise in weird and wonderful 'ge-cko'
calls. Two huge geckos once landed on my head when I was in the
middle of the act of brushing my hair, plastering themselves firmly

on my face before I was able to shake them off. Perhaps the most scary drop attack I have heard of, though, was when a friend reported a visit from a cobra in her lovely fashionable open-air bathroom. I am not easily scared off, coming from the land of the greatest number of lethal animals in the world, but I must say the thought of a cobra drop while showering does rather send a shiver up my spine. We have had snakes in the garden, dropping from the bamboo and slithering through the grass—even a couple of cobras hiding in our living areas—and that was freaky enough.

More domesticated varieties of household visitors have also, like the local cows, often dropped in unexpectedly. Nancy had once brought a whole family of chickens back from Java on a bus after visiting her family *kampung*. Unfortunately these animals went missing one by one, and we're still not sure to this day whether they were kidnapped, went walkabout, or were eaten.

We did reach the point, at some stage along the way, where we were ready for a more permanent pet, and Andrew came up with the idea of getting a guard dog. Next thing I knew he'd turned up with a tiny little mixed mutt he'd found on the beach—a puppy barely six weeks old. Guard dog? I wasn't so sure about this strategy myself. Bali must have among the most extensive and most pathetic-looking stray dog populations of anywhere in the world, so you can imagine how thrilled I was at the prospect of having to share our living room with one of these scraggy specimens.

Zoe chose the name GC for the puppy (which stood for Girl Charlton—don't ask me what it actually meant!). She was cute—and she became a great guard dog as she grew up—but it would have been so much better if she had been able to distinguish between friend and foe. Small children, Zoe included, were soon terrified to walk around our home, and eventually GC had to be banished to her own quarters in one of the other abandoned houses on the property. She met a tragic end one day, however, after escaping and being hit by a car, and so the search for the best domestic pet began again.

Along came GC No.2 (Zoe insisted on giving him the same name, even though Girl Charlton No.2 was a boy). He was also found on the beach by Andrew. I couldn't believe it! Both GCs actually had lovely temperaments, but their bite was as bad as their bark. GC No.2 threatened any other potential pets, and a fluffy white rabbit rescued from a busy road by one of our staff lasted only a few weeks before being crushed to death in GC No.2's jaws.

One day three kittens were literally dropped into our house by a neighbouring cat and left with us when they were only a day or two old. After they recovered from the initial shock of such a cruel introduction to the world, the kittens took over the house, jumping around fearlessly and hiding in every little nook and cranny. GC No.2 thought they were live toys, and happily chased after them wherever they went. They did survive, but the kittens were eventually abandoned at an unknown location in the local village by Nancy, who apparently interpreted my instructions to 'help find some good homes for the kittens', as 'choose a random house somewhere in the neighbourhood and drop them outside'. I know my Indonesian's not crash hot, but I actually suspect that she was only too pleased to have an excuse to get the kittens out of her underwear drawer!

There was a fish that lasted one night—who knows what that animal died of (although we're fairly certain in this case that GC was not responsible!)—and another tiny baby chicken that was accidentally mauled by a child. Of all those animals, only GC No.2 survived more than a few weeks, and he was the hardest to handle!

Of course we'd still get plenty of those surprise drop-in visits from a range of local animals—no Balinese village household would be complete without them—but we tried to ensure that it was the humans who had the balance of power in the house.

We certainly learnt something about the sensible Balinese approach to dealing with animals, though. Simply learning to live happily alongside them. Probably a good way to foster harmonious relationships with all creatures.

Ibu Gendeg walked her cow towards our front door. She led the large brown animal to the tap at the far side of our hut, and gave it a drink. She then sauntered up to us and showed us her wares.

Ibu had a few brooms for sale. The brooms here are not the

same variety we'd have used in Sydney. They are basically a collection of long, thin sticks (actually large, dried leaf veins), bound together at the top with string. There is no handle, so the sweeper has to bend over—one hand tucked up behind the back, one hand in action. We bought the few she had, as we always did. We had a large collection of them ready for emergencies (though I'm not really sure what sort of emergency requires twenty brooms!). At other times she'd bring a young coconut (it was only possible for her to carry one of those at a time), or some bananas.

We chatted about the price of fruit in the markets, we chatted about her grandchildren. She shared with us her concerns about her cow's health, and how she felt old age was catching up with her. While we chatted, the cow nibbled on the potplant just inside the front of the house and Zoe tried desperately to shoo it away.

Ibu's face cracked up as she chuckled at the sight of a little girl trying to control a cow. She swept her up into her arms and talked nonstop to her. Zoe could not understand what she was saying, but her lyrical tone and incessant smile were all that needed to be communicated. Ibu then walked off with Zoe, pulling the cow behind her, taking them both to see the sights of the village.

I was so touched by the moment, by the natural and loving way Ibu had picked up Zoe as if she was one of her own grandchildren. Something deep inside me melted, and I was overcome with feelings of both pride and humility. It deepened the sense of this village as being a good place to make a home.

The Balinese love children, and give them so much special attention and care. Even outsiders' children are accepted and welcomed into the community in such a giving way. I was so grateful for that.

I have heard it said that it takes a village to bring up a child. It certainly took a village to begin to transform our modern, stressed-out family.

Chapter 8

Cultural Nomads

Nearing the end of our experimental year, we decided it was time to explore the island more. It might have been a 'let's take a trip around the island just in case we don't end up staying' decision—but it also might have been an 'if we are staying then we should get to know the place better' resolution. Or perhaps it was just a great opportunity to make another escape and put off the decision for a short while longer.

We had begun weighing up our options. Should we stay, or should we go back to Australia? Were we being totally irresponsible by trying to opt out of society, or were we simply creating a positive, alternative lifestyle for ourselves? We had let time slip by, enjoying the chance just to live in the moment and make the most of our freedom. It was time to think about taking some responsibility again, time—soon—for decisions.

I think my mind was already made up. I wanted to stay, and I hoped Andrew would want to stay too, of his own accord. I thought he was probably ready to make that decision with me, but I was also sure that some time away together, totally immersing ourselves in the therapeutic countryside, wouldn't hurt either. Whatever the outcome, the island circumnavigation we planned would be the perfect opportunity to reflect on what we had been through together, for thinking about where we had come from and where we were going, as we absorbed the beauty of the unfolding green, the magic of the unwinding rural scenes.

The need to explore was still within me, too, and I embraced the chance to discover more about the place where we had set up a home. Andrew didn't seem to be concerned about my adventurous spirit this time around; I guess he could sense my newfound contentment and inner security. I was no longer the ever-searching traveller with an insatiable appetite, never satisfied until the next destination is reached, never content until all experiences have been experienced. And interestingly enough, it was becoming apparent to me that Andrew's own adventurous spirit had been reawakened. He had taken the huge leap with me into the unknown, and we had landed on our feet. We had given ourselves the chance to enjoy the freedom we had enjoyed as young teenage lovers. I had the feeling that Andrew, like me, was ready to continue that wonderful rediscovery process.

As we prepared for this trip we both became excited about the prospect of getting a broader, deeper feel for the way the island is and always has been. We knew we'd also get a glimpse of what it might become. Past travels in Bali had been very limited—one tourist spot to the next, only in restricted slots of time—but on this occasion we were going to take our time and drink it all in.

The first step for the journey was strapping Zoe into the car—a normal experience for any western family, but a totally alien practice to Indonesians (who don't use seatbelts at all). A group of local villagers who were visiting the temple in front of our house watched in apparent awe as we loaded up the car and I firmly tied Zoe into her special child car seat. The seat was then lashed to the frame of the car in a makeshift manner. I imagined my Balinese companions were marvelling at the wonders of modern technology, at how safe and secure we were able to keep our child, but as we were about to leave I discovered that it was a totally wrong assumption to make. The look I had interpreted as admiration was in fact one of horror.

'How could you entrust your children to bits of metal and plastic?' One elderly woman exclaimed as we were just about ready to make our getaway. 'Children need to be in their parents' arms!'

She was right. I would much rather have held Zoe in my arms, but safety consciousness was the overriding issue in these situations. I thought she wasn't going to let us go until we had released Zoe from her straitjacket. She continued to watch in horror, flabbergasted at our thoughtlessness, as we confidently drove away, the others in the group left laughing and chattering at the scenario. I'm sure our curious foreign family gave the villagers plenty to talk about in our absence.

We were travelling in style. Our getaway vehicle was the old VW Safari, the basic box on wheels with a soft convertible cover and no windows, completely rusted up and falling apart. It moved at a snail's pace, and regularly had to be pushed up hills, but it would have been criminal to try to see Bali at any other speed.

It was a cheap deal, and a marginally safer alternative to a motorbike. Having done the motorbike thing when in Bali five years before, there was no way I was going to go anywhere near one again. I've got a large ugly scar on my heel as evidence that trying to negotiate those contraptions on the crazy Bali roads is downright dangerous. Being stitched up in some dirty backyard surgery by a half-blind doctor who needed assistance with finding the wound, and later watching the wound fester in the humid climate . . . I can think of less risky ways of having fun.

The Safari had an ancient instrument panel. Even the speed dial (and kilometre gauge), the only dial on the dashboard, had seized up. As for a petrol gauge? None in sight. Which meant that we constantly and unexpectedly ran out of petrol. Luckily, the countryside is dotted with small roadside *warungs* that sell petrol in glass jars for motorbikes (and the occasional stranded Safari). We found we could usually walk to the nearest *warung*—or hitch a ride around the corner—to pick up enough petrol to get us to the next petrol station.

Running out of petrol became such a regular experience that almost three-year-old Zoe assumed that it must be a pretty standard thing. So much so that shortly after our countryside tour, when in an aeroplane, which suddenly slowed down and came to a halt just prior to take-off, Zoe exclaimed 'Oh dear, we've run out of petrol again.' She looked back down the runway to the main airport terminal. 'I hope there's a petrol stall here somewhere!'

100

It may have been a primitive way to travel, but the open-air design of the car made it quite a fun way to see and experience everything, sights and smells. It did also put us on show a bit, though. Just as we were busy staring out at what was strange and new, there were many people interested in checking out the strange aliens inside the unusual contraption, especially the white-skinned, white-haired little one in the back. Although Bali may well and truly have been saturated with tourism by the time we made this trip, our choice of out of the way backroads made us more of a novelty. Outside of the major tourist centres, we discovered, life had a whole different shade and tempo. We were definitely out of place in those areas.

Of course Zoe did all she could to draw attention to us. Totally oblivious to the stares and snickers of passing motorcyclists and pedestrians at intersections, she would fill the air with semi-melodious song. Her own compositions. Commentaries on travel-ling and life in general. Sung at top volume.

I luv go'in in the car
Wid my mummeee
And my daddeee
And I see the doggeee
And the roosta
And the roosta is lowd
And the car is lowd
And I smell the treeeees
And I s-i-i-i-i-ng
Cause I love my cuzins
And they are in Auscheleeea
And I'n in Baaali
But I will go on the plane to Auscheleeea . . .

And so the song continued, ad infinitum. Great entertainment for the world at large, and it did help to pass the longer stretches of driving.

Despite the dubiously tuneful soundtrack, the lively colours of rural village life in the centre of the island became a fascinating cinematic experience. Scene by scene, sometimes frame by frame, we found ourselves witnessing the unfolding of a Balinese drama depicting life at the end of the twentieth century:

. . . Patches of fluorescent green rice paddies with rigid mud walls. Skinny farmhands with bamboo hats threshing out the last of the grain. Golden cornfields. A tinkling streetcart selling *bakso* fishball soup. A few customers squatting by the road devouring the soup hungrily. Some youngsters with bleached hair lounging in a roadside bamboo hut, grooving to rock music, making sly comments as the girls saunter by . . .

. . . A group of topless women bathing in a roadside drain, laughing and shouting, twisting long locks of glistening black hair behind their backs. A little further along, some men washing a car in the drain, dressed only in their white y-front undies. A handful of muddy ducks making rainbows as they splash the drainwater up in the air . . .

. . . A young couple riding by on their Suzuki motorcycle. Both in traditional ceremonial gear. The guy with the latest surfing sunglasses. The girl with the latest trend in makeup and accessories. She is daintily perched on the back of the motorcycle, riding side-saddle. She is also performing the not inconsiderable feat of carrying a basket of ceremonial fruits and cakes on her head. They stop at the traffic lights. The young man pulls out his mobile phone to make a quick call . . .

The images were strange blends of opposites. This was a land that had been forgotten by time, but was simultaneously very much up with the times. Sleepy volcanoes towered over misty clouds and commanded respect from the island's centre, as if warning the constant stream of descending air passengers to pay homage to the ancient spirits guarding the island. Lush jungle patchworked with the ancient rice paddies, while clean paved streets weaved their way down to thriving contemporary commercial precincts.

This was a place, we now well and truly discovered, where the people worshipped the spirits of the earth, land and sea—as well as showing great faith in modern technology. You could join a remote village for a traditional *wayang* puppet play, or catch the blockbuster movies in modern cinemas with luxurious velvet seats and Dolby Surroundsound. You could witness the local magic of the highly revered *balian* priests, as they went into trances and delivered the weak and the sick from demons—or you could gain access to modern medical equipment.

It was still possible to sample the sorts of delicacies that the Balinese had enjoyed for many generations at any number of ceremonial occasions throughout the year—such as the delicately spiced *sate lilit* made of turtle meat, or *arak* rice wine—or choose from the best (and worst) of western-style dishes. En route out of Kuta I had spotted several McDonald's restaurants—including the latest drive-through version—along with Dunkin' Donuts, Baskin Robbins and Pizza Hut. But surprisingly I discovered that Bali was also home to some of the best chefs in the world, who offered first-class dining experiences from a range of international cuisines.

All aspects of life appeared to combine ancient traditions and modern practices, and this intriguing blend of old and new was what had made Bali so unique and so fascinating, worldwide. Bali had not left behind the important traditions that had shaped its culture, but had also been open to change. The people had not forgotten where they had come from, but they were also very conscious of where they were going.

I could see that this idea of the need for balance was so much a part of the religion, and so much a part of the way of life. The *sekala* and *niskala*, the seen and unseen forces, helped to define the island as a place where all things could be experienced from all perspectives.

We were now more conscious than ever of where we had come from and where we were going. Of the forces that had shaped our lives. The positive and the negative. The good and the bad. Of the need for continuing balance in our own lives.

As we navigated towards the centre of the island, we began to sense the heart of Bali. We could feel the pulse. The road climbed up a steep ridge, bordered by the distinctly carved mud walls of vibrant rice terraces. As the road levelled out again, it divided into two branches.

'Which road do we take?' asked Andrew, who was driving at the time.

'I have no idea!' I replied, snapping back into consciousness. I had become so mesmerised by the brilliant scenery that I had lost track of time and place. Zoe was asleep in the back, and the humming engine and calming visual images had put me in a trance.

Andrew pulled over to the side of the road and I opened the guidebook to examine the map at the front.

'So, where are we?' Andrew peered over my arm to get a look at the map.

'I haven't been paying attention,' I admitted. 'What was the last village we passed through?'

'You're the one directing us at the moment. You should be on the ball. You should know,' Andrew scolded, obviously a little amused and a little annoyed at the same time.

'You're the one driving. Heaven help us if you're not paying attention!' I responded. 'Anyway, it doesn't really matter where we are, does it? We're here to enjoy the journey, to immerse ourselves in the experience. Whatever road we choose to take I'm sure it will take us somewhere interesting.'

We had been cruising along, following a reasonably sized road for a good half-hour or so. Every so often we had ducked off to check out interesting little detours, but I thought we had returned to the same road each time. As I could see no fork in the road on the map, I now wondered if we had inadvertently gone off on another tangent while exploring.

I had a quick look around. There was no-one in sight, no-one we could ask directions from. Unusual. The island is so densely populated that although it doesn't look crowded, there is almost always somebody somewhere. It felt eerily quiet.

The map gave away no clues either. The heavily rippled contour lines and numerous winding road markings and river tributaries were cryptic. I knew we were somewhere in the north-east mountains, but was unsure precisely where. I could recognise the major names on the map: Tampaksiring, where there is a temple with holy springs said to be flowing with an elixir of youth; Besakih, with an enormous temple complex—the mother temple of all

Bali—reaching up the side of Mount Agung volcano; Tirtagganga with its elaborate water palace; Sideman, famous as a place of quiet retreat for European artists. I could recognise the region, but not the precise location. At this point the best way ahead was no longer clear.

Grabbing a coin from the dashboard, I flipped it and asked, 'Heads or tails?'

Andrew cocked his head and raised an eyebrow, then looked back at the fork ahead. 'Tails,' he said.

I had the coin resting on the back of one hand by this time, the other hand covering it. When I checked how the coin had landed I had no idea which side was the head and which was the tail—both sides had pictures of birds on them, an eagle on one side and a cockatoo on the other.

'Well, it's birds or birds!' I concluded.

We laughed for no real reason, the way you sometimes do when the sublime becomes the ridiculous and you'll crack up at anything.

'Well, let's pull out the full-sized map, then, and see what we can make out from it,' I said when I could catch my breath again, when we had calmed.

I reached down to the pocket in the side of the car door to pull out the super duper large map we had bought at a petrol station on the way. After I had unfolded it carefully, it almost filled the whole front of the car. We looked at the expanse of land represented diagrammatically, and it immediately struck me what a range of different characters the island held in such a compact area.

After travelling up from the isthmus at the bottom, where the land can be quite dry and arid, there had been a dramatic transition to greener plains and then lushly vegetated hills. 'I remember reading something about that,' I told Andrew. 'It's quite interesting. We should just have a look at the guidebook.'

Andrew glanced at his watch—perhaps out of habit, as the next minute he looked at me with a wry smile and proclaimed that, of course, we had no deadlines, no schedule to keep to! Yes, I agreed, we should just continue to relax and enjoy the exploring as a learning experience. He turned off the car engine and opened the guidebook, reading out relevant bits of information as we studied the map in more detail.

The book told us there is a distinct geographical line—known as the Wallace line—that lies across the section of Bali that we had just come from, cutting off the southern tip of the island (metaphorically) and grouping it with the islands to the east, which show more Australian and New Guinean influence. Even though Bali is only 5,000 square kilometres in all, we went on to read, it encompasses a whole range of different environments. That had already become obvious to us in our journey north. We had passed, in turn: seaweed farms and water-logged mangrove swamps at the ocean; coconut groves and cow paddocks over the plains; cultivated rice fields from the plains towards the mountains; then contrasting patches of crop growth; and finally tropical rainforests as we climbed ever higher.

We had wondered about the dark, fertile soil that produced the wild sea of green we now saw before us, but we only had to lift our eyes to be reminded that the volcanic mountains in the island's centre had enriched the land with volcanic ash. The map showed a whole string of these active volcanoes dominating the central region, the alluvial slopes spilling down to the coastal plains. The rice paddies were also well watered, I knew, by an intricate irrigation system leading from the mountains down to the plains.

'It all makes sense, now!' I exclaimed, reminded of a nagging question I had had about why the culture in Bali was so complex. 'The rich landscape has produced a rich culture. These people have the time to explore the arts, and have the inspiration from their fabulous environment. No wonder their spirituality is so intricate and they're so devoted to their religion. I guess many other cultures need to focus on survival.'

I turned the map over out of curiosity, the whole interior of the car absorbed in the rustling movement, and on the other side the island of Bali was shown in context with the 13,700-plus other Indonesian islands. I knew that Bali was the only Hindu island out of all of them. A small dot in the ocean, but significant.

We represented but a microscopic speck on that page, but we felt like we were in a place of incredible importance.

At that moment a duck herder emerged from the fields on the left fork and started to cross the road. His herd of squabbling ducks crossed with him, chattering and squawking as they went, waddling along in unison. We were brought back to the moment.

'How about we go and ask that man for directions,' Andrew suggested as he started up the engine and put the car into first gear.

It sounded like a sensible idea, but as soon as we got to the place where the man had crossed the road, he and his ducks had already disappeared down one of the small tracks between the paddies.

'Never mind. We're on the left fork now. It leads further into the mountains, by the looks of it, so it should be worth exploring.'

And so we continued on.

'Are we there yet?' a little voice piped up from the back seat.

When you explore an island with no particular destination in mind you are free to follow the wind. You can allow yourself to be drawn into any experiences that cross your path, to make decisions on a whim. But almost-three-year-olds are often inclined to believe that there should be a start and a finish to a journey.

'We're just enjoying the beautiful scenery, darling. There—did you see that cow eating the flowers? Oh—and there's a man at the top of a coconut tree—he's going to cut the coconuts down with the big knife so his family can drink the coconut milk and eat the yummy coconut meat.'

'But I'm hungry, Mummy.'

Kids can be pretty easily distracted most of the time, and we did want this to be a wonderful educational experience for her, but it eventually gets to the point where you need to stop and get out of the car if you want to really enjoy the experience. We looked for somewhere to stop and take a break. Fortunately, there were plenty of choices.

Back in Australia, travelling from one part of the island to another had meant jumping on massive freeways dotted sparsely with institutionalised petrol station cafe stops. In Bali all countryside travel was on small roads, and was low key. There were literally thousands of tiny roadside *warung* stalls—the small bamboo huts offering a few basic snacks and drinks for sale.

'I really am hungry, Mum; I want something to eat!' Zoe wasn't going to give up.

'Okay, then, we'll stop and buy some food.'

At the next *warung* we came to, the owners were sitting on a bench at the front of the stall, apparently content to watch the occasional passing car, while their small child played in the dirt. The man was without a shirt, and it was difficult not to notice his taut chest, the scorched brown skin stretched thinly over his protruding ribs. The lady wore a loose cotton shirt and an old faded sarong hanging limply from her fragile frame.

As we slowed to a stop I had a quick look at Andrew, who also had his shirt off. The air was hot and sticky, and without airconditioning it was the most comfortable way for him to travel. Somehow, though, it felt inappropriate. Andrew is by no means fat, but I was worried that those few extra kilos of white paunch sitting around his waist might seem like an insult to these people.

'Here, put your shirt on. You need to cover up your gut.'

'What's wrong with my gut? Everyone goes without a shirt here. What's the big deal? Even the guy in the *warung* doesn't have one on. Chill out.' Andrew's hand was already on the door handle, ready to get out.

I desperately called him back, 'Andrew, he obviously works very hard in the fields and has very little money. Look at how thin they all are. Please, it's embarrassing that we're so well off and can eat so much.'

'But it's so hot. I can't bear wearing a shirt. I'm swimming in sweat. Come on, they wouldn't even notice something like that.'

A bit more pleading and the shirt was put on, reluctantly— although still unbuttoned at the front. Oh well, that's what marriage is all about, isn't it? Compromise.

Perhaps I was being over-sensitive, but I knew exactly how we would be perceived by these people. In the western world, the ideal image is to be muscular, thin and brown. If you are successful, you are in control of your life. That means you can control what you eat, and have plenty of time for exercising and plenty of money for doing it in gyms—where your muscle development can be carefully sculpted. You also have lots of leisure time to soak up the sun, while you're sitting on your yacht, or at least at the beach or by your private pool.

In Indonesia, as in the rest of Asia, the ideal is to be pale-skinned and overweight. Pale-skinned, because white skin has for a long time represented the wealth of foreigners, and it also means that you are well-off enough to avoid working in the fields or walking around in the sun. Overweight, because it indicates you are not working hard physically and you have lots of money to spend on rich, fatty foods. I still get a shock when I see the round pale-skinned models cheerily advertising superfluous products on the TV or in magazines here. Rich Indonesian kids are often overfed, their servants running around after them shovelling in as much food as they can. Cakes, sweets and soggy fried foods can feature heavily in their diet. Probably the most popular beauty products currently on the market are skin whitening creams.

While we're busy trying to get brown in the sun or resorting to fake tan creams and solar salons, the other half of the world is desperately trying to whiten their skin. The more we try to push our bodies physically in an attempt to whack them back into super-slim shape, the more others are dreaming of being able to rest, relax and eat enough to add a bit of gristle to their bony frames.

I was contemplating the unfairness of it all as we approached the *warung* and greeted the stall owners.

'Selamat sore Ibu dan Bapak.'

'Ya, selamat sore.'

'What would you like, sweetie?' I asked Zoe.

She looked overheated and sweaty, but enthused by the prospect of open choice at the *warung*. She eyed the dusty rows of jars with little sweets and peanut packets in them, the baskets of fruit at the front, the sacks of rice and corn by the side, and then eventually looked up to the brightly coloured chip packets hanging from a hook. Finally, she pointed a sticky finger to the brightest of all the packets, the one that looked like it had the least nutritional value. Oh well, that's the idea of a treat.

'How much are the Chitos?'

'One thousand rupiah,' came the weary reply.

'What? One thousand rupiah? You can't be serious! We never pay more than five hundred rupiah for these sorts of snacks. Come on, I'll pay what I usually pay. Five hundred only.'

'It's one thousand rupiah.'

'Hold on, maybe that's what the tourists pay, but I'm not a tourist. I'm living here in Bali. I know what the regular prices are.' I pulled out a five hundred coin, and offered it to the lady, speaking the Indonesian language, of course, to give the impression that I was virtually an Indonesian native. 'Here you go, here's the five hundred I usually pay.'

The lady barely moved a muscle. She looked at the coin in my hand, then slowly moved her gaze up to my face.

'I think you are rich. I think you eat well,' she said, emphasising the point with a gesture at Andrew's stomach.

I cast Andrew a quick, harsh see-I-told-you-so . . . how-could-you-ignore-me-and-trivialise-the-issue . . . I'm-always-right look. He knew that look well. He'd seen it plenty of times before. It must be pretty annoying to have a wife who thinks she's always right.

'An extra five hundred rupiah is not so much to pay.' The lady was stuboorn.

Andrew glared back at me. 'She's right, what's it to us? Just give her the extra five hundred rupiah, for goodness sake. Don't make something out of nothing.'

Time for a reality check. He was right. Five hundred rupiah (about ten cents) was just not a huge amount. In fact, it was nothing to us, while to these people it could mean the difference between being able to afford their next meal or not. Sometimes you're so busy focusing on the principle that you get everything out of perspective. I was being the obscenely stubborn one. Wasn't I the one originally worried about flaunting our comparative wealth?

I was instantly ashamed, and dug deep into my purse.

'Okay, here's the extra five hundred. And we might have some Sprite as well.' I decided I should try to make amends. 'I wouldn't want my husband's stomach to shrink too much from starvation.'

(I thought it was a clever way of trying to turn the situation around, but woe betide Andrew if he ever tried to make the same sort of joke about the state of my stomach in front of others! That right is strictly one-way!)

The woman stared at me for a good few seconds more, and then she started to chuckle and mutter under her breath as she turned to reach for the Sprite bottles. I couldn't understand what she was saying, she was speaking the Balinese dialect, but I could easily tell by the way she was saying it that it was something to do with the tourist's insolence and pettiness. Her husband's face softened too, and he looked at us as if we were cheeky children.

'Chubby baby, too,' the lady said.

She no doubt thought she was complimenting us on how healthy the child looked, but I suddenly started worrying about whether my daughter might be carrying around too much extra weight, whether I should try to change her eating habits.

'How old is your daughter?' asked the lady.

'Almost three years old.'

'Ohhh!' That was the most expression I'd seen on the woman's face the whole time we'd been there. She bantered excitedly in Balinese to her husband, and he too nodded and exclaimed.

'Very big, your child. My child already more than three years old, but only half the size of your child!'

I turned my attention to the little girl forming large circles in the dirt. She was a tiny thing, her arms and legs almost as thin as the brittle stick she was using to trace the shapes. My daughter ate chips while she stood next to her, interested in the other child's drawing. Zoe did look about twice the size.

'My child is just like her father,' I said, 'very big and strong. I feed her up so one day soon she will be the one looking after me!'

That was it, we'd broken the ice. The couple thought that was hilarious, probably for a few reasons. They would have thought it was funny that I was still poking fun at my husband—the Balinese enjoy that sort of slapstick humour—but there was another, deeper reason it was funny. In Bali, a boy child is prized much more highly than a girl child, because the son would stay in the family home and help to bring income in for the family, eventually providing for

111

his parents. I was breaking the taboos a little by daring to suggest that my daughter might be the one to care for me, that she was valued as a first child.

The thought had obviously crossed their minds, as the man finally spoke up, 'I don't have a son to take care of me when I get old. Perhaps you can tell me what the secret of fattening up your child is so my daughter can also be the strong one in the family.'

Sitting ourselves down on the bench beside this man, we too started to watch the world go by, and we shared our different life experiences. The children interacted on a silent level, the way children often do when they're not inhibited by social expectations. Even language is not a barrier for children.

Time began to evaporate and lose its meaning.

'Hey,' Andrew said, when he could see the day slipping away in front of our eyes, 'we need to think about where we're going to sleep tonight.'

Our shadows were stretching across the road, interrupted only by the occasional passing car or motorbike. The volcanic mountains lifting from the paddies on the other side of the road had turned a burnished bronze, and were fading away into the late afternoon mist.

'You come to my friend's house. She has a special room for tourists. You will be very happy there,' the lady said.

It was a statement of fact, not a suggestion or even a request. We had shared so much in the short space of time we had spent together—talking about our cultures and customs, our friends and families, our different ways of life—that she was now treating us like long-lost friends who must be taken care of. Oh well, that was the beauty of an open ended-car trip. We were free to take up any opportunities that came our way.

Pulling the essential belongings from the car, we followed the lady through a maze of laneways until we reached her friend's house. As always, it seemed surprising how the microcosmic compound opened up before us as we passed through the narrow stone gateway. While standing at the top of the steps at the entrance, we had time to survey the area. It was carefully oriented according to the traditional Hindu prescriptions: the family temple and main living rooms facing *kaja* towards the sacred mountains, behind where we were standing, and the kitchen and garbage disposal area and animal pens at the back of the compound closest to the sea, which was considered to be the profane direction, *kelod*.

Descending the steps and into the compound, we were led past the household temple in the corner of the compound, the afternoon's offerings already in place at the entrance to the temple. Next, past the *bale* hut, where coconut leaves and knives lay as they always lie, ready for action, evidence of the never-ending process of making the delicate *canang* offerings. These offerings would be fashioned from coconut leaves made into small trays, filled with coloured flowers, leaves and fruit pieces—sometimes also other odd objects of offering, such as money or a cigarette. Placed in important positions all around the compound and surroundings, the *canangs* would be prayed over with incense to ensure their efficacy in appeasing and honouring the various spirits.

Finally, we reached the sleeping rooms, all in a row, with shiny white-tiled floors and whitewashed walls. More Balinese chatter ensued as the house owner emerged from the kitchen building opposite, and our new friend discussed us and our need with the Ibu of the house. Yes, her friend looked pleased with the prospect of a few guests for the night and a little extra pocket money. She rushed to us, pinched our daughter's cheeks firmly, made her howl, and then enthusiastically fussed us into the guest room, where we placed our belongings.

No sooner had our bags hit the floor than we were ushered out to the kitchen, where, it was believed, any evil spirits that may have followed us into the compound would be purged from us. The evening meal was already set out. Huge bowls of rice, and some veggies and meat smothered in red hot chillies and onions. The kitchen was a sooty black from the wood-burning open fireplace, still used for cooking along with the gas burner benchtop stove, and there were all sorts of interesting things hanging from the rafters. Dried and twisted animal body parts, it looked like. I dared not ask exactly what they were.

We nibbled on the fiery meat and vegetable preparations cautiously, drowning them as much as possible in rice and the smoky water boiled on the open fire, but our daughter had to stick with plain rice for dinner. She complained, but that was that. Nothing else to be done at that time of night. While we ate together all the other members of the extended household scattered around the compound to eat their meals, mostly in solitary silence. The Balinese are very shy about eating around others, being accustomed to coming in from the fields when they have finished their chores, and helping themselves to the food prepared earlier in the day and left waiting in the kitchen. Even in urban settings, we had discovered, the custom had remained.

Before long it was time to get ready for bed. We managed a smoky-water teeth-cleaning session, with considerable resistance from Miss Almost-three-years-old, and then it was time for the toilet.

Well. You would have thought we were about to torture the poor child. As soon as she saw the Indonesian-style squat toilet in the dingy bathroom, she freaked completely.

'No, Mummy, NO!!! I *cannot* do my wees in that toilet! I might fall into it.' Tears of utter distress streaming down her cheeks.

'Don't worry, we'll hold you.'

'I'm *scared* of that toilet, Mummy. I will not go to that toilet!'

'Well, where else are you going to go? Out in the garden?'

'NO. It's dark and scary out there.'

After a long and teary discussion, she eventually settled on us holding her a good few feet off the toilet while she shut her eyes. Toilet travelling experiences are always traumatic, but we had seen much worse. The child was just going to have to toughen up a bit.

Meanwhile, Zoe had provided the evening's entertainment for what was otherwise destined to be a regular quiet night in for the household. They were amused by the flash of blonde hair that swished this way and that with her unhappiness. They laughed at her incessant chattering—obviously not what they were used to with their own kids. They smiled at our frustration.

Once the toiletting dilemma had been solved, we were off to the bedroom. A three-quarter sized mattress, and a bedside table with a fan. What more could you want? Only a mosquito net, and luckily we'd brought our own.

The three of us were quite used to sharing a bed, as I had always believed in keeping close contact with my child, so the small bed was no problem. But the small fan was. I realised we were usually exposed to the fresh sea breezes in the evening where we lived, and that the pocket-sized room with no windows we now found ourselves in was stiflingly hot. It meant that we tossed and turned all night, each taking turns to wake the others with our incessant restlessness. Finally, the night was over and dawn bleached the sleek dark sky. Andrew and I emerged from the small oven, dishevelled and bleary-eyed, our nightclothes damp with a hot sweat.

Aaah . . . but it was so beautiful outside. There was a very low-lying morning mist, a steam rising slowly from the heating ground. The women were busy sweeping the whole area clean, and wore their flashy ceremonial *kabaya* dresses, obviously in readiness for one of the myriad ceremonies that are both their duty and their life. With all the different ceremonial occasions—the temple blessings, the full moon blessings, the births, deaths, marriages and numerous others involving the cycles of life—the Balinese seem to end up having to dress up in this way and perform the necessary rituals at least once a month—often many times more.

Despite the delicate, lacy long-sleeved tops, the hip-hugging sarongs, and the long slinky hair curled up in an oversized bun (often a separate hairpiece these days), the women worked hard and still managed to look like graceful goddesses. The men were wearing their white overshirts, more masculine sarongs, and the traditional white headbands, pulled out like table serviettes at the front. I had seen people dressed and ready for these ceremonies before, so many times, but this time I felt like I was getting an insider's impression. No matter how traditional or how modern the area may be, the religion still dominates. Tucked away in this little hidden valley, though, there was less contrast with the new, more immersion in the old.

Even Zoe—who already had her own ceremonial dress by this stage, and who had learnt to pray on her knees with her hands delicately raised above the head—seemed overawed by the surreal ambience. After emerging from our cocoon, fuzzy-haired and obviously disoriented, she took her time rubbing her eyes before slowly and carefully checking if all the colours and textures were real.

'Mind your manners,' I told her, with a quick reminder of appropriate Balinese household etiquette. 'Don't touch the other children on the head [the head is the top, the sacred part of the body], don't step over anybody [at the bottom, closest to the demon underworld, the feet are considered to be profane], and don't give or take anything from your left hand [which is used for cleaning after defecating].' There. I thought I'd just about covered the main points.

'Don't you use toilet paper in your house? Do you wipe your bottom with your hand?' Zoe promptly asked the first person she came across. Hmm . . . I didn't give her that instruction, did I?!

After a few days sloshing around the muddy banks of rice paddies, wading in the cooling river where the locals meet and wash, and hanging around the busy communal compound, it was time to return. Journeying down from the mountains, we slowly eased our way towards the decision we knew we would have to make.

As the Safari negotiated a particularly sharp turn in the road, we suddenly found ourselves confronted by a dramatic vista stretching over the vast plains and ocean below and then south to our village. Stopping the car on a small verge, we took in the broad panorama.

'I want to go home now, Mummy and Daddy,' Zoe suddenly announced. Out of nowhere. I knew this time she meant our beach hut—not Australia.

'Yes, let's go home,' Andrew said. And I knew he meant our beach hut, too.

I was so relieved that we were all thinking the same thing in harmony, that we were all ready to enter the next phase. We floated back down to our current reality, to the dream under construction. The decision had been made, and we had made it together—just as I had hoped we would.

I had a very
normal, happy
childhood – and
I've always had
a hearty appetite
for new
experiences.

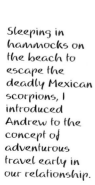

Sleeping in
hammocks on
the beach to
escape the
deadly Mexican
scorpions, I
introduced
Andrew to the
concept of
adventurous
travel early in
our relationship.

As young idealistic newlyweds, we were ready to take on the world.

On our search for paradise, we reached the highest peaks and lowest depths. Here in Nepal – en route to Bali – our toddler Zoe is with me contemplating the spectacular view.

My dream hut on the beach in Bali – found after thrashing through the tropical foliage near a quiet village – was as perfect as I had imagined it would be.

Before long we were drawn into village life. As a young child Zoe learnt to make the delicate flower offerings in the Balinese tradition and join in on the colourful ceremonies.

Opening up the front
roller-door of our
renovated hut, we could
sit in our living area and
look out through the
coconut trees to the
ocean. What more could
you want?

As part of our
new island
lifestyle,
Andrew started
training Zoe as a
young surfer
girl.

In Bali, even domestic duties became a wonderful learning experience, especially when in the company of our extended Balinese family.

A laptop in the attic bedroom. During our early days in paradise, I was able to finish the therapeutic writing projects I never had the time for in the city. Bliss.

Our son, Kallen, was initiated into the Balinese way of life from birth.

The basic grass-walled office in our hut had all the necessary electronic gadgets to connect us to the corporate world.

Have kids – will travel. The children often came with us on our international work expeditions when we needed to journey out from home base Bali. Kallen grabbed a free ride at the airport on my suitcase whenever he could.

Even ten minutes on the beach at the end of each day is enough to relax and re-energise us as a family.

Life on our
Balinese patch
of paradise has
brought
incredible
contentment to
all of us. We have
found a balance
between our
corporate work
and family life . . .

. . . and will always
benefit from the
healing energy of
the waters
surrounding our
island. Life is good!

Chapter 9

Taking Care of Business

At the beginning of our second year in Bali, after we had made the big decision to stay on, we finally relaxed into the feeling that perhaps we could live like this long term. We were in our paradise hut, and had significantly adapted our lifestyle. Now we needed to consider the next step. It was time to think about what direction our careers were going to take. We couldn't survive or thrive on odd jobs forever.

Andrew and I had both had similar careers in education before moving to Bali. Although we had loved the challenges of our work, we had also become drained by the phenomenal amounts of energy that needed to be invested in these positions. As much as we really believed in what we were doing, and felt committed to it, education was a heavy responsibility. Andrew had responded to the stress by giving as much as he could through the work and then taking off surfing as often as he could. I had responded by exploring other interests and avenues. Writing and publishing curriculum resources. Teaching college courses at nights. Starting new uni courses for myself. Running the bed and breakfast guest house cum spiritual retreat cum English language homestay from home.

Through our travels we had ended up working with people at all extremes and in all sorts of locations: with adult students in colleges and academics in universities, with indigenous people in hill tribes and street kids in war zones. Through everything we had done, we had built up a wide range of experiences and skills that stood us in good stead as we considered our future now, but we began to wonder exactly how we could find a new and positive challenge—and make a decent living—in Bali.

The problem was, now that life was so good, we didn't want to risk what we had by sliding back into the same work stresses that had encouraged us to make the break in the first place. We wanted to set some strict rules to ensure our work would fit into our new lifestyle.

A great new revelation came to us one night—some time during that second year (I was already losing track of time!)—as we were sitting at a table in an elegant outdoor hotel restaurant perched on the edge of a cliff. We had been invited to dinner by Peter and Anne, whose child had started at the playgroup in our compound. We had spent some time with each of the parents at pick-up time, but had not really had the chance to get to know each other. A lovely dinner without the kids around was the opportunity we needed.

Peter was, we now found out, the sales manager of the hotel we were dining in. Anne also had a background in hotels, but was currently taking the time out to look after their children. After discussing the interesting challenges of bringing up children in Bali, the inevitable question came up about what work we were involved in. Andrew and I both looked at each other, unsure of how to answer. We had been doing so many different things since our arrival, mostly on a casual basis. We had dabbled in tutoring, part-time teaching, writing articles, working with a local tourism magazine. Our answer finally came out in bits and pieces. It was obvious that we were merely happily ambling along, experimenting with one thing or another. I think it was at that point, as we were attempting to justify ourselves and our existence, that the lack of direction struck us. Sure, we had opted out, we had chosen a different direction—but a total lack of direction wasn't really ideal.

Peter had come to Bali for a specific work contract—a nice package with expensive western-style accommodation (swimming pool, satellite dish for TV, full airconditioning), car, and schooling for the children all included. He and his family would stay for a few years, save up some money, and then move on to another lucrative position with more career advancement opportunities. Our situation must have seemed insane to them. Anxious to give the impression we were not merely layabout beach bums, we told him about our deliberate lifestyle change, about how coming to Bali had allowed us to slow down and re-focus. But, I ventured—casting a sideways glance at Andrew—perhaps it was time to think more seriously about what we were going to do next. After all, Zoe would be nearing school age before too long, and the international school required a more permanent visa and exorbitant fees—more than any top private school back in Australia. It would also be personally and professionally satisfying to find a career niche to settle into.

What work would we be interested in, he asked?

Hmmm . . . A protracted silence as we took the time to think. We had a gorgeous seafood platter in front of us that we had hardly yet scratched the surface of. The palms above us were swaying ever so gently, the flickering candles spread around the perimeter of the dining area creating a warm fuzzy glow. The working world was thousands of miles away, and we had to reach deep into our conscious minds to find the right language again. But we had to do it. We had to start thinking about the future.

Although we had loved the work we did in Australia, we told him, we just couldn't cope with the stress. We explained that the challenge would be to continue the work we enjoyed, and at the same time maintain the right lifestyle to balance it out. Our most recent work, we went on to explain, had been running courses and developing resources for adult groups in a number of different personal and group development areas. We had taught communication skills—such as conflict resolution, negotiation, active listening—as well as individual and organisational psychology, including leadership, team development, change management, and so on.

Have you ever thought of doing that sort of work here in Bali, Peter continued, with groups that come to run conferences in hotels?

The suggestion came out of the blue for us, but it had immediate appeal. As a salesman, Peter was very good at what he did. He went on to sell to us a key piece in our new life puzzle. He described how the hotels often have a lot of conference organisers approaching them, looking for good resources.

Having been drawn into the concept, we wanted to know more. Apparently these organisers often needed to run business sessions—and were always on the lookout for keynote speakers, workshop leaders, seminar coordinators. People who could offer valuable input on personal- and group-development issues. They could also be looking for more fun input—like team-building sessions, where they could get outside and enjoy Bali's great environment as a group.

Just then an unassuming waiter refilled our glasses, a calm-looking man with an open face and the slightest glint in his eye. Everything about the meal was impeccable, and his service was friendly and smart. The waiter's presence reminded me of the enduring positive presence of the Balinese. Then I suddenly recognised him as someone from our village, his irrepressible mischievousness lying barely repressed below the serene surface. He was well trained and professional, but somehow once I realised who he was, the prominent image in my mind was of an easygoing, cheekily smiling fisherman's son sharing a joke with his mates. This hotel was only a few kilometres away from our hut in physical distance, but worlds away in terms of experience.

Though we had been living between these two contrasting worlds to some extent for some time by this stage, we were now overwhelmed by the way we were being stretched to think in both directions at once. It was important to start thinking in terms of the realities of the working world we had temporarily left behind, as well as keeping in mind our new simple community priorities. Having been lulled into a different space in time by the fine food, the good wine and, at a deeper level, the relaxed Balinese approach to life, it was going to take time to readjust to the expectations of the modern working world.

This was also a whole new league for us. We were experienced in teaching seminars in the education and community sectors, but the general business world had remained a bit of a mysterious never-never land. It would be a curious challenge. Our discussion flowed around the possibilities and practical details as we gradually became more and more excited about the prospect. By the end of the main course we had a clearer picture in our minds of what this opportunity could involve and where it could lead.

Finally, third course arrived—a wonderful dessert-sampler plate crammed full of all the most rich and tasty treats the chef could come up with—poached pear and chocolate torte, mango and coconut mousse, hazelnut cream brownies, vanilla bean crème caramel with double cream, white chocolate melts and brandy snaps. Instantly the focus was on the food. As we cleaned up the plate, though, our conversation returned again to the everyday experiences of expat living in Bali—as expat conversations often do. When we eventually prised ourselves out of our seats and prepared to waddle away, we took with us a taste for life at the higher end and a keenness to explore the work prospect further. Food for pleasure, and food for thought!

Andrew and I took some time to wander around the cliff's edge before leaving for home. It was a good chance to discuss everything that had come up and at the same time somehow try to hold on to that unreal ambience. This time Andrew was the one to bring up the idea for serious discussion, and he enthusiastically described the possibilities with me. Caught off guard, I listened carefully and enjoyed the dramatic role reversal. At last I had the chance to play the devil's advocate against him as the idealist.

The buzz of anticipation and excitement became palpable, and we kissed on the verge of the cliff. With only the sound of tumbling waves and the shifting orange candle flames lining the clifftop as a backdrop, we took great pleasure in yet another slice of heaven. As we held hands, we looked down together at the dizzying rocks below—then, looking up towards the horizon, our focus broadened to include the full expanse of silvery water. We had come much further than even I had dreamed of. There were so many more possibilities than I had originally anticipated. But only now, finally, were we ready to be able to move ahead with a firm commitment and mutual trust and respect.

I could sense that we were both ready to jump—this time completely together. It was an exhilarating moment. One that cemented our future path as both business and marriage partners. We were about to enter a new era in our careers and in our relationship.

I felt like a criminal. I had never had to give so many fingerprints in my life! In fact I don't remember ever having to give fingerprints before this, at all. Now, in order to get the proper working visas for our business, we were dealing with the necessary bureaucratic procedures, and numerous fingerprints were but one of the requirements.

Left thumb. Left forefinger. Left middle finger. Left ring finger. Left pinky. Each finger on the left hand was independently stamped in separate little boxes individually allocated for such purposes. The whole process was repeated three times for three different forms. Then we moved on to the right hand . . . and we went through the procedure again. There were no tissues in the immigration office. We were left standing with our black inky fingers stuck up in the air. Worst, though, was when it was Zoe's turn. Apparently it didn't matter how old she was. Even newborn babies are fingerprinted in the same way. It must freak them out completely.

'Who's next?' The iron-faced immigration officer with the grey uniform was functioning on automatic.

Getting the right visas actually felt more like processing a police crime report. It appeared that nothing was computerised, and that all the forms were going to be handwritten, hand typed, and individually copied—with carbon paper. 'What are those funny computers?' Zoe had asked when she saw the 1950s-style typewriters lining the immigration office. The whole procedure seemed so antiquated and slow.

Another requirement was mug shots. We had to provide lots of little photographs. All with a red background. All different sizes. One hundred and eighty photos in total!

After the long traumatic exercise, we eventually emerged from the office with black smudges all over ourselves and a developing weariness for Indonesian administration. Setting up and running a business in Bali was, we learnt the hard way, a weird and convoluted process. By the time we'd completed all the requirements, and prepared the thick wad of documents, we could probably have passed any CIA test. The Indonesian government certainly knew absolutely everything about us.

I should have known it would not be a straightforward affair. We'd actually had some immigration officers turn up to our house to interrogate us one time early in our stay, before the new visas had been sorted out.

There they were, on our doorstep. Two men with major moustaches and attitudes to match. They invited themselves straight into our house without being asked. Both men were looking very serious, and we wondered if we were about to be arrested. Pak No.1 lit up a cigarette and sat on our lounge, enjoying his powerful position, taking his time. Pak No.2 lit up next.

I was horrified. I can't stand cigarette smoke in the house, and I asked in my most polite Indonesian if they could possibly put their cigarettes out. They looked at me as if I was an impertinent schoolchild, looked at each other, and then I guess it registered that they were, after all, in our house. They stubbed out their cigarettes on the doorstep and sat down again, the slightest bit sheepishly. I felt like I'd won a minor victory. In these situations, I believed, it is important not to be the victim, not to get intimidated too easily. Having travelled through police states before, I was not scared of confronting military bravado.

'Is there anything we can help you with, Pak?' Andrew eventually asked.

There was quite a long stretch of time before Pak No.1 finally spoke up.

'We are from the immigration office, and we believe you have violated article number 72365 . . .' Out came a large manual with thousands upon thousands of regulations listed inside. Pak No.1 flicked through until he reached article number 72365 and thrust it triumphantly in front of our faces.

'There is quite a substantial fine for this sort of violation, you know,' added Pak No.2, keen to look important, too.

Zoe began to cry. Painful, ear-piercing cries. It was time for her afternoon nap, and she could somehow sense the tension. Her crying increased in intensity and volume, threatening to turn into a tantrum. Soon we couldn't hear each other speak. Rather than taking her outside to try to settle her, I stared at the men defiantly as if to say, 'Now look what you've done! You think you can just waltz into someone's household and cause havoc!'

Sitting in stalemate for quite a long time, Andrew and I were just not exactly sure which laws we had violated—perhaps there was some sort of problem with the playgroup running in our compound, in the house behind ours, I figured. Or there may have been a problem with processing our papers. We had no idea what was going on. We waited for the immigration officers to make their accusation directly, so we would know exactly what we were dealing with. They wouldn't come out with it. I was starting to suspect they may just have been looking for a bribe opportunity.

Eventually, Andrew made a breakthrough. 'Sorry,' he said, 'but we're not sure what the problem is. Perhaps it would be best if my sponsor dealt with this.'

Great idea. Why didn't we think of that earlier? The Indonesian man who had sponsored our visas was pretty influential, and had lots of friends in immigration. He'd know how to deal with this, we figured. All it took was one phone call, a quick visit from our sponsor, and then the men were sent scurrying from our house like frightened mice. As it turned out, our sponsor discovered that these immigration men were actually off-duty at the time, and were looking at getting a bit of extra cash on the side from any apparently vulnerable newcomers to the island.

Eventually, step by step, we managed to get through the bureaucratic nightmare and strange peculiarities of setting up our business in Bali. As we had already learnt right from our first days, it's usually more a matter of who you know, and we had been incredibly lucky to make the right contacts at the right time.

In the end it was worth all the hassle. Setting up the company was an amazingly long, protracted process, but it gave us what we needed. Before we knew it we had set up an office and had written up a list of possible programs. Boasting a nice colour brochure, we went around to visit key people in the major companies. The work started flowing in from there, slowly but surely.

Once we got past the setup phase, we began to relax and settle into our new roles and expectations, finding the challenges incredibly fulfilling on many different levels. For starters, we had our own company—so we felt we had power over what we were doing and where we were going. Rather than being vulnerable to circumstances, we could control what was happening to us. Although we had put an awful lot of hours into getting the company set up, we were motivated to do it and could do it together from the comfort of our hut on the beach, with our child around. That made all the difference.

It ended up being a great opportunity to utilise all the different interests and skills we had developed. It was amazing how well our early years of work prepared us for this new challenge. We had developed skills in teaching, motivating, presenting, organising, creating, facilitating, counselling, hosting . . . the work we were launching into was merely an amalgamation of all these experiences, a natural progression. It was wonderful to have the chance to put everything into the one job, rather than trying to divide ourselves up into separate categories. Through the work there were also opportunities to contribute something valuable to others' lives without becoming drained in the way we had in the past. And we also found that we could share with others a little of the paradise we had come to enjoy ourselves.

As we learnt and grew through our experiences, the small husband and wife company that had started in a thatched island beach hut continued to expand—not into a large multinational corporation (which wouldn't fit with our new life direction) but into a very strong, personally committed, international team operation.

Our village hut continued as our main office base, as the heart of our company. It became symbolic of both where we had started from and where we intended to go.

On a day-to-day basis, we had never before experienced such a flexible and satisfying approach to work. We had always enjoyed our careers and had worked hard at whatever positions we had been in, but had never before felt quite this sense of freedom.

We were working in the office one day, a few months after we had settled comfortably into our new roles, when I looked across to where Andrew was sitting. It was just one of those moments that remains distinctly filed in your mind. There was nothing at all extraordinary about this segment in time, which is perhaps exactly why it stood out. A day not unlike any other. A project with an established client. Nothing remarkable.

Andrew was in classic concentration mode, his left hand smoothing over his brow, his right hand alternating deftly between rolling the computer mouse over the raw wooden desk surface and tapping briskly on the springy computer keys. For quite a few minutes he was looking focused and serious, clearly enjoying a concentrated creative spurt. Then, for the briefest few seconds, he shifted his gaze and looked out at the ocean.

I didn't need to ask what he was looking at, I knew. He was checking the wind and surf conditions. His eyes were expertly trained to pick up the slightest sign of wind—a small ripple on the surface of the water, a delicate movement in the highest branches of the trees. He could spot a rising swell from a good distance—the black lines of building mounds of water, the white lacy edges of a breaking wave.

Having obviously appropriately positioned his head—resting on one side, tilted at just the right angle—Andrew could take in both the computer and the window behind it in one sweep. A few seconds was all it took, and then his eyes shifted oh so quickly and imperceptibly back to the computer screen, his fingers hardly missing a beat as they continued clickety clacking away.

I couldn't help but smile to myself. Andrew was well and truly in his element. He was working harder than I had ever seen him work, producing so many good ideas and building so much expertise in the field so quickly, but not at all missing out on the leisure focus that he needed. We were together, enjoying the comfortable companionship of a trusting working relationship, and our child was downstairs, popping up to visit every so often to give us some big news or show us a painting.

I felt so proud, right then, of where we had come together.

'What are you staring at?' Andrew eventually called out, still happily clickety clacking away. Eyes in the back of his head, the sign of an experienced teacher.

'Just you and your little information-gathering strategies. Got yourself all set up there perfectly, haven't you?!'

'My word. I've got my priorities in order. Now stop distracting me and get back to work!'

Not yet ready to get back to work, I started to think, instead, about what this whole new venture had meant for us. There were times when we would sit no more than a metre apart, each of us totally focused on our own task, totally oblivious to the other person. There were other times when we shared a good joke, or a deep insight. There were definitely also times when we were frustrated with each other and with the close working conditions. We would argue over our different approaches to teaching, our different management styles, our different ways of running the office— even what we were going to eat for lunch. And yet stronger always was the conviction that this was the best possible partnership we could find ourselves in. That this was right for us.

I checked my watch, and it brought me abruptly back to the day's schedule. Our conference call was due to start in the next few minutes.

'Come on,' I said. 'Get your mind off the surf and back on to your work. We need to be really prepared for this conference, you know.'

'I'm ready,' he came back, quick as a shot, now turning around to face me for full impact. 'You're the one who's been sitting around daydreaming!'

I stuck out my tongue at him.

He feigned utter shock, screwed up a piece of scrap paper, and flung it towards me with great precision. I copped it in the right cheek, predictably slow to respond.

I was about to start an all out war when the call came through.

'Good morning, Stephen. It's nice to have the chance to speak to you,' Andrew began, the consummate professional.

Retrieving the crumpled paper, I glared in his direction (indicating that the war would continue after we had dealt with the business at hand) and picked up my phone.

'Hello, it's Gaia here on the line also. So glad we could get this opportunity to talk,' I said.

Andrew reclined casually in the grey office chair, his feet up on the antique carved wooden bench from eastern Java. He began consulting with the senior executive from Singapore, choosing his words carefully and listening appropriately. He was in board shorts without a shirt, I was in shorts and a singlet top. I couldn't think of a better way to conduct a meeting. Though the tone of the discussion was very proper, appropriately formal, we could still relax behind the scenes in our own beach hut hideaway office.

At various stages throughout the hour-long conversation Zoe burst into the office and had to be quickly and quietly ushered out again, the power cut and we were left without our computer records to refer to, and someone outside started singing loudly not more than a few metres from where we were sitting (noise travels easily through grass walls!) It was barely controlled mayhem.

The most enjoyable way to do business!

It was hard not to keep pinching ourselves, to check if it was really true. No-one could have come up with a better job description and working conditions for us.

We had the flexibility of modern technology to be able to work from our beachfront office, and before long we also had the chance to get out and travel. At least once a month we'd find ourselves in some exotic location in some beautiful five-star resort or classy city hotel somewhere in Asia. We would then return to our quiet island hideaway.

When we later went to Singapore to deliver the program we had been negotiating in that conference call, the client invited us up to his office, obviously proud to show us around. We took note of the lift up to the twenty-third floor, of the main working area with its cubicles and partitions, of the junior offices with a couple of desks crammed in to each section, of the more senior offices with only one desk in each, and of the boss's larger corner office. The bright blue synthetic carpet throughout, the spick and span melamine desks and partitions, the artificial plants. The generous coffee and tea making facilities, the latest office equipment, the efficient office design. Nothing was really able to impress.

All we could think of was our little thatched hut on the beach. Of the way our simple but warm office environment connected people rather than cutting them off. Of sitting, looking out at the calming ocean while waiting for the phone lines to be reconnected . . . the water to come back on . . . the power to start up again. Of watching our Zoe play computer games or bring us paintings to decorate the office walls . . .

Just so long as we put up with the little day-to-day idiosyncrasies of running a business in Bali, we were able to continue to enjoy the benefits of the tropical corporate life.

Chapter 10

Sacred Life Cycles

Our second child was conceived in Bali, on a magical night when the moon was full and ripe, under the sacred watch of the affable island spirits. As he grew in the womb, from the tiniest life form into a clearly defined little person, he became a constant reminder of the wonder of life.

By the time Kallen was born we had been living in Bali for over a year and a half, and bringing another child into the world we had come to love seemed the most positive and natural thing to do. I'm sure he gained many of the benefits of our island life even during those early months of my pregnancy. I had been making the most of our second year: enjoying the restorative value of fresh island fruits, inhaling the vigorous sea air daily, and generally continuing to de-stress from the previous years' build up. That must have created a positive environment for baby Kallen. I don't think you can get a much better start to life than that. I believe our little boy had somehow absorbed something of the island's serenity, too. A friend told us his fortune soon after he was born. He would be a spiritual child, she predicted. His numbers were blessed.

It would have been nice to have introduced Kallen to our Balinese world immediately, but we actually decided to leave the island when it was time to give birth. There were no international-standard clinics at this time, and the medical facilities in Bali were simply inadequate to cope with emergencies. I was fairly confident of a healthy birth, but you never can tell, and if anything did go wrong, it would be one of those things you could never forgive yourself for.

I could relate many stories about the dangerous birthing procedures in Bali—about the excessive number of caesarian births given here (perhaps a good money-making exercise for the doctors?); about the knack the staff have of introducing complications when there shouldn't be any (like the time the nurse literally pushed the baby back inside the mother's womb because the doctor hadn't arrived yet, and the disproportionate number of times babies get brain damage from poor use of the forceps); of the poor postnatal care for both mothers and babies (like the mother who was told not to eat or drink for three days after the birth while her child was put on milk formula, as most children are as a matter of course); about the high rate of deaths of mothers and babies while giving birth; the list goes on—but I wouldn't want to be accused of exaggerating. Suffice to say we didn't feel it was a worthwhile risk.

Conceived in Bali, born in Australia. Like the labels—Italian design, made in China. I'm still not sure which has the greater significance.

Sneaking back on the aeroplane at the last possible minute, I was absolutely huge and ready to drop at any time. We had been back to Australia once at the end of the first year—to spend time with our families for Christmas—but now that we were already well into our second year they were keen to see us again and to be involved in the birth of the baby.

Zoe was almost four at the time her brother was born, and she travelled with me and our ten bags (Andrew had to continue working and came later). We somehow survived the dreaded overnight economy shuttle run, and I managed to get the huge belly and the rest of myself off at the other end, with an entourage of airline staff pushing the ten bags on trolleys and Zoe in a wheelchair (nobody could wake her up).

It was a relief when we arrived on our friend Rita's doorstep: myself, my belly, the three-year-old, and the ten bags. We had tried to ensure the basement flat in our own house would be free when we returned, but the rental timing just didn't work out, so we took the option of staying with friends instead. I don't think these lovely, kind people, who had enthusiastically offered for us to come and stay at their place, anticipated exactly what was coming . . .

'Hi! Come in. So good to see you again!' Rita said as she opened the door for us.

'Great to see you, too.' A peck on the cheek and a warm hug. I went to do the double cheek kiss that I had become accustomed to in Bali, but was left in mid-air feeling a bit like a goose. (There are obviously too many European expats in Bali, dictating the social etiquette.) I recovered my dignity as soon as possible, and turned my attention to Rita's little boy. 'And look at you, Danny, my goodness—you've grown so much. He's gorgeous, isn't he?'

'Gosh, your little one's not so little any more, is she? And I can see you're ready to drop at any time, aren't you? Well, let's get you all inside and settled.'

It is always nice to see old friends after you've been living away. I was looking forward to having some time to hang out and catch up. I realised it was a big call, though, having us come and stay. I wondered if she was beginning to think the same thing as we all shuttled backwards and forwards so we could set ourselves up in the small bedroom that had been vacated to accommodate us. The reality of inviting a birthing family into an already established household would not be easy for anyone. And this was actually no ordinary household. This was already an extended family group made up of two brothers and their wives, one couple with a two-year-old and a five-week-old, the other couple with an eight-week-old. The house was already operating like a hospital nursery ward even without us around.

'So where's the bub?' I asked. 'He must still be tiny . . .'

'He's sleeping, but come and have a look.'

There were only three bedrooms on the top level of the house—one for each of the two families, and we were placed in the centre one. Baby was in the far-end family room. He was so gorgeous. Tiny pursed lips in perfect angelic formation. Miniature fingers with miniscule fingernails clasping the wrapping sheet tightly. The softest, downiest hair, fluffing up ever so slightly in the breeze from the window. A gentle, rhythmic breathing, only just perceptible. I was getting clucky all over again.

After retreating downstairs together to drink peppermint tea on the large old floral lounge, Rita and I reminisced over the lives that had been lived since we were last together. The kids reacquainted themselves, slowly and politely discussing the toy collection. Our own conversation was casual and relaxed, nurtured by the warmth of the late afternoon sun as it snuck in from the courtyard through the bay windows. I thought about how much I had missed the comfort of old friendships, what I had given up in my quest to find a new lifestyle.

The very moment that thought crossed my mind, the peaceful scene was interrupted by a heart-wrenching newborn scream. Rita jumped up and ran up the stairs to rescue her little one. As that happened, Danny walked to the bottom of the stairs calling after her, scared to be left in the company of virtual strangers. I then heard another tiny baby scream start up on the second floor, somewhere down the other end of the house.

We spent the next few hours juggling babies' and toddlers' needs, feeding, bathing, changing, entertaining. Everything moved into a higher gear as we ran through the childcare motions. Our catch-up chat became somewhat stilted and stuttered, little chunks of conversation lost in between the present practical realities. I was being reinitiated into newborn family parenting. It was a jolt back to the reality of how hard it can be—and how my friends were able to support each other and help each other out in practical ways. It was so difficult, I remembered, to have to focus so completely on a child's needs. And that was only with one child!

As the time for our own baby's arrival approached, Andrew now back with me ready for the forthcoming event, we were feeling both exhausted and elated. Exhausted with the various demands of sharing a household with another family. Elated because, after all, it's always different with your own child, isn't it?!

Our precious package decided to indicate his imminent arrival in the dead of night, as many babies do. It really does have to be a grand entry into the world. Nothing else is good enough. I waited through a few more increasingly painful contractions, then I decided I couldn't wait any more. After waking Andrew, we discussed (as reasonably as anything can be discussed—considering I was feeling like I was being repeatedly skewered with a huge hot poker) what we were going to do with Zoe. We had wanted her to be with us during the birth, but weren't sure if it was going to be worth it in the middle of the night. Why not wake her and give her the choice, I suggested—ask if she wanted to come with us to the hospital, or whether she would rather go back to sleep and stay where she was.

She was quite firm in wanting to come, so we decided it would be worth it to have her there. Finishing the packing in a mad rush, we crept down the long, dark hallway, being careful not to wake anyone else.

'Everyone won't know what's happened to us,' a sharp, clear little voice reverberated up the corridor.

Hmmm . . . somehow I was sure they would. We continued to the kitchen, where we shut the door so we could finish dressing without waking anyone else. When we were almost ready, Andrew went to get the car.

'I don't want to wear these shoes! I want the other ones.'

But could we find the other ones? Of course not.

'Just put these on quickly. Mummy's going to have the baby soon, and I'm in a lot of pain.'

'I'm not wearing these shoes.'

No, she certainly wasn't going to. Not without a lot of fuss and bother. I carried her out to the car with no shoes on, stopping to double over in pain every few steps. Great idea bringing the child, I thought to myself. The funny thing was that it actually distracted me from my misery between contractions. I was not able to dwell on the pain, and realised that I could, in fact, remain quite functional in the pocket of time when the pain ceased.

A fleeting thought skittled across my mind. I had heard that in Indonesia women will sometimes give birth in the rice fields during a lunchbreak and then return to finish their work for the rest of the day. Perhaps that image came more from times past, but it was an interesting little subliminal reminder. Western women are just not tough enough, I thought to myself. If we would only stop focusing on ourselves and just get on with it, perhaps giving birth wouldn't be such a big deal. But the noble thought was rudely interrupted by another contraction, this one even more intense and painful than the last. I doubled over with pain, and cursed myself and my high ideals. It's easy to forget just how incredibly bloody painful the whole thing is. There can be no rhyme or reason when the sledgehammer hits.

At the hospital, Zoe held my hand through the pain. I failed to notice that she was looking a little in pain herself. Andrew suggested I didn't squeeze her hand so tightly.

'Make sure you smile between contractions,' he simply said, 'to show her you're fine.'

Sure. No problem. Easy for him to say. We both smiled for the camera just before I started pushing. The photo I looked at afterwards shows an angry grimacing witch rather than a positively blooming pre-birth mum.

The screams increased in volume and intensity.

'Can someone take me outside for a little while?' Zoe asked very quietly and most politely.

Wonderful timing. Grandma had just arrived, and she took Zoe out for a snack and a short walk while we concentrated on focusing energy in all the right places. She was back in time to see the head coming out. We all snuggled together on the bed with excitement and relief when baby finally emerged. At that moment, we definitely belonged together.

But we did pay the price. Our poor little girl was simply exhausted by the all-night ordeal, and I think Andrew's patience had worn pretty thin after coaxing me through the exercise. He struggled with her through a succession of tantrums back at the ranch, while I tried to adapt to having a needy little thing constantly around in the hospital. I moved out of the hospital and back to the house after forty-eight hours. I think it was all too much too soon.

While I was happy to be with my family and in relatively comfortable homely surroundings, our host families realised they had taken on more than they could cope with, and we were asked if we could make other accommodation arrangements. I couldn't blame them, but it was very upsetting. Your hormones are supposed to send you into a nosedive a few days after the hyped-up post-birth elation, and I was feeling shattered.

As has probably already become quite obvious, I am usually a very strong person, always determined and often iron-willed. When I gave birth the first time around, I actually walked the half-hour walk up the steep hill to the local hospital. I came back home to a pile of office work three days after giving birth to Zoe and sol-diered on with that, the baby and the housework. But this time it was all too much. I had wanted to simulate the Balinese open com-munity environment by moving in with friends, but I should have remembered from my previous city communal living experiments that it is very hard to achieve in an urban context.

We then stayed with different family members and at friends' houses—a couple of nights here and a couple of nights there, shifting all over the eastern part of the state, wanting to see everyone and spend time with everyone, but conscious of not over-staying our welcome. I worked out afterwards that we moved eight times. I did pride myself on being a very relaxed and flexible mother, but by the end even I was feeling like my axis was spinning just a little too fast. I was more tired and stressed than I had expected, and Kallen was more unsettled than I had hoped.

There had been a distinct period of satisfied contentment—espe-cially after getting over the initial culture shock of arriving back in a city—a contentment that can only be experienced in the company of your family and oldest friends. But the pace of life was starting to catch up with us again, and when it was time to leave, we were ready. Kallen's passport photo had been taken the instant he could open his eyes, and as soon as we had the passport finalised—when he was about three weeks old—we were excited to be once more on our way 'home' to Bali.

Giving birth in Bali is probably just as painful—and definitely a medical risk—but somehow there seems to be more of a social

136

buffer zone in place for the Balinese that helps to cushion the impact. Made Sri and I had delivered our baby boys only months apart, in the same region of the world—but we may as well have been living on completely different planets and during completely different ages, considering the social gap between us. I was glad I did not have to put up with her simple medical conditions and restrictions, but envied her strong ready-made social support system.

I was motivated to research what I could about birthing and bringing up children in Bali. That motivation had been there, too, when Zoe was born; in fact I was so keen to find out about how different cultures bring up their children that I ended up writing a whole book on the subject! But now I felt the need to know more about the Balinese way.

Because each stage in life has a deeply religious significance for the Balinese, I discovered, there are rites and rituals in place that help give structure and meaning to the otherwise unfathomable mysteries of life. Even before birth the foetus is protected ceremonially by a ritual that empowers the four spirits standing guard over the child and ensures a long and healthy life. After that there is a series of elaborate ceremonies at the time of birth, when the umbilical cord falls off, twelve days after the birth, one month and seven days after the birth, three months after the birth, and six months after the birth—or for the 'first' birthday according to the Balinese.

It is only once the baby is six months old that it is actually allowed to touch the ground. Pretty amazing, considering that by that age we have our babies actively in training with little plastic kindy gyms—even at special baby gym clubs—rolling around on the floor with myriad toys, and experiencing the world from the ground up. In order to join the regular world (babies are, up until this point, considered to be like gods—having descended from the heavens at birth), the six-month-old child is usually placed under a cock cage and then released from it, given a metal cap, made to put his hands in a fish bowl, shaved (with just a small tuft of hair left at the front), and ritually 'bought' by the mother and father—and these rituals are only the last installment in the series of complicated babyhood rites! The important thing is that all this brings the community together, often for colourful and noisy festivities, always supported by the extended family.

When I went to visit Made Sri soon after our return from Australia, to show her my baby and to see how her small child was getting on, the contrasts were more clearly highlighted. In Bali, the mother is not permitted out of the house for the first month—probably not a bad thing considering how wrecked I was feeling, and how unsettling it was to be racing around trying to get a hundred and one things done when I was already physically depleted from breastfeeding and little uninterrupted sleep.

My baby was crying. I was chided by the many women in the household for coming out myself, and for bringing my baby outside my house.

'No wonder he is crying,' they said. 'He has probably been affected by the wind.' (The cause of just about all ailments, according to the Balinese.)

Made's baby was happily sitting in someone's lap, eating packaged mush mixed with warm water from a spoon.

'How long has he been eating solids?' I asked.

'He already started eating when he was two months old,' Grandma Gendeg announced proudly as she wiped some soggy dribble from his mouth.

It was my turn to do the chiding. 'Two months old! You must be very careful,' I responded sternly. 'In my country we are told not to give solid foods until at least five or six months. The baby can get infections very easily, and really needs as much of the mother's milk as it can get, for as long as it can get it.'

With two children and having read plenty of books about childrearing, I felt like I had become an expert. But Grandmother smiled at me politely, knowingly. She had many more years of experience behind her, many more children and grandchildren. She was sure of her own methods. I had my culture and she had hers.

I read the babyfood package, dismayed to see that sugar was second on the list of ingredients. And the stuff was expensive for local people. He also drank formula milk from a cup, to supplement his mother's milk, which dries up in the afternoon, they said.

Well of course it dries up in the afternoon, I thought to myself, without actually verbalising it. The supply is decreasing because the demand is decreasing. Isn't it obvious?

No. It was not obvious. Whatever you have not grown up with or been educated about always seems strange. There was no point in each of us judging the other: we could merely share information and ideas across cultures, and learn from each other what we could.

We shared some lunch together—a mix of white rice (naturally), tiny salted whole fried fish, and spicy condiments. There were lots of people in the compound at that time, and while my baby slept, Made Sri's baby was busy being entranced by the bright movements and happy chatter. That was something I could definitely learn from the Balinese. About creating a healthy social environment for children. The stress and fuss of looking after a baby is minimised by the sheer number of people willing and available to help out, and the dense human contact.

Although I had wanted to create that sort of communal environment for Zoe while she was young, I had continually felt frustrated about my inability to do so. But here, second time around, I could tell Kallen was already starting to enjoy the benefits of Balinese communal living. I was already slowing down, winding down again, and I could feel the tension in Kallen's small, wiry body gradually easing.

Yes, the Balinese way sure made a difference in the parenting experience. I didn't need to study books to see that.

Days had turned into weeks, weeks into months—and before I was able to stop and think about it, Kallen had grown and passed a few developmental milestones. It was now birthday party season, too— I knew that when my children received four invitations to four separate parties all in the one week.

The first party was for a friend of Zoe's, Leila, a half-Vietnamese, half-American child. The second was for Peter and Anne's child— Zoe's friend Michaela. The third was for another of Pak Gusti's small sons. And the last was for Made Sri's child, baby Wayan.

Leila's party was in a beautiful Balinese-style house, but with marble floors, expensive teak furniture, an intricately landscaped garden with waterfalls which tiered into ponds. The children played games in the garden, but it was a real fantasyland compared to the parties in the quarter-acre suburban backyards I had been used to back in Sydney.

Peter and Anne's hotel party for Michaela was even more elaborate. Hotel staff in white uniforms waited on the children, who were served fancy miniature hamburgers and hot dogs from silver serving dishes, fruit punch ladled out of large crystal bowls, ice-cream cake modelled into a fancy cartoon character—all on a central buffet table decorated with huge ice carvings and delicately fashioned fruit and flower displays.

Pak Kadek held his second son's party in KFC—yes, exactly the same KFC that you'll find anywhere in every corner of the world, except that the children were served chilli sauce alongside the tomato sauce, and rice as well as the sugary buns. There were moulded red seats, and there was a plastic playground that the children happily descended on. The children were served the wonderfully preserved pre-packaged food and bright coloured soft drinks out of styrofoam containers.

The first two parties were truly international, with the children's parents coming from Malaysia, Switzerland, America, France, Canada, Italy, Austria, Scotland, Algeria, Germany, Indonesia . . . and Australia. The families at the third party were all wealthy Indonesians, apart from us. But the party language in each case was universal. All of these parties followed the standard birthday party formula. The games included: Pin the Tail on the Donkey . . . Pass the Parcel . . . Treasure Hunt . . . Apple Dunking . . . sound familiar? Yes, exactly the same games as when we were kids. They all candled, cut and eagerly devoured a birthday cake. A frantic present opening followed in all three cases, and then they had the final ritual of the giving out of balloons and lolly bags as the children departed. Although the children and their parents had come from the four corners of the globe, every child present at each of the parties knew exactly what to expect, and eagerly launched into the next phase as it was announced.

At little Wayan's party, the hyperactive children were there, as were the decorations, games, foods, and present giving and receiving. But it was a totally different birthday experience. The family compound was decorated with streamers and balloons, but the finely patterned hand-cut decorative coconut leaf strips were also there as a reminder that this was different, it was also traditionally Balinese. Even though Wayan was still small, the compound was filled with well-wishing family and neighbours of all different ages.

The program was not scheduled, so it was up to the children themselves to improvise and create their own entertainment. The older children played chasings and took turns at miming traditional Balinese dances: the little boys moved their limbs with the stiff jerky movements of the masked male dancers, the little girls curling their fingers, swaying their hips and tilting their heads demurely.

We ate white rice (as always!) and fried soy bean patties, along with spicy chicken deep fried in coconut oil (*ayam goreng*, the original Balinese version of KFC), fried noodles with egg and green vegetables, and the popular *krupuks*—or fried prawn chips. All out of bright plastic dishes or served on banana leaves. We finished up the feast with the green and purple coloured sticky rice sweets flavoured with coconut and palm sugar.

The whole ceremony was much simpler, but it must still have put a dent in the family expenses. The present giving was quite a bit less lavish—a small packet of chips or a tiny plastic toy was about as much as most of the guests could afford, and obviously a birthday cake was too much of an extravagance, but still, all those visitors expected to be well fed, and went straight to the table laden with food the very second the announcement was made.

Next was the Balinese 'Happy Birthday' song, '*Panjang Umurnya*'—which gives best wishes for a long and successful life—and then everyone suddenly disappeared, the food gone, the main attractions over.

But this was only the secular birthday celebration. The relevant religious ceremony had already been conducted in private with the family (which still adds up to a significant number of people!). Wayan had been blessed by the priests so that he could touch the

141

ground and begin to walk upon the land of the living after his recent descent from the land of the gods.

It was nice to think that these special transitions through life were being so carefully marked and commemorated. It made us aware of the need to consider the significance of the milestones in our own children's lives. To take the time to celebrate and enjoy each one. Recognising these was going to be a first step in finding the rhythm in our new Balinese-based lives.

For every step along the way in Bali, for every important change in life, it seems there is constant support and recognition. The first early childhood ceremony comes when a child loses his first milk teeth—in the same way that we recognise the loss of milk teeth by bringing in the tooth fairy.

Going along with the tooth fairy myth with Zoe when she was young, we slipped a few coins under her pillow whenever one of her teeth came out. It was a simple but special occasion for her, but we weren't really sure ourselves exactly what we were celebrating. Actually, we had a little trouble working out what would be a reasonable amount for the Indonesian tooth fairy to deliver—especially considering the dramatically fluctuating exchange rate and all. On subsequent tooth losses, which became more and more frequent as she grew, the tooth fairy became a little erratic, sometimes forgetting to come, sometimes changing the amounts she gave without realising it. But it was, nevertheless, a nice phase in life, when magic and money were the simple ingredients for immediate happiness.

The occasion of the first tooth falling out is not one of the most important life ceremonies in Bali, but is usually commemorated nevertheless. After descending from the heavens in the form of a god, the child will have completed the transition to regular run-of-the-mill humanity when permanent teeth start to appear. Teeth actually feature significantly in the Balinese life cycle. Teenagers, for example, usually become fully fledged adults when they have their teeth filed to make them straight and, apparently, attractive.

Anyway, with this first tooth-loss ceremony there will be

prayers to the gods for clean and strong teeth that also look good. (Unfortunately, it doesn't seem that the gods can do much about the sweet milk formula and baby food, and later lollies and sticky sweets that most Balinese kids consume in plentiful quantities. Many children's teeth are brown and rotting badly.) At this stage, now that the child is no longer considered to be a baby, he or she is thought to be capable of studying; hence most Balinese children don't start their schooling until they are six or seven years old. From here on the child learns and grows towards adulthood until that really decisive phase of development—in our western world at least—puberty.

Perhaps one of the reasons the child's transition into puberty can be so traumatic for so many western kids (and for so many parents) is precisely because we have no real way of measuring or celebrating the beginning of this new developmental step. In fact, our kids are usually shy and embarrassed about the changes, and will hide developments rather than celebrating them. They seem to become confused, frustrated, and resentful of what they cannot understand.

Balinese kids, on the other hand, are publicly recognised with elaborate ceremonies as soon as they have started menstruating (in the case of the girls) or their voices have deepened (in the case of the boys). Girls and boys alike are promoted as flowering virgins with sexual potential. The goddess of sexual union is called upon to bring health and success to the young teen, and the new weight of working responsibility in the household will be emphasised for the young girls. They will rehearse the regular cooking chores to demonstrate their readiness to contribute to the household.

There is no doubt, for these kids, of their changing physical and social status. They know what to expect. And—phew!—with the sensuous ceremony that acknowledges their growth, they are probably much better prepared to cope with their changing sexuality. Perhaps that's why so many of them seem to move so acceptingly on to the next stages of life as they arise.

So, that brings us back to the tooth-filing ceremony that usually marks the entry into adulthood—the ritual that aids the transition of the spirit through the channels of birth, death and reincarnation.

143

Quite apart from making the teeth appear more attractive, according to the Balinese way of thinking, the filing exercise also is a way of bringing the major personality traits into alignment. In contrast to the coarse fangs of evil mythological creatures, the Balinese like to show more refinement of character by having their teeth filed. As unpleasant as it is to have a priest sawing across the edge of your teeth, all individuals will desire to have the job done. It is a very expensive ceremony, but considered vital for spiritual safekeeping through life and into death. It is such an important event, in fact, that those who cannot afford to have their teeth filed while they are young will have it done in their old age. Even after someone has died, the family will arrange for the dead person's teeth to be filed to ensure the individual's health and wellbeing in the spirit world.

Ultimately, it is the death rituals that are the most important transitions through life in Bali. I guess it's death that really puts life into perspective . . .

Chapter 11

Lives in Transition

The streets were blocked. There appeared to be one long swarming stream of marching people clad in dark shirts and black and white checked sarongs.

We stopped the car to wait, not so patiently, for the procession to move past. As we were late for an appointment with a client, and were getting hot and flustered sitting in the car in our more formal 'work' clothes with the airconditioning broken. We were only a few minutes from home—just around the corner from our house, not yet out of our village and the procession looked as though it could continue for hours. Andrew pressed the buttons on the mobile phone, dialling the client's hotel number to let him know we'd be late.

'Hello, yes. Can you put me through to room 718 please—Mr Waltman? No, not Waterman, *Walt*man. W for Whisky, A for Alpha, L for Lima, T for Taxi—and 'man' for 'man and woman'.'

Beads of sweat had formed on his forehead, threatening to become rivulets. I was holding my arms up in the air, to ensure I didn't get wet patches under my arms.

'No—*Walt*man. Like Walt Disney. Like waltzing.'

Of course these concepts probably had little meaning for the poor confused front-office lady on the other end of the phone. Andrew rolled his eyes one more time, and was about to loudly launch into another attempt at explanation when he suddenly pulled the small black object away from his ear and stared at it furiously.

'God, I don't believe it! The stupid phone's cut out! The battery's flat!'

That was it. We were stuck. How unprofessional. We were late for a meeting for legitimate Balinese reasons, but we had no way of explaining it all to the client.

'I'll see if I can get to the Wartel [public telephone station],' I offered unenthusiastically. I knew it was only a little further along the road.

As soon as I got out of the car, though, I was back in the real Bali, away from the artificial stress. The momentum of the lively procession dragged me along for the ride. I was swept alongside the jaunty youngsters, the limping old ladies, the proud men. I could feel the spiritual gust blowing through the mass of people, driven on by religious purpose and a strong sense of social responsibility. I couldn't help but be drawn along with them, as if I was part of a Mardi Gras procession myself. I forgot that I was on a mission, and started to allow myself to enjoy the rhythm and energy of the humming throng. There was a large sarcophagus just ahead of me, balancing on the mens' shoulders, an oversized papier-mâché bull with a nose ring painted in gaudy colours and positively glittering with gold leaf patches. Near that was a tower, swaying precariously on tall stilts.

It was a Ngaben ceremony, the ceremony of all ceremonies that celebrates someone's death and his or her passage through to the next life with a dramatic cremation. The corpse was being carried to the cremation site in the tower, then at this special site it would be placed inside the hollow animal before being set alight. Apart from the dark clothing, there was nothing especially sombre or grave about the event. I had heard that the community prepares for and contributes to the ceremony, so I guess it really is a joint memorial to the life lost. The family must feel very supported. There is usually so much colour and energy, that it is hard to compare it with the funerals in our own society.

Many weeks or even months and thousands of dollars would have been involved in the preparations. In fact, it is such an expensive and grand event that quite often the bodies of poor people are buried until the family has saved up enough for a cremation ceremony, after which time the body is dug up for burning so that the soul might finally be properly released.

I stopped suddenly in my tracks. There ahead, hanging on to the side of the coffin, were Nyoman and Made Sri. Pak Gendeg was walking in front of the sarcophagus. As I watched I could gradually pick out more and more people from the Gendeg extended family compound. An unpleasant sickly feeling rose in the pit of my stomach as the realisation struck me that Ibu Gendeg had died. I felt guilty that we had not been to visit for a while, that we were not up to date with what had happened. Perhaps we were starting to get into the busy work trap again and as a consequence had started to lose touch, to miss out on important connections. It was sad to think that she had left without us having the opportunity to say goodbye, but I was now unsure about the most appropriate way to express my condolences. Ibu Gendeg had been frail and unwell for a long time, but had always maintained her strong will and determined manner. It occurred to me that the family did not now look upset about her death. This was probably just seen as a necessary part of the cycle of life.

Before long, I caught a glimpse of the Wartel sign between the bull's legs, and then it disappeared out of sight just as quickly. That brief sighting was enough to jolt me back to my present reality, to the need to get to the Wartel to make a call. I would have to catch up with my village friends later, when the time was right. Easing my way to the side of the crowd, from where I could more easily break out of the relentless flow of people, I then jumped up onto the pavement as soon as I got the chance, as if trying to clamber ashore on a mossy river bank, fighting against a strong current.

Inside the Wartel, there was the chance to shut myself in a booth and block out the noise. All was quiet and calm. Shielded from the mass fervour once more by the double glass windows, I took a few minutes to come to terms with what had happened and gather my thoughts again. It was going to be difficult to switch straight into business mode.

Soon, though, I was thinking about my own father's death. He had died at a young age, only fifty-four, due to the stress that had driven him to achieve so highly in his chosen field, I suspect. His health had deteriorated little by little, until he had passed away—peacefully at home with his family around him to care for him. We all cried until it hurt. The extended family and friends had gathered together for a quiet, calm ceremony where Dad's body was kept out of sight until it disappeared into the dark incinerator vault, only the slightest flicker of flame reminding us of what was happening to his body. Later we had scattered his ashes from a high cliff into the ocean, feeling confident that his spirit would feel free in the open watery expanse. It had been a special time of family and community support.

Very much my father's child. I had the same drive and passion in me, and I became conscious of the need to be careful not to allow myself to get sucked into the same over-committed vortex. Eventually, I was able to pull myself away from the past and into the present. By this time I had calmed significantly, so much so that my priorities once more became crystal clear. What was a mere business deal in the context of life and death?

When I was ready, I made the call to Mr Waltman, no longer worrying about the consequences. Instead, I described the whole experience, going into great detail about the nature of our delay, describing the people, the colour, the ceremony. We chatted for a while—after all, I wasn't going anywhere in a hurry, and by the end of the conversation I actually felt pleased that I had been able to inject a dose of reality into what may otherwise have been a more impersonal business interaction.

We reached our destination a good half an hour after the arranged time and began apologising profusely to Mr Waltman as soon as we met him, but it soon became clear that he was bemused about the nature of doing business in Bali, and touched by the island's cultural vibrancy. His interest gave us the chance to draw out the uniqueness of Bali as a possible location for his conference group, and it eventually dawned on us that a potential negative had been turned into a real positive. We joined him for lunch at his invitation, and this meeting ended up being the start of a long-term relationship—with us, with our work, and with Bali.

As we drove home later in the afternoon, we passed the field where the cremation had taken place. Ribbons of smoke were peeling off the mountain of ashes. There were still piles of fruit and flowers fringing the funeral pyre, and the thinning crowd was looking much more subdued and reflective.

This time we stopped voluntarily to absorb the ceremony. To join in with the farewell. We arrived home with a new sense of awareness, with a new appreciation for the buoyant Balinese celebration of every stage of life, even death.

These ceremonies often help to put everything back into perspective, in the way that Ibu Gendeg's had done for me.

It was only a short space of time—but quite a significant spiritual leap—before Easter was upon us: the time for people from the Christian tradition to be thinking about life and death. Unfortunately, it was also the time when the spirit of death began to invade our own house.

We were keeping in our house a small chicken that the children at Zoe's playgroup had befriended as part of the lead-up to their special Easter program. His constant cheeping was a cheery reminder that he was with us, and we often held him and played with him. One night, though, things seemed remarkably quiet for an extended period of time. I didn't think much of it until I was in the bathroom where the chick had been boarding, and noticed the bucket—which was his temporary little home—ominously positioned under the floor tap. As I cautiously crept closer, my fears were confirmed: the bucket was full of water, and it appeared that there were some clothes in there as well.

A dreaded investigation uncovered the limp and sodden baby bird under a few heavy layers of clothing. No autopsy was needed—death by drowning was quite apparent. It turned out that Andrew had arrived home after playing sport and put his sweaty clothes in the bucket to soak. It was, after all, the bucket we usually used for dirty washing.

What would I tell Zoe? I wondered whether she was old enough to understand what had happened. If I told her the truth, would she be permanently emotionally scarred? I decided to take the tough option.

'Look at our poor chicken,' I told her. 'He's not alive any more, he's died.'

She didn't get upset at all. She was more fascinated with the poor little limp body than anything else.

'What happened?'

'He was under the water for too long so he couldn't breathe.'

'So he can't go "cheep, cheep" any more?'

'No, he can't go "cheep, cheep" any more. It's like he's gone away . . . or gone to sleep. He died.'

'Why?'

'Because he couldn't breathe, so his body stopped working.'

'But why?'

I gave up.

We both contemplated the chicken's sad demise for a while and observed a brief period of mourning. I felt this should be an important learning experience for her, to learn to express grief and all, but she was more interested in the circumstances that led to the chicken's demise than anything else.

When Dad came home, he got the full story in graphic detail, with the concluding lesson for the day: that the chicken couldn't go 'cheep, cheep' any more. This event subsequently became the benchmark for future discussions about death.

Just a week or two later I was looking with Zoe at a wedding photo, one of Andrew and me standing with my mother and father.

'Where am I?' Zoe asked.

'You hadn't been born.'

'I want to be there in the photo.'

'But you couldn't, because you hadn't been born.'

A few seconds of deep thought, then: 'Was I still in Mummy's tummy?'

'Oh, well—yes, sort of. So I guess you were there in a way.'

'Who is that man with Nanna?' She squinted at the photo to try to get a better look.

'That's my daddy. He was your grandpa, but he died.'

'Like the chicken who couldn't go "cheep, cheep" any more?'

'Yes. Just like the chicken.'

'Why?'

There it was, the constant young child's question.

'He got very sick and very weak, and then one day he couldn't breathe any more and his body stopped working.'

She stopped to contemplate this idea momentarily, resting her head in my lap pensively, before returning to her investigation in earnest.

'But why did his body stop working?'

'He got cancer, darling, a dreadful disease that eats away at your body and makes you very sick.' I had tears in my eyes, remembering the painful slow process of my father dying. My daughter noticed and patted my hand as if she was the mother and I was the child. But curiosity drew her questioning on . . .

'Where is he now?'

'His body has gone, but the person inside is in a special place.'

'Like a special hospital?'

'Kind of, only much nicer than a hospital.'

Andrew's father was dying at this time, so I figured it could be the ideal opportunity to try to explain what her other grandfather was going through. We ran through a similar conversation, and I explained again how Papa would stop talking, moving, breathing—like he was going to sleep.

'But can't I just hold his hand to wake him up?' Zoe asked. She had seen him in hospital when he had been sick and weak, sleeping through the day, waking only when roused for meals or for family visits. She had assumed the special task of holding his hand, and had taken her part seriously, somehow knowing that a young child has the power to maintain hope and light through darkness.

'No, darling. This time he won't wake up because his body will have stopped.'

'Will he go to a special hospital too?'

'He will go to a special place, and he'll be much happier there. He won't be in pain any more.'

Zoe was with us in our Balinese home when we heard the news from Australia that Andrew's father—her Papa—had died. She cuddled her dad and held his hand to help him to feel better. He buried himself in her small frame, crying onto her delicate shoulder. She continued to be the epitome of hope and innocent love.

We were all on the next plane home, feeling choked with sadness that we were so far away from Andrew's mother at this time. Of all the things I had found tough about living so far away from home, not being able to be there at times like this was the hardest.

Our young daughter and baby son were there at the crematorium, and at the funeral—to 'say goodbye' to their Papa. They were with us as his ashes were scattered in the church garden.

'I know I can't see Papa any more. I wish I could, but I can't,' Zoe said.

She was so strong and had such a great vision, an incredible inspiration. Perhaps, in some ways, children really are gods incarnate, just as the Balinese believe.

They say that when one life ends, another begins.

At the time when Kallen was born, Andrew's father had already been hanging on to the last threads of life. Seeing Kallen had given him a real spark in his frailty. He had been overjoyed to have a grandson to follow his granddaughter. He had chosen Kallen's second name—a good Scottish name, Thomas. It was so important to us that we could share the joy of new life. Perhaps that was one of the last things that kept him going.

Do I believe in reincarnation? The eternal cycle of life? I must admit the eastern Hindu tradition is still strange to me. I still find it hard to believe that one being could evolve to become so many other forms. But I do like the concept of hope for the future. Of the possibility of rebirth for hopes and dreams. The Christian tradition is more familiar to me. There is the same belief that the spirit lives on after death, that even through death there can still be life.

Whatever happens, it helps to trust that the wheel of this cycle of life must continue turning so that new hopes can rise out of apparent despair. We were continuing the process of transition from one world into another ourselves, and for us this lesson was a pivotal step.

Chapter 12

The Changing Shape of Paradise

It felt like it had happened overnight. It was unquestionably the fastest moving construction project I had ever seen in Bali.

No sooner had we really settled into our magical beachside existence than our little patch of paradise was invaded and transformed. Year three, day one—or so it felt. Troops of workers moved in, labouring day and night to clear away the gorgeous vegetation in front of our hut. The chainsaws started up, the landfill trucks charged ahead. The whole stretch of land between us and the beach was almost completely cleared to make way for beachfront restaurants and a huge car park. I mean restaurants—plural. And I mean huge. They were up and running in no time at all.

In typical Balinese style, a concept that had worked well had been copied and multiplied. The three original beautiful small cafes that had been positioned much further down the beach were moved directly in front of our house, and sixteen other brand-new cafes were squashed in beside them to fill in the space. The original cafes had been lovely. A few wooden tables on the sand, lit by bare candlelight, the barbeques at the back burning the coconut husks that would be used to cook the seafood. With the new setup, the rows of barbeques belched heavy smoke and the tables stretched as far as the eye could see. Cows and coconut trees made way for stray dogs, ramshackle buildings, and large dirty spaces.

Nineteen cafes! With busloads of tourists being brought in each night, the buses, taxis and tour cars turning around and parking up against our house!

But that wasn't all. Once it was realised that there was still room for more, twenty-one tourist 'art shops' (designed to sell sarongs, bamboo chimes, painted decorative surfboards, and so on) were squeezed in as well. Just in case you didn't catch the maths, we now had forty new restaurants and shops plus the car park in front of our house!

Our hut was no longer right on the beach. We weren't on our own any more. We were no longer surrounded by lush vegetation—a peaceful green buffer zone from civilisation. We had enjoyed three years of relative peace and isolation in our idyllic little spot, but civilisation had now well and truly encroached on our patch of paradise. We were mortified. A part of the dream had died, and our hopes were significantly dampened as a result.

But perhaps the timing was right. We had been learning about the cycles of life, about the inevitability of change. We knew we were just going to have to learn to live with it.

One morning, not so long after the restaurants had opened, the sky was shifting from black to pearly grey when my personal alarm clock invaded pleasantly bizarre dreams.

'Mummy,' baby Kallen screamed. 'Come on, get up. You're so lazy. It's almost light, it's a new day. I need milk, I need changing. I need to get out of this room and get some action!'

I cuddled Kallen closer, just in case I could convince him to snuggle back to sleep, but it didn't look likely. I needed to be careful, too, not to let him wake his sister. We all shared the top single room of our three-level hut, usually with no problems, but every so often someone would be woken unintentionally.

Squinting, not wanting to allow too much light in until my eyes had adjusted, I could just make out some pinky strands of sky filtering through the bamboo outside the window. The thought of having to get up and out of bed at this unearthly hour of the day was not inviting, but then the promise of an early-morning beach panorama was almost incentive enough to get me moving. Carrying Kallen, I tiptoed carefully down the two flights of narrow stairs. He was wide awake and happy now. Gorgeous and googly eyed. How could I possibly resist sharing these private morning moments with him? Even if I could barely focus on putting one foot in front of the other!

Rather than sitting around and waiting for the day to formally begin, I popped Kallen in the special super-duper hiking baby backpack, and off we trundled to the beach for a pre-dawn walk. A great idea, I thought. Killing two birds with one stone (so to speak). Baby was happy, and I was getting my daily exercise. I had always believed in carrying my children while they were young, staying physically close to them, sleeping with them, being near while they need the extra care. My earlier travels had been inspiration for this, and watching the Balinese women carry their babies around in simple sarongs and stretch out with them on bamboo mats at night had only strengthened my gut feeling about it.

Zoe and I had been on long walks on the beach together when she was a baby—crossing busy roads and braving the late afternoon pedestrian traffic of the city. Our Bali beach scene had always been markedly different, but now the similarities between my new beach walking experience and the old one were growing disarmingly close. Coming out of the house early in the morning, my mind still half in a dream state, the grey sky only just clearing enough for us to see easily, Kallen and I were immediately confronted again by the apocalyptic devastation. It was a rude awakening. I had almost forgotten the cafes were there.

The wounds were still fresh, and I felt cheated. We walked over the bare dusty ground of the carpark, over the leftover building materials strewn around carelessly: rusty nails, bits of metal, wire remnants. Past the endless row of shops, rollerdoor shutters all clamped down. Past the open kitchens at the back of the restaurants, with dirty boxes scattered around, tiles already looking cracked and old. Past the open beach huts, piled high with the plastic and vinyl tables and chairs that would soon be positioned on the sand.

We had enjoyed our total peace and isolation for a decent period of time. I guess we should have been grateful for what we had been able to enjoy. But development was ruthless. Funny thing is that I'm not sure many of the locals were aware that in the process of trying to increase tourist capacity, they may actually have been turning the tourists off.

There's a classic example from the east coast of Bali. The popular tourist area of Candi Dasa, well known some time ago for its beautiful beaches and great snorkelling, was avidly developed by the locals. They bombed the reef to get coral for building tourist roads into the area, and ended up destroying the very opportunity they had set out to develop. The beaches were eroded away, and the smashed coral was no longer attractive to snorkellers and divers. It became an overdeveloped ghost town.

I really couldn't complain. Once we had passed the new developments on our beach we were stepping onto the cool morning stretch of sand and looking out at the broad ocean vista. It all fell back into perspective. Wow! The beach was absolutely glorious at that time of the day. It was so calm and clear, the sand fresh, the air soft. As the night lifted and cleared space for the rising sun, very subtle tawny colours pierced through the sky's misty canopy.

Although it was barely light, I could just make out the shape of a lone figure, slightly stooped with age but still very strong and capable, finding his way up the beach and back to the road. I eventually recognised the shape as belonging to an elderly American man who lived in the neighbourhood. This sixty-plus-year-old man had lived in Bali for more than half of his life, had made it his second home (perhaps he now considered it his real home). He had studied Balinese customs and ways of life intimately, and had published volumes about every detail. His books had actually been my source of information about the Balinese culture, and through these books he had taught me so much about the place and the people. He spoke Balinese fluently, had converted to Hinduism, and had adopted a local family as his own next of kin. This man's enthusiasm and genuine love for his adopted home was a real inspiration. Embracing the day at the break of dawn, it appeared that he had already walked the full length of the beach and was on his way home.

What an incredible amount of development he must have seen during his time on the island. And yet, there he was, continuing to enjoy the positive side of what the island had to offer, dedicated as always to simply taking pleasure in each day as it came, making the most of what he had.

After he left the beach, Kallen and I had the place to ourselves. We stopped and stared out at the expanse of water, and then I began to walk, enthused by the reminder I had been inadvertently given that there is always a bright side.

'Hey, look, bubba!'

Talking to Kallen helped me deal with the unfamiliar early morning silence. (And talking to your young infant positively is supposed to make all the difference in language development, isn't it?)

'I can see some fishing boats out on the water.'

It wasn't difficult to see the large triangular sails, bright swatches of colour against the steely water. Kallen had no idea what I was talking about, but he did seem to be transfixed by the colour and movement. Most often, whenever I saw the traditional *jukung* fishing boats they were high and dry up on the beach, lazily sleeping the day away. They were usually creatures of the night, bobbing spots of light in the pitch black—but in the day they became beautiful works of art, installations on the sand, with determined slashes of paint along the hull, expressive eyes and a long snapping snout at the front. They were sleek and slim, the bamboo poles balancing the boats at the side giving them a proud self-assuredness. On the boats we could see, some men were leaning over the sides, dragging along their fishing nets. Others were coming in to shore further up the beach, bringing in their catch from the night.

Starting our trek up the shoreline, we headed north towards the fishing area. The section of beach near the front of our house was quiet and relatively clean—the hotel next door made sure of that. It was carefully raked over each morning, appropriately by a cow with a plough, in the traditional way. Everything in the hotel grounds bordering the beach to the north was carefully positioned and neatly trimmed. Thatched grass umbrellas over reclining beach chairs, representing the ultimate holiday luxury, greener than green grass like a lavish soft carpet reaching down to the sandy edge. Hammocks slung casually between two tall palm trees in the background further embellished the tranquillity of the scene.

We continued walking until we reached a stretch of vacant land beyond the hotel. Here, the first locals of the day were sauntering down to enjoy the peaceful morning. It was now light enough to see up the beach clearly—even as far as the spectacular volcano that was perched on the horizon at the top end of the beach, usually well hidden by heavy, misty clouds.

'Gosh, bub. Can you see that incredible volcano? You've never seen that before, have you? We're usually still at home when that fellow makes his early-morning appearance.'

I stumbled over a stick protruding from the sand, an unseen vertical obstruction. Some cloth had been hanging slackly from the stick as a warning of its presence, like a minimalist scarecrow—but I was too busy looking at the horizon, mesmerised by the majestic volcano, to notice. As the cloth was knocked to the ground, I heard a disconcerted yelp rise from the water. A man, small, with a sunken chest, was calling out from where he had been bathing waist deep in the water. I realised now that I had evidently knocked his clothes off their hook. Wanting to save the embarrassment of him having to emerge from the water naked to rescue his clothes, I quickly bent down to salvage them. In the process, forgetting that there was a precious bundle on my back, I knocked baby Kallen around a bit and started him crying.

Well, if the beach was empty before, it suddenly now seemed crowded. People gathered around to see what the cause of the commotion was. The owner of the clothes strode out of the water to see for himself what was going on, and I quickly averted my eyes, focusing on soothing my crying child. He marched up and gathered his clothes, brushing the sand off them as he put them on. I was still trying to avoid looking directly at him, but fortunately by this time Kallen had almost settled. Next thing I knew the man from the water had grabbed Kallen and was putting a mark on his forehead. He was dressed in a white loin cloth wrapped around his groin, another white cloth around his head, and I could now tell that he was a priest.

Perhaps he had been praying on the beach before taking time out for bathing in the ocean. Or perhaps he had first been soaking in the natural springs that flow from between the rocks at one end of the beach—enjoying the healing properties, as many older men did.

The priest muttered something under his breath, in the Balinese dialect, and somebody translated for me into Indonesian.

'He is worried about your baby being exposed to the wind and the elements. He says no wonder your child is crying. He says the bad spirits from the wind can enter the child. He is worried that silly tourists don't know how to look after children.'

Apparently the priest had forgotten about my carelessness with his clothes. More important matters were at hand. Instead I was in trouble again for being so careless with my child, bringing him out and exposing him to the elements at such a young age.

'Please tell the priest that in my country we believe that the outside elements make the child strong, just as long as they are not too harsh. Please apologise for the inconvenience I have caused, and tell him the silly tourist woman was a bit rough with her own baby.'

The group smiled in unison, and then broke into laughter as they discussed the situation at hand. They obviously agreed with the silly tourist woman's assessment of herself. The priest gave a final blessing and a few fatherly words, then we were on our way again.

Walking for a while before we reached the position where the boats came ashore, we then spent some time watching whole family groups sort through the fish, check the net for sticks and seaweed, and then haul the heavy boats up the beach above the high tide marks.

'Look at all the fish! There's lots of fish in the boat. We must bring some money next time so we have a nice fresh fish to bring home for dinner.'

The fishermen had been too involved in their task to notice me up until then, but at this point they looked around to try to identify who I was and who I was talking to. 'So, the silly tourist women talk to their small babies,' I could see them thinking. 'No wonder they're all visiting psychiatrists by the time they reach adulthood!'

159

Although the village used to be a fishing village, the locals had quickly discovered they could make much more money from selling fish at their barbeque restaurants than from being responsible for the tiring task of catching the fish for themselves. The restaurants had actually started at this end of the beach perhaps five years before, and now there were seventy-seven in total, strewn all the way along the lengthy stretch of beach around the bay. Obviously the motto is, 'When you're on a good thing . . .'

As the local community started to pull out of fishing, fishermen began coming over from Java in their relatively small boats, many perishing in the rougher conditions, ironically because of a general fear of the water—so pronounced around Indonesia that even the fishermen cannot swim. In Bali the oceans have the power to purify and sanctify, and they can also be a channel for preparing the dead for their afterlife, but there is still an anxiety about the sea as the great unknown. The Javanese fishermen would sleep in small shacks on the beach or in a district settlement at the northern end of the beach after coming in with their catch. There were some brothels over the road to cater to their every need, too. Under the cover of semi-darkness, they would complete their morning ablutions at the waters' edge. On this particular day there was a foul steaming trail on this section of the beach along the path I had intended to take.

'Okay. Time to turn around,' I announced enthusiastically to baby. 'Time to head for home.'

One last look up the beach to the mountains—I could see all three volcano peaks now above the expanse of the bay. Amazing, so dramatic. You really had to be there at that time of day to appreciate what lay behind the scenes in Bali. The sun had already begun to appear above the tips of the coconut trees, casting its bright light over the mountains. Where the first rays reached us on the tops of our heads, small beads of sweat had already formed.

No sooner had we made the about-face decision than we were immediately greeted by a white dog bounding up towards us. Because Bali has such a limitless motley collection of no-breed mutts, many of which have grossly deforming skin diseases, my first reaction was to look for a stick to have ready in case of the need for self-defence. It actually took me a few minutes to recognise that the dog was in fact our own—GC No.2. The little rascal had jumped over the wall and gone for a nice wander all the way to the village to meet with his mates. Because he was a Bali beach mutt himself, he blended into the local dog scene perfectly, but I was not happy that he was mingling freely with his now lower-class cousins. Who could tell what nasty diseases or bad habits he might pick up?

I negotiated for a bit of rope from the fishermen, called GC No.2 to me for a pat, then quickly wrapped the rope around his neck. But the hardest challenge was to come. This was a totally untrained animal that had inherited the wildest of genes, and the walking-the-dog concept eluded him completely. He was well and truly taking me and Kallen for a ride. As we moved along I tried to absorb as much shock as possible in my arm, to make sure my son's ride was not too rough, but we both ended up zig-zagging behind him erratically. The beach was now alive with morning activity: school kids who'd come down for PE races, fathers keeping their babies happy while the mothers prepared the day's meals, the odd soccer game, tourists out for a bit of a local experience or some fresh tropical air. They were all busy, but they all seemed to have time to stop and stare or snicker at my strange predicament.

'I can see your dog's taking you and the baby out for a walk this morning!' A friend that lived nearby, cruising along in trendy jogging shorts and Nike shoes, ran alongside me for long enough to make this encouraging comment and then shot off ahead. Confident, in control. He had a well-trained and obedient German shepherd that had been imported into the country at great expense.

'How're you going there bub?' I yelled in a general backwards direction when the pace had slowed a little.

All was quiet on the passenger front, so I checked over my shoulder to see if he was okay. I could just see out of the corner of my eye that his head had lolled to one side, and he was snoozing quite contentedly. Babies can sleep through absolutely anything! By the time we reached the cafes in front of our house, I was exhausted. At least I had benefited from some exercise, and baby Kallen seemed to have enjoyed the adventure.

Our new neighbours were now laying out the cafe tables for the day. Because the tables were stored under cover at night, each morning they found a new position on the sand—always, it seemed, just that little bit closer to the breaking waves. I had seen shoes washed away, tables slide, and customers shriek when the tide had been misjudged and that one extra large wave swept up onto the shore.

The cafe families and staff crowded around me to fuss over the baby, waking him up by giving him a few of those good old hearty cheek pinches.

'Very good you have a little boy, Ibu. One girl and one boy. Enough.'

Many people in Bali have paid attention to the strong government family planning messages, and now most couples only have one or two children, unless they are still trying to have a boy . . .

'Yep, two children is plenty. I don't know if I could cope with any more babies. It's hard work. I'm not used to these early morning adventures.'

'Oh, but you're a strong lady to carry your baby all the way down the beach, Ibu.'

Just then GC No.2 jerked my arm forward and pulled the rope out of my grasp, picking a fight with the nearest cafe dog. Kallen started crying so I gave up on GC. I would have to disown him and hope he would eventually decide to come home.

'I'm obviously not strong enough . . . I'm not sure that I'll ever really understand babies and animals. They always seem to get the better of me!'

'They have their own spirits, Ibu. Don't try to understand.'

The Balinese must think it strange the way westerners try to control children and animals. There's no such thing as walking your dog for the Balinese. The dogs are simply free to come and go as they please. Children, too, are not usually strictly disciplined in the ways western children are.

After chatting for a while, I headed back towards the house, thinking about the way the Balinese adore children and give them so much positive attention. I reached the front door of the compound without even realising I had passed the ugly cafe post-construction site. Somehow, even through the onslaught of development, the beautiful Balinese environment and culture had continued to persevere—as always—and once again turned my own perspective around.

As soon as the trucks had moved in, we had started to think about the possibility of moving out. We were attached to the place and the people, so we were reluctant to give up what we had already benefited from, but opening up our garage door and looking straight out on the unsightly development couldn't compare with opening up to a coconut field. Then a great compromise solution came to us. At about the same time that we were getting concerned, Amelia told us that she was planning to move the playgroup to a larger purpose-built property. By that stage the group had grown from a small casual collection of friends into a more serious preschool business, and it needed room to continue to grow.

The timing was right. As soon as we found out the preschool was moving on, we contacted the owner about renting the building ourselves. By transferring to the back house—which was tucked in behind the compound walls—we would be in a lovely garden setting totally separate from what was happening in front of our house—and yet we would still have direct access to the beach. The timing was perfect in more ways than one. As it was we had already well and truly outgrown the house we were in, and the way our business was growing we would be more than bursting at the seams if we didn't find a solution soon. We had really loved our hut—for sentimental reasons as much as anything else—but it was time to expand.

The owner was asking $80 a week for the larger house at the back, so together with the front house we would only be paying $120 a week for a large property with two separate functioning buildings. After some basic improvements on the house at the back we moved our living area into it. Our original hut at the front was converted into storage, an office and a guest room. At the same time we decided to celebrate our growing commitment to our Balinese home by upgrading our facilities just a little.

We replaced the second-hand fridge that had been working more as a heat box than an ice box—but that had at least helped to keep the ants away from the food. Up until then we had mostly survived on fresh fruits, vegetables and fish bought daily from the local markets, along with powdered milk, rice and dried packet noodles—eating the way the locals do. After the arrival of the brand-new fridge we finally started enjoying cold drinks and limited deli items for a change. It then didn't take long to start to reintroduce foods that brought us back to our western eating habits. Although it had been near impossible to enjoy any real western food delicacies when we had first arrived, a few imported food shops had sprung up by this stage, tempting us with all those familiar tastes from home. Butter, fresh milk, Coon cheese, muesli bars, real chocolate. There are certain foods that it is hard to do without long term. (The local Indonesian margarine is designed to sit on a shelf without refrigeration in 40-degree celsius heat, as is the local chocolate—so you can imagine the wonderful chemical taste and oily texture they have!)

The next step was buying some shelves and cupboards for our personal belongings rather than relying on baskets, and proper beds with inner-spring mattresses. A little while after settling in to the new house we decided to upgrade to hot water for showering in, and cold airconditioning for sleeping and working in (for the office and bedroom).We suddenly felt like we were living in utter luxury.

Throughout the process of expansion and development we made some firm decisions about what we wanted to do without, though. We chose not to have a TV or VCR, for example. Although it had initially taken quite a while to get used to the deafening quiet, we found we really enjoyed the psychological space. The day remained less cluttered, and we continued to discover more ways to relax and unwind. Like walking along the beach. Like playing music and reading books. Like talking to the other members of the family!

Surprisingly, the children never asked for a television. Each day was already full, and so much of what they did was outdoors. A friend of my daughter did once comment to her that, 'Your family must be very poor if you don't have a TV!' But fortunately Zoe merely laughed about the funny point of view rather than feeling the pressure to conform.

It's amazing what you can do without when you really have to, or when you really want to. The way the Balinese culture had persevered through rapid change was an inspiration, a reminder that there are some important values you must be able to hang on to—no matter what.

A bigger property to take care of, a bigger business to run, and Heni was moving on with the preschool. We needed new staff—and we now had the space for them. Before too long a new household community evolved and took shape, which developed into enduring extended family relationships.

Ana was the first to arrive. Originally employed to help with the domestic chores and childcare, Ana was a simple, happy soul who kept us easily amused with her genuine but frustrated attempts to learn English. We would spend long periods of time trying to explain that we're going to make 'toast' rather than grill our 'toes', or that we were looking for our 'shoes' rather than someone called 'Sue'. But, although only young, Ana had an uncanny ability to find and choose other good staff. She had plenty of friends with a range of gifts and abilities, and I often found myself acting as a go between for other people I knew who were looking for staff. She married not long after she arrived, but rather than losing her to her husband and his family, her husband moved in and started working with us. Mustafa soon became a valued member of our household, too. The more the merrier, we figured!

Mia was an older friend of Ana's. She apparently needed a family to adopt. The children loved her like an aunt, as she mollycoddled them and always responded caringly with an infectious smile. She sang Indonesian songs and lullabies, and brightened the house like an early morning ray of sunshine. She was enthusiastic and efficient with both domestic and business demands.

Ketut—or Ketut No.1 as we came to call him (there were soon two Ketuts in the household)—was our other live-in male companion. He had been employed to be a driver for our business and help with maintenance. He was a young lad with large dark eyes, long lashes, and an innocent and willing attitude to match (also, incidentally, found by Ana). We would often find young Kallen perched somewhere playing a Balinese drum while Ketut played the bamboo *gamelan*. At other times I caught the two of them jumping at a newspaper ball wrapped in rubber bands and hanging from the ceiling, two cheeky little kids. As Mia was the aunt, Ketut became the big brother.

More staff also started to come in on a daily basis—such as Ketut No.2. A dependable, loyal friend, Ketut No.2 lived in a compound nearby. Like the others, she would slip into any role we needed her most for at the time—domestic or business. Our children often went to her compound to play with her extended family and friends.

By the way, there's an interesting reason why our Ketuts shared the same name. Most people in Bali have one of four names according to their birth order. Every first child is called Wayan (pronounced something like Why-yahn), regardless of whether they are male or female. Every second child is Made (Mah-day), the third is Nyoman (Nee-oe-mahn), and the fourth is Ketut (Ke-toot). And the fifth child? From then on the names are repeated, so the fifth is Wayan, the sixth is Made, the seventh is Nyoman—and so on—ad infinitum. The only exception to this rule concerns those of the upper castes and royalty, who have special names. Just as well most families only have two children now. But it does mean nearly every Balinese person you meet is a Wayan or a Made! In one extended family living together, you'll always have a few cousins and aunts and uncles with the same name.

Nina came on board next, helping out as a supervisor in the business. With good English and organisational skills, she was able to cope with the demands of the growing international company. Her ability to coordinate the roles of the other staff—and to generally get things done efficiently and effectively—made her a valued addition to the clan.

Then there was Yulia, our key Bali-based associate. By the time Yulia came along we had a number of excellent associates based in Australia and all through Asia—with management teams in Sydney and Singapore—but Yulia was a godsend for our work in Indonesia. We were very lucky to come across someone who had both international education and experience and appropriate local knowledge. She had been a neighbour, had lived for a while in the other solitary house near ours, and we had got to know her through helping out with her magazine work. A beautiful woman with stacks of charisma, she also had a good deal of practical sense. An unusual combination. She was so good at the social niceties, but also developed into a very astute teacher and program organiser. In no time at all she too became one of the family, as well as an incredibly invaluable team member.

All of our staff family, live-in and live-out, shared roles and responsibilities. We were all busy together, all helping each other out. The compound became a hive of activity, with many people coming and going each day. There were by this stage six adults living on the property, plus our two children. It was the closest I had ever come to cosy communal living. The kids really enjoyed having company at all times of the day, and we were never short of companionship and conversation ourselves. It was a great way to live.

At times I wondered about whether it was fair to have become reliant on so many different people, but at those times I would remind myself that it was actually reasonably close to the traditional Indonesian way of life—where large groups of people live and work together. The western nuclear family concept is really a relatively new social construct. Only in the last hundred years or so have families been defined as mum, dad and the kids. And even now that idea has been redefined—with single-parent families becoming so common.

Most of us in the west find it such a struggle to get through each day and to cope with all the expectations of modern city living. But I came to believe that we're just not meant to live that way. It became clear to me that we were meant to have the support of family and friends who are attached to us in some way, and who share mutual cares and concerns. It is not normal to have to employ staff to come and assist you with your daily requirements, but neither is it normal to have to try to cope on your own.

The sense of harmony and balance we experienced—of mutual assistance and appreciation—soon calmed my fears about employing staff in this different cultural setting. I felt so lucky to have the opportunity to share in these people's lives.

No sooner was our enlarged household set up and running smoothly and the business doing really well, than disaster struck. Indonesia erupted in a mass revolution.

Tensions had flared up in Jakarta, involving extensive demonstrations and the threat of the president being overthrown.

This first taste of violent crisis Indonesian-style came after some student protestors were shot. The oppressive Soeharto government of thirty years was losing its firm grip, and the possible implications were unimaginable. Nobody was sure how far-reaching the violence was going to become, and when it was clear that a revolution was imminent, the stakes were raised much higher. Even distant Bali, the eternal holiday island, started to feel the political fallout. By mid 1998 the whole country was suddenly in a state of emergency.

Just imagine, the same president for thirty years! If you get the same teacher for more than one year it can be a real bore. If you're stuck in the same job with the same boss for more than two it can get you down. If you can't change your country leader every so often, you're bound to start to feel like you're stuck in a rut—at the very least. Soeharto had brought relative peace and economic stability to the country, but only through a strict military dictatorship.

As soon as the lid was let off the box, there was an excited euphoria. Like teenagers who have just turned eighteen, the Indonesians were ready for a wild night on the town, ready to express their suppressed yearnings for political freedom.

In Jakarta, Australian army jets were flown in to evacuate expats, and Australian navy ships were positioned off the coast in case of further emergencies. In Bali there was a clear and strong undercurrent, an excited anticipation of change—but it was still very difficult to tell how that excitement was going to express itself. Some hotels evacuated their expat staff families, most families that remained in Bali stocked up the household with extra sacks of rice and tins of meat. We all had our passports and extra cash put aside, with evacuation plans in case the worst got to the worst.

After we had been living with the uncertainty for a while, avoiding going out too much, we braved the Kuta streets one night with some friends, tired of waiting at home for whatever might happen. It was spookily quiet. There was plenty of space to drive down the street, to park your car, to walk down the sidewalks.

'Please you buy a watch . . . look at my rings . . . have massage . . .'

The ratio of streetsellers to potential customers was now 100:1, or so it felt. They were absolutely desperate to make a sale. I've heard that most Balinese who work actually support another eight people in their family (apparently each worker has to support eleven others in Java)—so by this stage things were starting to look desperate. We couldn't spend long in Kuta that night. It was too depressing. How could an area so dependent on tourism possibly survive?

Our young fledgling company certainly felt the after effects, and we just had to sit it out to see what would happen next. We were learning the tough lesson that business in contemporary Bali can be so unpredictable. Many other local businesses, most of which also relied heavily on tourism, suffered badly. Hotels, which took the brunt of the tourism bust, were down to a fifteen percent occupancy rate when they should have been close to a hundred percent at that time of the year. They lost millions upon millions of dollars.

When the economy took a sharp nosedive, a lot of basic food commodities went up by three hundred percent or more. The price of petrol doubled. Large numbers of locals were out of work and out of luck.

In Bali the social support structures within extended families are so strong that no-one was ever completely down and out. But, although beggars and street dwellers had been virtually unknown, at this point in time there was a noticeable difference in the welfare of non-Balinese on the island. Suddenly, stopping at traffic lights could mean having a grubby forlorn child's face plastered to the window, hand pitifully held out in a pleading gesture. Washed-out mothers with tiny babies permanently attached to their breasts started knocking on the door of the house asking for handouts. The Balinese continued looking after each other, but victims of the revolution were flooding onto the island from other parts of the country.

One obvious change in the Balinese people was the awakening of the sleeping giant, the fierce and proud independent spirit of a tiny island of Hindus in the midst of a massive Muslim nation. The tribal roots of the Balinese people were also revealed in street demonstrations, as there was the realisation that for the first time freedom of speech was not just a dream, it was a right. In Kuta this translated into a sort of modern tribal war, where the soup carts of the poorer Javanese streetsellers were overturned and set alight by the Balinese locals. Their owners were run out of town, and for once the streets were completely devoid of the famous hassling traders. The area was now even quieter than that night we had gone into Kuta before the violence began. As much as the street-sellers can be a hassle, it felt even sadder to know that there were more people out there somewhere without an income.

Almost simultaneously, other giants were awakening all around the country. Conservative Muslim separatists in Sumatra stepped up their ongoing campaign, dramatically adding to the increasing death tolls. The Muslims and Christians fought in the Malluccas, sending thousands of homeless refugees fleeing from the small island. Freedom fighters in Irian Jaya intensified their campaign. Christian churches were burnt to the ground in Lombok, instantly turning the once growing tourist resort into a ghost town. And East Timor finally moved towards independence, after years of aggressive Indonesian occupation.

It was chaos.

I have learnt that the most important things in life can survive and even strengthen through any upheaval, so long as you keep looking for the positive.

In Indonesia's case, the country needed a dramatic overhaul to begin to deal with the many years of suppressed problems. Sorting it all out was going to be a very long, very involved process—so much had become ingrained in the system, but it had to happen.

And for us? We found ways to benefit from the changes, too. A Christmas trip back to Australia had already been planned, so we chose to spend more time there building up our business networks. We had the opportunity to develop areas of the business we hadn't yet had the chance to work on, and we had valuable time with family and friends, ensuring we didn't cut ourselves off completely. In the end we stayed in Australia for a good four months, making the most of prospects developing there.

As unsettling as this unexpected change in plans was, it gave us a reminder that all things change. They don't have to come to an end, but they will not necessarily stay the same. You can't hang on to the ideal forever. You just have to learn to adapt to the change, go with the flow. To find the positive where you can and make the most of it.

Chapter 13

Culture to Culture

We were now stuck between two cultures: not ready to give up all hope and move everything back to Australia, as we had invested too much in our Balinese home and business, but not knowing whether we could continue to live in Bali over the long term. Still so attached to our special tropical way of life, it was also clear we had to keep our options open, to ensure that we were covered if things did get more desperate. And, after all, Australia was our home. We didn't want to give up on that, either.

The timing was right for using the basement flat under our Australian house this visit (in fact, I made sure it was right!). After being away for three years, Zoe still had some sense of this house as her place of origin, so we were glad to have the chance to reinforce that feeling. Although it was small and dark, we needed to try to create a temporary home there. Unfortunately, we ended up with hay fever and then bad cases of the flu from handling the mouldy mattresses and bed linen stored in our garage, and from such a sudden and dramatic change in environment from an airy seaside grass hut to a cold, damp urban unit cut into stone. It took us a few weeks to regain our health, settle in and get ourselves organised . . . but it was still difficult to settle in properly.

It was hard to try to fit into everyone else's busy schedules. And no sooner had we readjusted to the money system, the driving rules, the social norms, the education standards, the times, shopping and eating . . . than it was time to change again. But we did try to spoil ourselves, to take advantage of some of the lurks and perks of the wonderful Australian lifestyle that we had been cut off from or had deliberately cut back on in our more simple Bali lives. TV and videos, ice-creams and takeaway fish and chips and hamburgers, theatre and children's playgrounds. Only having limited babysitting options meant that TV and videos were often relied on for childcare backup, and having to cook on our own again meant that takeaway was often a tempting option! The other entertainment choices were pure indulgence for us all.

Our time in Australia also happened to coincide with Zoe starting school. I felt that was a real positive, that it would give her the chance to get an Australian schooling experience and feel a little more in touch with her roots. I wanted to ensure she still had a sense of home.

Zoe began attending the local primary school as soon as the school year started. We bought the uniform and the school bag and lunchboxes, and she was set. Ready to go.

She was so self-assured on that first day, happily trotting off into a brand-new classroom in a brand-new school. I had a tear in my eye and a lump in my throat, thinking of how fast she had grown up and how independent she had become, but she seemed to be ready to be off on her own. I was sure that travelling and living in a supportive and secure environment in Bali had helped her to develop that incredible confidence, a willingness and enthusiasm to face new circumstances. She made several new little friends, most of whom we have managed to maintain contact with over the years, and generally got herself into the neighbourhood crowd.

Zoe's school hours gave us some parameters to work around, a daily routine. We would try desperately to shake her awake at around eight o'clock to get ready in time for school at nine. Even though there's not much of a time lag between the two countries, we all somehow stuck to Bali's time zone. So getting up at eight was like trying to get up at five. Though of course Kallen was always up and cheery by then, as was his regular habit!

A quick breakfast of cereal, fresh milk and yoghurt. Complete luxury. We had bowls and bowls of the stuff in quick succession. Everything from then on was a mad rush, arms and feet flying everywhere as we all tried to get dressed and ready in time, assorted objects being scattered around the room in our wake.

When Andrew was off doing the business meetings and it was my turn to drive Zoe to school, I'd bundle both kids in the car and pull out of the driveway in a mild panic, knowing the bell was about to ring at any time. My driving had become a bit erratic anyway, since living in Bali. I forgot how to stick to lanes and stop at red lights and pedestrian crossings. But the added dimension of the last-minute rush made me pretty lethal on the roads.

Zoe was dropped at school with a farewell kiss, a last wave, and a pang of guilt. Was this the right thing for her? Was I expecting too much? Was she going to cope with all the changes? But she was always a happy, adaptable child. She was doing amazingly well. Next, Kallen was taken to his childcare place. Another kiss, another stab of guilt—especially since he was still so young and didn't have much of a concept of what was going on. It was much harder to judge how he was coping.

From then on it was a mad rush to get as much done as possible while the childcare hours ticked away, then it was pick-up time. We followed the same procedure, except in reverse. There would often be some household errands to run with the kids in tow—bank, post office, grocery shopping and so on—and then back to the house to try to get the children bathed, fed and dressed for bed by a decent hour. Not that they were able to get to sleep straight-away. Because their time clocks hadn't adjusted, we spent ages trying to cajole, coerce or compel them to sleep.

Everything was so much quicker, more straightforward and more efficient than in Bali, but the daily routine still became very tiring and wearing for us all. It was a wonderful 'back to our roots' time, but it was tough, too. It reminded me of all the things we had tried to leave behind, and provided a window on to how life would have been had we continued to live in Australia.

I became particularly concerned when Zoe started to feel the effects of being in a large urban schooling environment. She was one of a class of thirty. One kindergarten class out of five. One hundred and twenty children in all in her kindergarten level, almost 900 in the whole school. She loved the lively and stimulating environment, her warm and caring teacher, but little by little she started to feel lost and overwhelmed by the sheer number of children. When she had a change of teacher the pressure was on. She started getting anxiety attacks about going to school, refusing to get out of bed, complaining about stomach pains.

As soon as the dust had settled after the political crisis, we knew it was time once again to get back to our community household and lifestyle. We were relieved that our time in Bali had not been brought to a premature end, that we had been given a second opportunity to live in our paradise.

Back in Bali we began to appreciate the time and space we had created in our lives more than ever before. Just as your senses are more alert after being in a contrasting physical environment—we were now all the more keenly aware of the special qualities of our Balinese life. We threw ourselves back into it with renewed enthusiasm and vigour.

We reunited with our Indonesian household family, who had been patiently awaiting our return. I could tell they had really missed the children, and we had all really missed them. Bali seemed to have survived relatively unscathed, and we were relieved to find everyone was doing fine.

Business was picking up again slowly, but I still had some time on my hands, so I decided to start doing correspondence lessons with Zoe at home. It was very difficult and frustrating at times, probably due to my high expectations and the intense nature of a one-on-one learning experience between mother and daughter. But it also gave me a wonderful opportunity to be involved in her early learning experiences, and Zoe gradually relaxed back into the enjoyment of it.

As business continued to improve I soon found I no longer had as much time for the lessons, so Zoe joined a small correspondence group with a supervisor. There just weren't the schooling options at that time. It was a very special learning time, where education was very flexible and personal, but it was not a secure arrangement for the long term. When the need arose we reconsidered the possibilities. By this stage at least six schools for foreigners had popped up in the tourist segment of the island, so there was more choice. Zoe ended up attending the island's first established international school.

The return to more formal schooling brought routine and structure back into our lives, particularly since the school started so early in the morning and was so far away. With an eight o'clock start, and a good half-hour drive to get there, we were often left scrambling to get ourselves together in the mornings once again. I continued reflecting on the two lives we had lived in the two different cultures in close succession. On the similarities and differences. We had developed similar structures and routines in both places, but somehow the flow was different. The day began in much the same way in Bali, but there were also marked contrasts.

Breakfast was the first point of both similarity and contrast. They say you can tell where a person comes from by the breakfast they eat, and we were obviously still very Australian. We were quite happy having rice for lunch and dinner nine times out of ten, as is the typical Asian custom, but we couldn't quite get into the three times a day habit. No thank you. For breakfast we stuck to the good old western traditions of cornflakes, porridge or vegemite toast. But we made one major concession to our tropical environment—fruit salad. Mmmm . . . seasonal tropical fruits . . . fresh and tangy first thing in the morning . . . there's nothing better. Juicy mangoes were always the favourite, when they were available, followed by the deep orange papayas, full-flavoured bananas, succulent crimson watermelons . . . rambutans, mangosteen, melons . . . all with squeezed lime on top. Heaven. Throughout the day we ate more fruit than a fruit bat would—apart from breakfast, we enjoyed fresh mixed juices, fruit lassis with yoghurt, fruit snacks. Nothing wrong with our digestive systems!

The Indonesian members of our household had quite a different morning routine. Mia was always up and praying at five o'clock. The most religious Muslim member of our household, she donned her special headscarf and petticoat-style dress, and spent a good half-hour or so bending to the ground in prayer. She would then spend some time on the beach, enjoying the freshness of the morning, before returning to the busy household. An inspiration to us all. Our Hindu neighbours would also be awake and active preparing their offerings, cooking food, and visiting the markets to avoid missing out on the early-morning bargains of the day. Most Indonesians would only have a snack soon after waking, and then a more hearty meal at around ten or eleven in the morning. Something like a brunch, but always with stacks of rice.

Ana chose to take on the market shopping responsibilities for the house, and she usually liked to leave nice and early to get the freshest produce. That was another point of difference. Where I would have been doing the shopping late in the afternoon in Sydney, after everyone was already exhausted, the shopping in Bali is an early-morning activity. Yet another major difference was the prices and quantities—we could spend as little as $400 a month on food for our household of six adults and two children, and that included the thirty-five kilos of rice required to keep our Indonesian family members happy! Ana absolutely insisted we didn't go with her as we completely spoiled her bargaining power. On the occasions we or our children had gone, the process was slowed down considerably by the extra chatter about who we were, where we came from, what we did for work, where we lived, etc, etc . . . And the prices were definitely higher. It was always a lively and fun experience at the local markets, finding the best fruit and vegetables and the best bargains in the tiny intricate laneways. It was colourful and noisy, but it is definitely hard work haggling over every item.

'Three for six.'

'Three for six? No way. I got six for six last week!'

'This week they're three for six.'

'How come?'

Here are some of the typical answers:

'Galungan coming up . . .' (big religious festival)

'It's going out of season . . .'

'Petrol prices have gone up . . .'

'I'm bankrupt . . .'

'It's rainy season . . .'

'This is a special kind . . .'

There's always some reason why the prices continue to fluctuate.

'How about five for six?'

'No, three for six.'

No budging. A final desperate offer . . .

'Okay, then four for six. Here take the money.' You get it out and waggle it in front of the stall owner's face.

'Okay.' Deal sealed.

Of course when I talk about 'six' for the price, I am not talking in single digits, I am talking in thousands of rupiah. That is another tricky part of the negotiations, checking you're talking in the right number of zeros. Just to give an idea of the scale: a small packet of chips is worth hundreds, paying for a kilo of fruit or vegetables is in the thousands, clothing prices are usually in the tens of thousands, monthly wages are in the hundreds of thousands to low millions, cars are in tens or hundreds of millions, and house prices can be in the billions and billions. The highest note until a few years ago was the 50,000 rupiah note, which is worth about $10. Even now Rp100,000 is the highest note. Imagine what it's like dealing with these quantities of money on a daily basis. You need to take a large sports bag with you if you want to change money or pay for a car in cash.

Whenever you do change money or pay for something, you have to have the patience to count and recount large amounts over and over. Then there are the additional problems associated with working with tricky money changers. After being duped several times over, we compiled a top six tricks list for the majority of money changers' operations in Kuta:

1) The ledger book cover-up trick: Covering up some of the piles of money with the ledger book, and slipping a few notes away from underneath.
2) The rapid disappearing act: Counting nine notes and dropping the tenth behind the counter.
3) The tampered calculator con: Using a calculator where the symbols on some buttons have been rubbed out and changed so that the total amount is incorrect.
4) The total confusion scam: Relying on the possibility that you

will confuse the number of zeros on the end of the note, the money changer passes off a 10,000 note for 100,000.

5) The patience pusher ploy: Counting and recounting the money till you simply run out of patience, grab the piles of money, and walk out without half of it.

6) The hidden charges hoax: Adding taxes onto the cost of changing the money after you've spent hours and hours counting and checking it, even if the money changer displays a sign saying 'No commission'.

Nothing like simply queuing up at the local ATM back in Sydney—or making electronic payments at the cash register! On the positive side, though, getting used to dealing with the local currency, our daughter learnt to calculate in thousands and millions and to handle conversions between three currencies by the age of seven—which can't have been a bad thing for her maths development!

There's a humorous angle, too. Andrew was once with a client in Sydney when Nina called from Bali on the mobile phone to check some payment details:

'No we don't have all thirteen million ready to go,' he said casually. 'Just pay the ten million now, and the extra three million will come through in the next day or so.' Little did the client know, Andrew was talking in rupiah, not dollars! Andrew said he was suddenly taken a lot more seriously by this client after that phone conversation!

Basic shopping and money-handling procedures and negotiations can be so much quicker in Australia, while they can drag on forever in Bali. And yet, in a strange sense, it's another of the things that makes Bali special. It reflects the emphasis on taking the time for interpersonal transactions.

Now, back to our daily routine—and the not inconsiderable task of getting Zoe to school. As I've mentioned, in Bali—just as in Sydney—we were often in a bit of a rush to get out the door. But unlike in Sydney, in Bali we had wonderful Ketut to drive us.

I always thought having a driver would be unnecessary—we could drive perfectly well ourselves and often enjoyed doing it—but I found there were certain benefits to having someone else help out with driving. One was that whenever we got pulled up by the police there was someone else to do the negotiating, in the local language. And we were less likely to be pulled up in the first place because there was not a white person driving the car!

Another is that we could actually get a lot done while travelling in the car as a passenger. When I was on my own with Ketut I could scan proposals, prepare notes for a meeting, catch up on my daily newspaper reading—or continue my study of the Indonesian language. Ketut became my Indonesian teacher, helping to explain signs we came across as we were driving, and words or phrases that I heard regularly but hadn't yet learned the meaning of. We had long conversations in Bahasa Indonesian about the current political situation, the Balinese way of life, the weather. And when I travelled with Zoe to school, we were able to spend that precious travel time completing whatever morning tasks had not yet been completed. We finished homework, studied spelling, ate fruit salad, cleaned teeth, plaited hair, read books. For two reluctant early morning risers, it could be a really valuable catch-up time.

Ketut was a great driver, too. He was only eighteen when he started working for us, but he had already spent a year after finishing school driving a truck around Denpasar city doing deliveries. He knew how to weave his way in and out of the lanes between motorcycles, cars, vans and trucks. But he also had that notorious Indonesian habit of tailgating the car in front.

'Is your girlfriend in the car in front?' Andrew always asked him if he was in the car when it happened, which inevitably brought on fits of laughter, stretching that permanent grin even further.

'No rush, Ketut,' was all I would say when he had to stop suddenly behind a turning car, and my fruit salad ended up half on my lap, half in my hair, the remnants squashed under my feet.

'No problem if we're late, Ketut,' I would say a few minutes later when a sudden jolt tugged Zoe's plait out of my hand, making her shriek in pain.

Of course Ketut's job was not made any easier by the strange traffic conditions in Bali. You couldn't, for example, turn right out of or into a main bypass road. You had to do u-turns instead, which meant that there was always one vehicle or another suddenly pulling up in front of you—or, if it was coming from the other direction, suddenly trying to turn around across both lanes. The idea was so absurd that any vehicle longer than a Tonka truck needed all four lanes of the road to turn, and even then it often had to end up doing a three-, four-, or five-point turn while the traffic on both sides banked up for miles around! I couldn't tell you the number of accidents I'd seen at these u-turn intersections.

Then there were the roundabouts. Now, in Australia we have a rule for our roundabouts. Vehicle in the roundabout has the right of way. Simple. It took a long time to work out if there was any rule for using roundabouts in Bali. I think it was something like: The biggest and/or most aggressive vehicle needs to be given the right of way. At roundabouts, as on any part of the road system, it really was the law of the jungle. And they often became gridlocked, for some strange reason, so that all intersections became blocked for miles around. We had a whopper of a roundabout intersection halfway along the school route, with five feeding arteries. It was the central hub from which roads led west to Kuta, north to Denpasar, north-east to some other suburb, east to Sanur, and south to Nusa Dua. When that intersection became blocked, just about the whole of Bali stood still.

People always asked how we could possibly drive in those conditions, but it's funny how you adapt. Possibly even scary how quickly you adapt. You can survive if you learn to check in front, behind, and on either side of you before you turn the steering wheel even the slightest amount. The other rule is to be assertive and confident; use the horn as much as possible to let others know you're not intimidated and you're coming through, or flash your lights at everyone if it's night-time.

'Negotiating the traffic in Bali is like travelling with a school of fish,' a long-term expat once explained to me. That simple bit of advice kept me sane on the roads, even allowing me to appreciate the free-flow concept.

Anyway, Ketut would eventually deliver us to school and almost in one piece. After removing the tufts of hair from my hands and cleaning the squishy bits of fruit off the other parts of my body, Zoe and I would get out of the car and walk to her classroom together.

Zoe's classroom was tucked away in the corner of the school, in a small garden haven. At one time, she and her classmates had been busy building a small terraced rice paddy right next to the classroom. They'd dug into the ground, shaped the terrace, formed the simple irrigation system from a small fountain placed at the top, and sloshed in the mud to plant the rice seedlings. They'd observed the standard Balinese customs for growing rice and had participated in the required blessing ceremony in full Balinese dress. Then they waited for the rice to grow so they could harvest it. While they waited, they helped build a bamboo *bale* hut near the paddy, for rest breaks during harvest time.

I don't remember my early schooling experiences being quite so much fun—or relevant. Of course Zoe still had to follow a curriculum not dissimilar to most countries in the western world, but somehow learning seemed more colourful and vibrant in this context—particularly when she was able to explore the wonderful environment in such practical ways.

Not far away, in one of the many local Indonesian schools, the kids would already have been seated inside and working diligently at their lessons. They'd sit on hard wooden benches, often four or five in a row, forty to fifty in a class. There would be no resources, at least virtually none—no textbooks, reading books, maths games, science equipment, art supplies, and computers were all extremely limited. The only interaction the students would have with the outside environment was when they were on cleaning duty, sweeping the yards with the stick brooms they'd all brought from home and digging the gardens with small improvised hand shovels, or when let out for short breaks.

By the time Zoe's school had started at eight, the Indonesian students in the school down the road would have already been working an hour. The schools are so overcrowded that they function on two shifts: seven a.m. to twelve p.m., and one p.m. to six p.m. And school runs six days a week. The teachers must be absolutely exhausted, and are definitely underpaid.

Learning is purely rote—copious notes scrawled on blackboards are conscientiously copied into exercise books. There is no real interaction between teachers and students, or between the students themselves. No discussion, no experimentation, no discovery learning. Discipline is very strict. How can you possibly teach creatively under those working conditions? Also, for a long time, education was a means of indoctrination and social control, so real freedom of thought has not been encouraged.

Exams are a way of life in Indonesia, too. A great money-making exercise for the government, I suspect, as you have to pay for your child to do the nationwide exam at the end of each term before he or she is permitted to progress to the next level. These exams are quite difficult rote learning exercises, often with bizarre irrelevant questions, and sometimes the answers are not even correct. For example, here's a question from a junior-school exam:

What is the national anthem of Australia?
(a) 'The Star Spangled Banner'
(b) 'God Save the Queen'
(c) 'Waltzing Matilda'

As Zoe stepped into her classroom, I'd call out those last-minute instructions: 'Don't forget to put your lunch in the fridge . . . And don't forget the money for the excursion is in the outside pocket of your bag . . . And wait at the playground after school to be picked up today . . .'

'Yes, Mum.' She'd sigh. 'Okay, okay, okay . . . I know what to do. You can go home now.'

They grow up and become independent so fast.

Zoe would then skip off to join her class of fourteen kids, all seated on the carpet reading near the teacher, or in other parts of the colourful classroom, finishing off individual projects. I'd blow a last kiss as the door closed, always conscious of how incredibly lucky she was to be able to enjoy such a positive learning environment.

Looking at my watch—usually just as the school bell rang—I could confirm it was now eight a.m., right on time. I could now get back to the office by eight-thirty, ready to start work. The day was really only just beginning!

Once the children were happily occupied for the day, we could focus on our business. After settling back in Bali, our work picked up so quickly that we were inundated with proposals and programs.

Having now spent some time developing the company back in Australia, it struck me how differently business was dealt with in the context of the two cultures. In Bali we could spend half the day on menial tasks or trying to get projects completed in between electricity failures and phone line disruptions. At times it would drive us insane, but we eventually learnt to make the most of the opportunity by switching off and relaxing. Every time something threatened to disrupt my busy work schedule, I would think about the way Ibu Gendeg's funeral procession had brought me back to the important priorities in life.

In Sydney, business had been much smoother, slicker. The boundaries for negotiations were clearer, but the expectations different. There was less margin for error of the local home-grown Balinese variety. The market was much broader and less personal.

Although we worked solidly in Bali, at the end of the day there was always the chance for a surf or a swim right outside our front door. We only needed ten minutes to get out there and unwind. And we made a habit of doing it almost every night, no matter how many deadlines were hanging over us. This was our chance to take time out for our family and for ourselves. Even when we took on those extra-curricular after-school activities that kids in Australia take on, with all the driving around that tends to go with them— at various times swimming, tennis, piano and ballet (and Balinese dancing)—we rarely missed out on at least a few minutes on the beach. Surfing or walking, chatting to our local friends, drinking fresh coconut, watching the fishing, catching crabs and collecting shells—there was so much to do. We ensured that each day we would get out there, sift our feet through the therapeutic sand, stare out to the mesmerising horizon, and enjoy the fresh, damp air. Whatever time we had available was enough to give us a good daily dose of the ocean's healing properties. And then at night we always slowed down that little bit more to enjoy the peace and quiet of a house without extra appliances.

We had lived between two cultures, and we had loved aspects of both. At the end of the day, though, it was good to come back to that serene space we had created for ourselves in Bali. We were so grateful that we had been able to reclaim what we had set up for ourselves, that our life in Bali could continue.

Chapter 14

Home Base Bali

Four years on.

Long enough to know that we could survive whatever new challenges might come our way; we were experienced enough now, too, not to be scared of making more of a commitment. The political situation had more or less settled down. There were still huge ongoing problems in other parts of the country, but Bali remained separate enough to be able to start functioning again as a tourist destination—albeit a more subdued tourist destination.

We took out a six-year rental contract on our compound in Bali. Looking back at the four years that had already passed and what we had already been through, it just didn't seem like a big deal to commit to that sort of time any more. It was so satisfying to know that we could really settle into our Balinese lives.

It was time to reassess the rental of our house in Sydney, too. I think we had wanted to be able to forget about the house for a while—to leave it to the agents. It was, after all, representative of the burden of responsibility we had wanted to leave behind. Now, though, we knew we had to face up to the responsibilities of ownership, and on our next visit to Australia, we intended to do just that.

Partly our fault, perhaps, that we had not been vigilant in keeping up to date with the property maintenance, but we had no idea that the house had been so badly looked after for the year since we had stayed in the basement flat. We could not believe that the place had deteriorated so quickly. The house had gradually been wearing down, but was now looking very old and tired. A lovely old renovated Edwardian-style house in its prime, with white shutters and diamond-shaped leadlight windows, it was now well and truly showing its age. The garden was completely over-grown, the paintwork peeling off, the plumbing rusting away.

The house had been rented out to groups of singles while we had been away, and was lacking that cared-for look that a young family or professional couple might have given it. A whole heap of ancient tatty or rusty furniture was scattered throughout the house and garden. There were cigarette butts everywhere. Taps, lights, appliances were all dirty, grimy, broken. I noticed an invitation on the fridge inviting all and sundry to a rave party, where 'anything is allowed', at—guess where—our house.

Great, just great. Our lovely family home cum guest house had turned into a wild singles drug den.

All of the agents who had been appointed to look after it had been hopeless—each one progressively worse than the one before. The latest agent hadn't sent statements for a year, hadn't collected rent for months, and most of the time we couldn't even locate him. The tenants were complaining of water and electricity being cut off because bills hadn't been paid by the agent, of problems with making rental payments and in receiving maintenance services. It was an absolute disaster. Quite a price to pay for being absentee landlords. For recklessly following the dream.

Apart from cleaning up the agency mess, and changing agents just one more time in an attempt to get everything back under control, we had our own personal clutter to sort through. The garage was piled high with any worldly possessions we couldn't carry with us when we left all those years before. At the time we'd thought they were of some value, but when we courageously ventured into the overcrowded storage space to attempt some sort of sorting process, we came out feeling overwhelmed by the moun-tains of dusty junk. For the first time since we had left Sydney, we realised we would have to be ruthless with our possessions. That it was time to let go of a past that we had been attempting to hang on to 'just in case'.

Zoe's baby clothes and accessories went out. Assorted kitchen utensils were ditched. A whole pile of old woollen jumpers, double-breasted suits, and one-time special dresses and shoes. All sorts of odd bits of furniture, old books and toys. Some items were sent off to St Vinnies, and then a large waste removal container was brought to the garage door. We defiantly dumped everything in, feeling like a significant weight had been thrown off our shoulders along with the piles of junk. All we hung on to was a few pieces of furniture that had real sentimental or practical value, and our precious photo, video and slide collections.

It turned out to be a wonderful cleansing process, which helped to prepare us psychologically for the next phase in our Balinese lives. We were not going to let go of our Australian home; we still all needed to feel a sense of our roots and to hang on to the friendships and family relationships that had been so important to us, but we had to face up to the fact that it was going to become increasingly difficult to keep our feet in both camps. We had to come to terms with the idea that Bali was now our main home base.

Home base Bali definitely continued to offer all the right ingredients for both our personal and our business development.

While we went on happily absorbing local community values and enjoying our positive lifestyle on the home front, our business continued to grow significantly. Even with the dips in the local commercial scene, there was increasingly enough work abroad to balance out our needs. As the company expanded, many long-term client relationships developed, and we were invited to travel round Asia more and more for work—sometimes to different conference destinations, but often also to the clients' company headquarters, to consult with and train executives and executive teams.

We could never have anticipated how ideal Bali would be as a base for business around Asia—even if we had deliberately planned out our whole company setup ourselves! Because the island is centrally located in the Asia Pacific region, we found it was very easy to get around. Only two hours to Singapore, three to Kuala Lumpur, five to Hong Kong or Manila—contact with clients was only a short phone call or flight away. We could easily travel around the region and hardly disrupt our daily schedule. Apart from the major city destinations, we travelled to many interesting and exotic places around Asia—to Borneo, Sabah and Johor in Malaysia, Phuket and Chiang Mai in Thailand, Bintan and Bogor in Indonesia, Cebu in the Philippines, to Vietnam, Cambodia, Japan and Macau. Always staying in beautiful five-star hotels.

Mind you, travelling around Asia and staying in exotic locations in luxury hotels was not quite as impressive as it may sound. Many times we would hardly get to see the resort, hotel, or location we were visiting. Most often we'd have to travel straight from the airport to the hotel and back again, with barely time to look out the window of the taxi at the passing views. Then at the hotel we'd be rushing directly from our room to the conference rooms on automatic with no real concept of where we were staying or what facilities there might have been. Still, every so often we could tack a day or two on to the end of a work program to take more time to enjoy the destination, and we were often given a glimpse into somewhere we may not otherwise have had the opportunity to visit—giving us the incentive to return there later when we could.

Perhaps one of the main reasons we really enjoyed the travelling was that while we could experience new places and meet new people, we could also maintain our secure home base, a sense of stability and continuation. Furthermore, because the living expenses in Bali can also be relatively low (as long as you manage to live without too many of those little western luxuries!), because the support is so strong, and because the lifestyle can be so comfortable and relaxing—we were in a great position to extend ourselves and meet whatever challenges lay ahead, in the greater world beyond.

There was always the chance to step out on the beach at the end of the day and feel that incredible sense of release. And it was always possible to find the balance we needed: a natural blending of work and home, personal and professional, traditional and modern, giving and receiving.

Sometimes Andrew and I travelled and worked separately, simply to cope with the different demands of our clients. But we were usually able to keep in close contact and maintain a unified management of the business during these times through emails and phone calls. There were also times when we could travel together for work, too, and we came to cherish those opportunities. When both of us were working on the same project, it often meant we were simply going flat chat together rather than separately, keeping each other awake with the small details that would need to be dealt with the following day. But it was always great to be in each other's company, to feel that we were charging ahead in top gear, together.

One night we were staying in an exclusive hotel in Shanghai—a spectacular glass highrise with absolutely every modern convenience and contemporary feature. We had retired to our room after a particularly heavy training and consulting program, stopping for the first time to relax and take in the dramatic surroundings. We were high on that post-program euphoria, having given so much and achieved so much. And we had done it together.

It was absolutely exhausting, though. The three-day conference had involved coordinating and presenting an intensive program for top executives from a financial institution. We had given one-on-one coaching sessions, group workshops, up-front presentations and had done the corporate social thing at night—the dinner cruise, the lavish theme dinners, the presentations and dances. To cap it all off, the general personal feedback and the evaluation sheets the participants had filled in showed that the program had been highly successful, so now we could unwind, satisfied that we had done our best.

We turned on the bath. It was soon looking very inviting, bubbling over with scented oils. A huge moulded tub, with the finest of fittings and polished marble edges; you couldn't ask for a more ideal spot in which to relax. Windows filled one side of the bathroom wall, reaching right down to the edge of the bath. When we slipped into it, and rested our heads on the side of the bath, we could see down about twenty floors to the street studded with bright lights below—or out over the bright cityscape to a distant horizon.

Sighing simultaneously, we shut our eyes and breathed in the moment. Gentle classical music was drifting through from the main stereo in the lounge area. The soft lighting was just enough for us to appreciate our surroundings without overpowering our senses. There was no need to say anything. All had been said and experienced together. We were in synergy.

I had just moved on to another level of consciousness when the phone rang. As low as the volume was, it was an annoying intrusion.

'I should have disconnected the phone,' Andrew groaned.

'We couldn't do that. We should never be out of contact in case someone needs to ring us about the children,' I reminded him.

'I guess so.'

'Well, are you going to answer it?' It was accessible from the bath at his end.

'Hmmm . . . guess so . . .' He reached over lazily and picked up the receiver. 'Yes? . . . We'll just have the dim sum then thanks . . . . Hang on, I'll check on that . . .'

Andrew covered over the mouthpiece and looked at me, 'They don't run the snack menu at this time of night. Is there anything else you want?'

'No, just dim sum is fine thanks. But tell them to bring it in twenty minutes, so we don't have to jump out of the bath too soon.'

He passed the message on and hung the phone up, before sinking back into the bubbly depths.

The phone rang again.

'I told you I should have disconnected the phone,' Andrew complained, but picked up the receiver immediately anyway.

'Hi, sweetie! What are you doing still up?'

I assumed it was Zoe, so I jumped out of the bath, threw on the plush white bathrobe and spongy terry towelling slippers, and padded my way through to the other phone in the main room. I picked it up just in time to hear her sad little voice say:

'. . . but I can't get to sleep, Daddy.' Enough of a whimper in it to tear at my heart strings.

'Hi darling, Mummy's here as well. Are you having trouble getting to sleep?'

'Yes, Mum. I've tried and I've tried. Can you come home now?'

'We'll be home tomorrow. But how about taking some camomile tea and asking Jane to read you a story?'

'Okay, Mummy. But can you just tell me the story about when I was a baby and we went hiking in Nepal?'

An abbreviated version of the story followed, after which we blew kisses all around and she seemed settled enough to attempt to get to sleep again. Sometimes I'm not sure whether the easy phone access is a blessing or a curse; I couldn't count the number of times we've been rung on our mobile by a little girl desperate to say just one more thing to Mum and Dad. In this case, though, I did feel relieved to know she was okay and that we had been able to give some form of positive reassurance at a time she'd needed it.

The dim sum arrived soon after that, and we settled into the lounge with the bathrobes on, feet up on the coffee table. We debriefed about the program, sharing thoughts about the people we had met, the insights we had experienced together, the possibilities for the future. We then talked about our upcoming schedule. I was keen to get the next few weeks straight in my mind so I could sleep easy that night.

'So, you'll go to Hong Kong on the twelfth, while I take care of the program in Bali, and then we'll need to make a firm decision on who should go for the program in Phuket on the twentieth.'

'Aren't you coming to Phuket?' Andrew was horrified by the suggestion that I might not be there.

'Just you and Alex should go. I don't want to be away from the kids twice in as many weeks.'

'Oh . . .' he pouted. 'But it's just not the same without you.' He batted his long, thick eyelashes. It usually worked—it had for more than twenty years. 'Please come . . . It's a beautiful place.'

'No, not this time. You're right, there's nothing like being able to do this together, but we have to balance that with the needs of the kids.'

'How about we take the kids, too, then?'

He threw me there. I hadn't thought about travelling with the children. I contemplated all the possible reasons why not, and couldn't come up with any decent ones, so I carefully answered: 'Yeah, okay. That could be a possibility.'

'Go on. Let's see if we can swing it.'

'It's going to be a heavy program . . .'

'It's a great hotel, and I'm sure they'll have fantastic kids' club there. All these places do. The children will love it.'

'Well . . .'

'Great. I'll book the tickets on Monday. If we take an extra day or two, we'll be able to make a good long weekend out of it.'

So, it looked as though Andrew had relaxed enough into travel that he was not fazed by the idea of travelling further afield with the children. And here he was trying to talk me into something out of the ordinary for a change!

We watched movies on satellite TV until the wee hours, shared our love on the crisp white sheets of the vast king-sized bed, slept heavily through the night, lay in delightfully late, and then enjoyed a lazy continental breakfast on the balcony, served on a silver tray. There was even time for a swim in the pool and a walk around town, before heading for the airport in the late afternoon. How heavenly. We arrived home refreshed and reinvigorated, ready to face our demanding work schedule again, enthused about the prospect of bringing our children with us on the next trip.

We must have looked a peculiar sight. Mum and Dad in their corporate gear, ready for their first meeting straight after landing, each loaded up with a briefcase containing a laptop and program materials on one shoulder, a child on the other hip or being tugged along at breakneck speed. Although we had travelled back to Australia plenty of times before with our children, the work factor added a different dimension again. Besides, travel is never straight-forward with children.

A few people did ask us why we would want to travel with the children. Travelling with a family can be difficult enough, as any journeying parent will tell you. But travelling with children while working is obviously considered absolutely suicidal.

'Families aren't meant to be portable,' my home-loving brother-in-law had always insisted with an indignant snort every time we whisked in and out of Australia. 'Families are meant to stay home.'

But of course children can be incredibly adaptable. And in the end it's usually worth any discomforts. In fact, I've found that so long as we can put up with the tougher side of travelling with the children, the rewards of sharing such a wonderful family experience far outweigh any hassles. For starters, it's always an incredibly mutual learning experience to travel with children by your side. Children can form an amazing link with people in other places, and particularly in other cultures. Many people are interested in your children, and in many countries families are warmly welcomed into local communities. Children also have an interesting, pint-sized perspective on life, and their knee-high observations can be absolutely astounding.

But now our main motivation for taking our children with us when we travelled was that we didn't want to be constantly taken away from them by our work. We wanted to use these work opportunities as opportunities to strengthen our relationships, too. I remembered back to our first experiences of travelling with Zoe to work on the India project, and knew how much we had all benefited from being together as we worked. I knew those new and different experiences had been amazing for her and had changed us in so many positive ways.

Regardless of our best intentions, on the journey to Phuket we had already argued with the children over how much luggage they could take before we'd even left home (we were already sure we were overweight with program materials). For any sort of journey—whether it was for work, for leisure, or for a home visit—there were always one hundred and one things to carry. At the check-in counter we'd cross our fingers, hoping that we'd get an especially nice attendant. Sometimes just by starting up a friendly conversation we could divert attention from our embarrassing predicament. Sometimes the sheer number of bags and articles we carried bamboozled the most diligent attendant. By the time we'd ferried items on and off the weighing machine, we were all confused about the weight. This time, though, having the kids with us was enough. Although the children's possessions were actually the least bulky and least weighty items we were carrying with us, there seemed to be an unwritten rule that travelling with children necessitates a whole lot more gear than usual. Fine by us. It almost worked out cheaper to bring them with us to get the extra weight allowance than paying for the overweight baggage!

The next hurdle was getting on to the plane successfully. Kallen had developed a habit of jumping on the small Samsonite suitcase we usually took on as hand luggage and grabbing a free ride. Pulling the weight of him plus the case along those long concourses could be quite a drag—literally! As soon as we actually got on to the plane, we argued about who was going to sit where, we wrestled with Kallen to keep him glued to his seat, and fussed over how many sweets it was sensible to eat during the flight.

It may have been a hassle in many ways, but we also had wonderful impromptu geography, maths, and English lessons: counting the seat numbers as we walked past them until we reached our own, looking at the world map together to trace our route, and reading all the important things that needed to be read on an aeroplane such as menus, immigration cards and flight safety information (okay, so the safety information is in symbols—but that is an important pre-reading experience for small kids, you know!).

When we arrived at our stopover point, Kallen decided it was time to go to the toilet for number twos, and took his time at it. We were worried we might miss our connection, but managed to get through in the nick of time. After finally reaching our destination, we were looking and feeling a little dishevelled—but a quick smarten-up in the hotel room and an efficient drop-off at the kids' centre, and we were ready for that first meeting.

The children often had to learn to look after themselves when travelling with us, and they usually did so very admirably.

A babysitter could always be organised through the hotel, but we often found that Zoe actually ended up being the boss. Zoe knew Kallen's routines, and usually acted as the responsible older sister, giving instructions and disciplining him appropriately whenever necessary. But then she also knew how to take advantage of the opportunity to take control. It occurred to me, yet again, that she was becoming more and more like her mother!

One day, we walked into our room between meetings to say a quick hi to the kids and to pick up some notes we needed. Zoe was on the telephone when we entered, and she urgently motioned for us to be quiet until she had finished. We sat obediently on the bed nearby, bemused and curious about what was going on. The babysitter was sitting on a chair in the corner of the room, apparently waiting for her next direction.

'Hello, is that room service? I'd like one Batman Burger, a Mickey Mouse Mini Pizza, and some Fred Flintstone Fries. Oh . . . and two strawberry ice-cream cones.'

Our mouths were agape, as we sat and watched. We were too stunned to say anything. We were not sure whether to chastise her or congratulate her on her confidence and excellent organisational skills. Not bad for a six-year-old! When she got off the phone, we just continued staring at her.

'We didn't know you knew how to order food,' I eventually said.

'Of course I do,' she replied. 'I've seen you do it lots of times.'

'But . . . you should have checked with the babysitter and she could have made something for you. We left you with some food so you could make your own sandwiches and have the healthy snacks we provided.'

'Come on, Mum. You know that's not fair. You're eating out at the restaurants all the time, and ordering room service whenever you want it. We can't be expected to survive on stale bread and boring snacks, you know.'

'At least the babysitter could have helped you.'

'She doesn't know how to ring room service!'

'I guess you are very clever to be able to organise it all,' Andrew ventured, 'but perhaps you should let us know before you do it again . . .'

'You guys are just not around at the right times. You'll have to learn to trust me, okay.' A simple defiance. Firm and strong.

Fair enough, I thought to myself. We were going to have to start giving her a little slack. Our little girl was growing up, and she was going to need a reasonable amount of self-determination and self-confidence to be able to cope with the constant change inherent in a travelling and working lifestyle.

Not long after the first incident, I turned up to the room unexpectedly and found Zoe on the phone again. Uh oh. I became concerned she was developing a bad habit. I was about to rudely interrupt and speak to her sternly about taking the whole room service thing too far, when she started speaking to someone on the other end of the line.

'Hello, is that reception?'

Hmmm, this was going to be interesting . . .

'We have lost our room key and would like another one delivered, thank you . . . . Okay, then, I'll be waiting for you.'

It sounded as though they'd taken this young child's request quite seriously. Sure enough, a new key turned up not long after.

'So, how did you get in to make the phone call?' I asked, astonished at her resourcefulness.

'Oh, I just called the housekeeping lady who was up the hallway. They always have keys to all the doors, you know.'

At the end of our stay, I noticed that there were a few extra pizzas and ice-creams on the bill, but Zoe generally appeared to have made her choices responsibly. She had also been a wonderful mother substitute, consoling Kallen if he was unhappy about us leaving, and organising activities for him. Zoe and Kallen had started playing together more, with little two-year-old Kallen taking more of an active role in initiating play. It was amazing for me to see how much my children had matured. I'm sure these unique 'coping with Mum and Dad working while travelling' skills will come in handy for them somewhere down the track. With the security of strong, loving family relationships, I hope they will have a firm foundation for exploring and surviving successfully whatever roads life may choose to take them down.

With all of these different experiences, our children continued developing a broader sense of what home was and what it meant to them.

By the time Kallen had acquired the language skills to express his own ideas and opinions, he'd developed his own sense of Bali as one of his homes. Whenever someone asked him where he came from, he would answer, 'Bali and Australia'. He would usually then hold up two fingers and say proudly, 'I have two homes!'.

We were sitting in the hairdresser's salon in Kuta one day when it came around to his turn to get his hair cut. (At only two dollars per cut—or an exorbitant four dollars if you wanted a wash, blow dry and head massage included—it was a common way for the family to spend a rainy Sunday afternoon. Not a great cut, by any means, but who really cared at that price?)

'Oh, he's so gorgeous, isn't he? Look at those beautiful big eyes and those long dark lashes!' the hairdresser exclaimed. (The eyes and lashes have been inherited from Dad, of course, and have been just as successfully utilised for winning me over to his requests or demands.)

The dozens of overtly gay men from Jakarta working in the salon were all over Kallen like a rash, they were often all over Andrew like a rash, too, much to his dismay!

'And blond silky hair . . . Too much,' the cutter squeaked excitedly.

'Where are you from, darling?' one of them asked my son directly.

Kallen came out with his standard response: 'Bali and Australia.' A quick, confident reply from such a little fellow. It sent ripples of girlish laughter through the whole salon.

'That's gorgeous, darling. But where are you actually from?'

Kallen looked at me for help.

'We live in Bali. But we're originally from Australia,' I replied for him.

'Oh, Australia, yes.' The hairdresser stroked Kallen's hair affectionately. 'But you live in Bali?'

'Yes,' I said.

'How long have you been here for?' (A very standard question.)

'Four years.'

'Four years! My goodness—did you hear that?', he announced to his cohorts. They all clucked and nodded their approval together. He commenced the cutting procedure with a grand flourish.

'So you like Indonesia, then?'

'Yes, we love it. It is a really beautiful place. It has become like a home.'

More clucking and nodding. It was the right answer to give. It also happened to be my honest response.

The hairdresser turned back to Kallen, who was by now covered in irregular lengths of hair clippings. The small thin Indonesian man, who was dressed in a tight black t-shirt and jeans—and with bright orange spiked hair—went on to ask Kallen some basic questions in Indonesian, to which he dutifully responded, and the ensuing conversation in Indonesian kept the whole salon amused for a good ten minutes more. As the last few strands of hair were brushed away from his shoulders and the powder puff liberally applied to his neck, Kallen stared at his reflection in the mirror for quite a while, obviously trying to absorb the concepts. It seemed like he was noticing, perhaps for the first time, some of the differences between himself and the Indonesian people all around us.

'How come I have white hair when all my friends have black hair?' he suddenly announced to us in quite a concerned tone. 'I come from Bali, too. I wish I had black hair.'

I tried to explain the idea further to him. 'We have found a nice place to live in Bali, but you come from Australia. That's where Mummy and Daddy come from, and where our family and a lot of our friends come from. A lot of people back in Australia have white hair, too.'

'Like Sam?'

'Yes, like Sam.'

'And Katie.'

'Yes, Katie has blonde hair, too, doesn't she!'

'But I have two homes, don't I Mummy?'

'Yes. That's right. We are very lucky we have two wonderful homes.'

So many times we were asked how long we intended to stay in Bali, as if it was some extended holiday we'd someday have to return home from. But although we were asked that question many times over, we never really formulated a decent answer.

Usually simply shrugging our shoulders, we would say something to the effect of, 'We've got no plans to move on at this stage . . . . We're happy where we are . . . We'll just have to wait and see what happens next . . . .' It was, after all, hard to plan ahead when we were living in a country in revolution, in a state of constant change. Not having to plan was a major part of the attraction of living in Bali, anyway!

We continued enjoying the lifestyle that had become so special to us in Bali and beyond, in the other parts of Asia we were travelling to. At this stage I had no desire to be based anywhere else. We were making the most of the opportunities open to us at 'Home Base Bali'. And that felt good. Really good.

Chapter 15

Island Life

Paradise has a wonderful way of sweeping you up and carrying you along. Life moves on. It's easy to relax, and drift with the tide.

Perhaps that's because time can move on a completely different scale in paradise. It can blow in and out with the seasonal winds, it can ebb and flow with the movement of waves on the sand. It often rises and falls with the changing shadows formed by the passing sun.

'Rubber time' they call it here. Very apt.

When there are no external time restraints, no school schedules or work meetings, you can lose yourself in the moment. That's why people come to Bali for holidays. That's why it began to feel as if we were on a permanent working holiday.

We knew that our time in Bali was precious, that it could end at any instant, so we became all the more determined to enjoy every moment. As each day progressed, we would allow ourselves the luxury of getting lost in that rubber time as often as possible, drifting with the flow, emerging only when necessary. Although we were working just as hard as we had ever worked, perhaps achieving more than we had ever achieved, somehow we didn't feel so trapped by time. And I think that this sense of freedom we enjoyed in the environment and our lifestyle helped us to regain our sense of health and vitality.

For so many years before we had come to Bali, we had tried to defy nature's laws. Because we could change our body clocks to suit our chosen lifestyle demands, we did. But our bodies paid the price. It became easy to see. While the Balinese look twenty-one years old for most of their adult life, and then only seem to start to show slight signs of aging when they reach their middle years, no sooner had I rounded the curve into the thirties track than I was already desperately trying to stretch away those wrinkles in the mirror and cover over the steadily encroaching grey strands in my hair.

Andrew and I have actually always led a relatively healthy lifestyle, despite our heavy work commitments: no smoking or drugs, limited drinking, plenty of exercise, and a pretty good diet. That kept us looking and feeling young right through our twenties. When we were high school teachers we were often mistaken for students. (You take that as an insult until you realise it's a much better alternative than being mistaken for the parent of a teenager!) We were Peter Pans for a while, looking and feeling good.

But I remember the first time I came to the realisation that the stress was catching up to me. Somehow, somewhere around that thirties mark, I started to recognise I wouldn't be young forever. Too many days spent staring at a computer screen, too many late evenings trying to meet work deadlines, too many sleepless nights sifting through the day's unfinished business. It does catch up with you. Before I knew it there was a haggard version of my once eternally youthful self staring back at me in the mornings, dark eyes ringed with evidence of sleep deprivation, skin etched with worry lines. I started to suffer from strange skin conditions, inexplicable headaches and diarrhoea. But there was no strange cause. No exotic bug.

'Stress,' said the doctor.

The first natural remedy to rapid aging and total body destruction has been the 'living on the beach' factor. Another has been the choice to stick with the simpler, fresher, less processed foods the Balinese have traditionally enjoyed. And yet another natural remedy has been making the most of the simple living concept that we have pretty much maintained throughout our time here.

But then there are also the fantastic leisure opportunities . . .

Sunday again.

Through those first few years of establishing the business in Bali we had worked a six-day working week, which was the Indonesian way, and which is probably fairly typical of anyone starting up a new venture. We often worked through much of Sunday as well. There would be Sundays when we promised to take the kids to the beach, but they would instead spend most of the day sitting in the office with their swimmers on, begging for us to get off the computers and get going. It was not at all ideal. I knew we were over the biggest hurdle in the business development, though, when we were able to reclaim Sunday as an official day of rest.

As Sunday developed more into a real day off for our whole compound, I actually made everyone in our immediate family do a bit of housework—to help even out our household contributions just a little, and so we didn't all end up getting totally domestically incompetent. Then there was piano practice for Zoe, some time spent lounging around and reading—unable to motivate ourselves to move much—before taking off to some other part of the island to make the most of the opportunity to be together as a family.

We'd load up the car—by this stage we were past the VW Safari, had finished with a tiny two-door Suzuki jeep, and were now on to a rather substantial 4WD-style Panther—which was just as well, as we had a stack of gear to pack in, and whenever the whole extended household went out together this car could accommodate us all quite comfortably. Now, I say a 4WD-style Panther because this car looked just like a 4WD. Any visitor to the island who got into it thought it was a 4WD. But the car didn't actually have 4WD capabilities. It was such a typically Indonesian thing to do—to copy the idea without really appreciating the concept. But it was a great, roomy car. You could just about camp inside it (and we should know, we'd camped in just about everything in our time!).

Once the car was crammed full of surfing gear, bikes, tennis racquets, swimming gear—and whatever else we might be needing for that particular day's excursion—it was on with the seatbelts (we had to install them ourselves—at great expense—and they still probably wouldn't even have saved us in an accident), and we would be off. By the time we ventured out of the house it was often already late morning and it would be hot. Really hot. We would try to salvage whatever cool puffs of air we could from the car's pathetic airconditioning (we paid a lot for that, too, and I swear it never, ever worked—no matter how many times we had it looked at by however many experts we could find).

On one particular Sunday we aimed straight for a beach on the opposite side of the isthmus to ours, not more than about fifteen minutes away, and then oozed out of the car like a handful of half-melted wax candle figurines. For the next few hours, we plonked ourselves on cosy lounge chairs perched on the carpet of white sand under a pandanus tree. The soft wind drifted over our bodies, as we sipped on fresh, iced fruit juices, buried ourselves in books, and passed in and out of sleep as easily as if we had not a worry in the world.

I was reading a book my mother had sent over to me for my birthday, *Life is So Good*. It was the memoirs of a 102-year-old black man who had only learnt to read when he'd turned ninety-eight years old. Any literature was like gold, as it had to be smuggled in from out of the country or begged out of the hands of unsuspecting visitors to the island. Apart from a few guide books and general interest Bali books sold in hotels and some department stores, there was nothing at all meaty and in the English language to interest the avid reader. There certainly weren't any bookshops with English language books.

Zoe curled up on my lounge with me, and asked me to read a section of the book to her. Because we had learned to share this special time off together, to go with the flow, we often shared some amazing discussions and experiences that we may not otherwise have opened ourselves up to, and this was one of those times.

'*I stared at the hard candies in the different wooden barrels...*'
I started reading.

'Why are they in wooden barrels, Mum?'

'This story was written about what things were like in America a hundred years ago. They didn't have plastic containers and plastic wrappings for lollies like we do now—they used to sell them in huge containers made out of wood. Did you know that in the past there were no plastic wrappings in Bali, either? They used banana leaves to wrap food in. That's why there's a pollution problem now, because you can't throw plastic around the way you can throw banana leaves around.' (I always tried to include an extra little moral lesson whenever I could, and it was often at these times that Zoe would be most receptive.)

'Oh, okay. Come on now, get on with the story.'

'. . . *The man behind the counter was white. I could tell he didn't like me . . .*'

'Why was he white? Why didn't he like the boy?'

Hmmm . . . how was I going to explain such a complex concept simply . . .

'Well, darling, in those days a lot of people had been taken to America from Africa in ships just so they could be slaves to the people that had already settled in America from Europe. Those who came over on the ships had black skin, and those who were already settled in America from Europe had white skin. Because the people from Africa had to work for the white Americans as slaves, a lot of the white-skinned people thought they weren't important and didn't treat them very well.'

'Oh, I see.' Zoe's eyes were growing ever wider as I tried to give a term's worth of history lessons in one short description.

We continued to discuss the details of the first few pages of the story, stopping at almost every new sentence; about the fact that the writer had to work to help his family from the age of four; the 'ribbon syrup' he and his father had prepared to take into town by horseback to sell; his family living and sleeping together in one room back at his house; the Ku Klux Klan; about the hanging they see in the main street of the town . . .

Soon we were in the throes of a different reality. I became aware, perhaps for the first time, that our children had lived a pretty charmed life. Really—to be able to enjoy an endless summer, to be able to frolic in the fresh air all year long, to be surrounded by quite a number of exceptionally kind, caring people—you couldn't ask for a gentler more forgiving introduction into the world for your kids.

Fascinated by the concept of hardships, perhaps by the sheer contrast between her own experience and that of the child in the story, Zoe insisted I continue reading, and continue explaining the peculiarities of this foreign world.

It was pretty heavy stuff for a six-year-old.

Eventually she said, 'Why is the book called *Life is so Good*? It doesn't sound very good, does it? If I was there, I would just go into that main square and let that man off the rope. I wouldn't let them do it.'

I looked at Zoe and saw myself at the same age. I had wanted to step in and change the world but had learnt, gradually, that the time needs to be right. That we can overcome problems and deal with unjust situations with persistence and conviction. That was how we were learning to deal with the underlying Indonesian crises.

'Yes, life doesn't always seem fair,' I told Zoe. 'We need people to help the people who are in trouble, but sometimes we have to wait for the best time. What the man who wrote this is trying to say is that we can always change things in some way . . . and we can always look for the positive.'

I paused, and took the conversation on a slightly different tack.

'People can get pretty nasty when they're just judging each other on the surface, like by their colour of skin. Do you ever think there are differences between yourself and people with skin of a different colour?'

'No. We're just the same people but with a different colour skin, aren't we?'

'Yes, of course.'

At that moment it occurred to me that Bali was becoming the central frame of reference for my children. They probably couldn't even see that they were different, that they had a different heritage and had been exposed to different values. In many ways they had learnt from us, and stood out from the locals in the same ways we did—but in other ways they had absorbed more of the Balinese spirit.

It was still a very turbulent time for Indonesia. I had communicated just a little of what was going on around us to Zoe; it was all very complex for a six-year-old. I wondered if we would reach the point where we would have to leave Bali permanently, how the children would respond . . . how they would be affected . . . how their perspectives would change . . .

They spoke better Indonesian than I did (certainly with a more authentic accent), shared more secrets with our household friends than I did, could dance and move like the Balinese. Even though the children still proudly called themselves Australian, their Australian nationality was becoming more and more of a textbook concept. I was glad they had developed a broader view of the world through our travels, but I did wonder about their future—whether they too would find the need to search for their own patch of paradise one day, whether they would think of Bali as their home or whether they would once more fully embrace their Australian identity and live in their country of origin.

I had to remind myself it was a Sunday. A little time for reflection and homespun philosophising was not a bad thing. The most startling truths and ideas often strike you when you're most relaxed, when you allow your mind to open up. But there needs to be time for recreation as well.

Dragging myself back to the present, I chased the kids into the ocean, which was as tepid as a baby's bath, and yet refreshing in the tropical heat. They surfed the small waves on body boards, delighting in trying to stand for a millisecond or two before the rolling foam caught them.

Meanwhile Andrew started setting up for a kite surf session, his latest hobby.

He had dabbled in a number of different watersports in his time, and had found Bali to be the ultimate venue for doing them all. Not only did Bali catch more swell and wind, but it provided the most glorious conditions for being in the water. Warm air temperature, warm water, beautiful beaches. Glorious scenic backdrops:

tall cliffs, misty volcanoes, swaying palms. In this environment it was possible to switch from the ultimate adrenaline rush to ultimate serenity, moment to moment.

Kite surfing was the zenith of the sports he had enjoyed to date—surfing, windsurfing, snowboarding, and wakeboarding all thrown into one exhilarating experience. And me? I had a brief fling with all of those sports for quite a few years after meeting Andrew, but by this stage was more content to be lolling in the water with the kids than trying to thrash around with the latest fandangled equipment.

Before long the kite-surfing gang had arrived, and they had all gathered together to discuss the prospect for the day.

'Owzitgoin', mate? Looks a bit on the light side, eh?'

'Yeh, reckon. Wots the reading, then?'

Cam pulled out his super-duper wind gauge, and the gang gathered around for a serious assessment.

'I doon't care about zis silly gauge. I'm just going to get oot zere for myseelf,' Francois retorted in that haughty French way. Before the slow Aussies had the chance to put two and two together, Francois was set up and ready to go. Once the kite had been launched off the beach, Francois hooked a rope from the holding bar onto his harness, grabbed his board, and walked out into the water, kite arching over the top, way up high. He was up and away, red and orange sail slicing through the air defiantly.

The huge fifteen-metre square kite on the thirty-metre long lines carved out a mighty big chunk of air space. It had to be kept moving through the sky in a figure-eight motion in order to build up the power needed to pull Francois along on his board. With enough power, the kite would pull him up out of the water so that he could do daring acrobatic twists and turns before landing on the water again. The sail sliced the air over the top of a few gorgeous sun-bathing beauties, coconut-oil slicked and well-browned topless torsos, and was swinging down towards a group of children just next to us before heading our way on the return loop.

'Quick. Under the water!' I yelled.

The kids and I ducked under just as the kite swooped overhead. It was actually a fair way above our heads, but the sheer size and speed of the thing was daunting. I noticed the mother of the children next to us had marched down to the edge of the water with an accusatory forefinger waggling in the air. Francois had conveniently managed to shoot out of hearing range, but I could see he was likely to get a good serving when he came back close in to shore.

I've heard that there have been some pretty horrific accidents with kite surfing. The kites reach so high—and the thermal winds can elevate the surfers so far above ground level—that one person actually ended up jumping clear over a four-lane highway near the beach. Another managed to get his kite tangled in a helicopter rotor blade!

Unconcerned by the possible dangers of the sport, however, the rest of the kite-surfing gang were soon out there with Francois, after having established a different launch point further away from the regular Sunday crowds. The sight of the massive crescent-shaped kites ducking and dodging each other against the clear aqua water backdrop was spellbinding. When Andrew came back into the beach, he was thoroughly exhausted, and completely relaxed.

We were all well rested and ready for another working week. Having our regular Sunday routine made all the difference in ensuring we had the chance to fully recharge, but it wasn't our only opportunity—Bali had so many leisure options that the working week was never really a huge burden . . .

Watersports are but some of the strange 'colonial' activities available on the island. Expats have found many more ways to re-energise in Bali.

Some may seem a little bizarre and out of context, but that's often the nature of the expat scene, where many attempt to recreate the comforts and choices of what has been left behind in the home country rather than making the most of the different opportunities available in the host country. Not that I'm complaining—I appreciate the range of choices just as much as the next person and could now not do without many of the little western luxuries I have come to enjoy—it's just every so often it strikes me as being a strange juxtaposition.

You can do tae kwon do, ballet, art classes, French lessons, reiki, yoga, cricket . . . you can go golfing, horse riding, hang gliding, canoeing . . . you can join Alcoholics Anonymous, Christian churches, New-Age meditation . . . you can get colonic therapy, chiropractic treatments and pedicures . . . the list is almost infinite.

During the strange waiting time we experienced when we resettled in Bali after the Jakarta riots, my outrageous actor friend Sarah started an amateur theatrical society for her female friends—perhaps subconsciously to take our minds off the ongoing uncertainty we were all feeling. It was actually great fun—some of the best release I've ever had—acting out absurd scenarios from different settings and losing ourselves completely in the moment. With bamboo and coconut trees as a visual backdrop and roosters crowing for ambient musical accompaniment, we took ourselves to Hollywood and Havana, to the moon and back.

This theatre group attracted quite a range of different women, including a school teacher, a business woman, and a few mothers. There was an alternative Ubud hippy and a beautiful Seminyak trendy. Amelia was there, and so was Anne. I think the different levels of the expat scene were pretty well covered. Women who may not have been friends, but were drawn together by a sense of fun and a willingness to make fools of ourselves. In this situation the unusual combination worked.

We would often be literally rolling on the ground in fits of laughter, unable to control the spontaneous humour. The climax was a production we put on in a convention centre. It was a murder mystery spoof set in a manor in England in the early 1900s. We wore large dresses, all flounces and frills, and had backdrops of dusty old libraries and grand living rooms. Inside the comfortably airconditioned convention centre we were no longer in Bali. We were in a time and space warp. It was a pretty bizarre feeling.

Mind you, the most bizarrely artificial scene I have seen was when we saw a Christmas production in India. As we walked into the hall where the show was to be held, we went through a dramatic transition from the baking stench of urban Calcutta to the cool sensation of an elaborate snow scene. There was fake snow everywhere, ice carvings, real fir trees, and Indians in sporty little snow outfits with fake fur trim on roller skates (pretending to be ice skating).

I'd never quite understood these sorts of contrasts in India, and yet there I was, acting out Edwardian England in the tropics. Strange—but weirdly comforting.

Of course the Balinese don't have any such elaborate leisure pursuits, but they sure do know how to relax and unwind.

They will happily sleep through the heat of the day. Sitting in the little roadside *bale* huts—those huts originally designed for resting during breaks from planting or harvesting in the rice fields—they will then talk the rest of the day away. Hours and hours and hours—apparently as much as twenty-five percent of the waking hours of the Balinese people—will also be spent leisurely preparing for ceremonies, making the coconut-leaf decorations and delicate *canang* offerings. And the men enjoy drinking and gambling as much as men tend to enjoy them in other parts of the world—although what they drink here is a particularly potent alcoholic *arak* rice wine or the strong *brem* palm liquors, and the favourite form of gambling has traditionally been cock fighting.

Cock fighting actually has an important ceremonial function, but has apparently been officially banned in Bali since 1981 because the gambling associated with it is illegal. You wouldn't know it. Several times we were sitting in our house or in our office, enjoying the usual peace and tranquillity, when we became conscious of an increasingly noisy chanting somewhere in the vicinity. The chanting would soon become a general mob shouting, which in turn would reach fever-pitch excitement levels—and sometimes this would go on a few times a day for up to five days at a time.

I wandered out the back with the children one such afternoon, curious about the excessive noise thundering in from the fields. Not ten metres behind our house, tucked away in a little cluster of trees, wooden benches and bamboo stalls had been set up for a grand cock-fighting event. We gently nudged our way through the crowd to get a better look. I stood Zoe and Kallen up on the end of a bench so they could see easily, and then immediately wondered if I'd done the right thing. It was a pretty wild and bloody scene. Hundreds of grown men were gathered there, working themselves into a lather over two chickens having a bit of a go at each other. Okay, they weren't officially chickens, they were roosters—and they did have sharp spikes attached to their feet, which apparently added to the action and drama—but I still could not really see the attraction of a couple of large birds jumping around a ring and spraying the spectators red!

You've never seen as disappointed a group as those men when one cock killed the other in about three seconds flat. They barely had the chance to get themselves excited, and there it was, the rooster already dead and out of the race. Suddenly, there was complete silence, a heavy despondence in the air. There would have been plenty of men in that ring who would have lost money on the bet, and the owner of the animal would have been thinking about all the time and effort that went into preparing the cock for the fight—only for the cock to end up as a feather duster!

I've since read that there are all sorts of interesting rules associated with the use of the *taji* blades the cocks fight with—particularly when the fighting is for ceremonial purposes, when the blood is considered a required offering to appease the evil forces. The blades can, for starters, only be sharpened at the dark of the moon. They must be forged from the charcoal taken from a tree that has been struck by lightning—and some even say they may only be forged at a time when there is lightning in the sky. Menstruating women must not look at or touch the blades, and neither can someone who has recently had a death in the family . . . These are but some of the many requirements for the sport that has become entrenched in the Balinese culture.

Although I was concerned about the children being exposed to the blood, guts and gore, they seemed pretty blasé about it. They must have sensed the sport of it. There were no other children there, though. I noticed I was the only woman present, too (apart from some ladies selling food at specially set up stalls), and clearly the only white one. But then the strange tourist women do seem to fit into a whole different category here—we are expected to stick our noses into the Balinese business, not necessarily following the local cultural norms.

Just when I was wondering about the appropriateness of us being there and was considering leaving quietly, Pak Gendeg walked up. He was with a young lady at least half his age. 'My new wife,' he proudly announced, 'from Java.'

I was quite surprised, it was not what I had expected at all. But then I realised there was no reason to be. After becoming widowed, he would have appreciated the attention and company. I shook hands with Pak and his new wife, congratulating them both, but I couldn't help continuing to look at Pak. I could tell something was different; I just couldn't work out what. Perhaps it was just the rejuvenated glow of a man who had captured the interest of a much younger woman.

Then I worked out what it was. Pak's silvery white hair had been dyed jet black! Now he looked like he belonged with his new wife. Guess that's one way to maintain your youth! We chatted for a while, me laughing with him about my startling discovery of his new hair and new wife. He picked up little Kallen and proudly took him off to meet some of his other friends, apparently unconcerned about our presence at the fight and helping me to feel more comfortable in that setting.

The raucous betting and wild crowd spirit during the fighting was pretty overbearing, but even I had become fascinated by the fight itself at this stage, so Zoe and I stayed on, wanting to see more. Zoe asked to see the dead birds in their bamboo cages placed on one side of the action, and happily surveyed the gore and guts with a surgeon's interest. By the time Kallen had returned from his walk around the area with Pak, though, I thought we had seen enough. We said our goodbyes and re-entered our compound— only to be constantly reminded of the spectacle for the next few days by the ongoing noise and commotion.

Apparently there's also a poor man's version of this bloodsport in Bali—betting on crickets! I have never actually seen a cricket fight, but it does sound like it's a step more bizarre again. In cricket fighting, I've read, there is exactly the same amount of attention to detail and serious commitment to this sport as there is in cock fighting, but it's all on a miniature scale. The crickets are exercised, tested by tickling, bathed, and fed special diets regularly. When they are finally ready to fight, they are placed in small cages hollowed out from bamboo poles with dividers between the cages that are lifted when the fight begins. A few karate chops later, one will retreat to his corner, and the fight is over.

Fascinating to what extent the competitive spirit will go!

Outside of the cock-fighting ring, the Balinese also enjoy the sports of soccer, volleyball and badminton. Beach soccer is a favourite, and on any afternoon we walked up the beach at low tide we would find at least three or four different games taking place. We would need to take care to duck the hard-kicked, sharply angled balls coming from would-be Maradonas. Each game was obviously casually organised, but they did seem to be clearly regimented into age divisions: there were the young boys who had barely reached puberty, competently dribbling and kicking the ball through goals marked by sticks in the sand; and there were the cocky teenagers who would take the time to send out a wolf whistle or 'I love you' comment to any passing girls; and then the serious, totally focused young adults.

Indonesia is badminton crazy, and has actually produced world-champion players in this sport. We went to the international championships in Denpasar one time, and the excitement level was amazing. It felt more like an international soccer game, the crowds roaring with every point lost or won by an Indonesian—cheering or jeering profusely.

The only other time I experienced that level of excitement in a large sports crowd in Bali was at an international women's tennis tournament. A sixteen-year-old Indonesian player, Angelique Wijaya had been entered into the competition as a wild card, and she ended up blowing everyone else off the court—even the top seed Aranxa Sanchez-Vicario was knocked out in an early round. Well, you've never heard such a wild crowd at a tennis match. Commenting on every move she made, and going absolutely batty over every single point the young star won, I was sure the whole specially built grandstand was going to come crashing down with the sheer force of their excitement.

Yes, the Indonesians certainly know how to enjoy themselves when they want to, how to really let go. For locals and expats alike, Bali is one of those places that invites release—and this is expressed in so many different ways. A laid back approach to life is certainly conducive to letting go.

This brings me around to what I eventually took on as my main form of physical release. Apart from the occasional adventure challenge, I wound up doing the typical expat thing when it comes to sport. I learnt that good old colonial game of tennis.

The tennis court was really the last place I expected to find myself when I arrived in Bali. I had intended to dabble in something more culturally relevant—to pick up a bit of Balinese dancing or painting perhaps. Besides, I couldn't even play tennis, and it looked like too much hard work to learn. But one day I was offered free coaching and before I had the chance to think twice I was out there with my whites on, sashaying around the court.

Our friend Greg said he'd teach me to play tennis if I could help him to record the impact of his unique teaching techniques. All I had to do was write about what it felt like to learn, how I understood and interpreted his instructions. Sounded easy enough. After all, how often do you get the chance to learn tennis from a professional who has reached number 300 in the world at the peak of his career? Not a bad opportunity for someone living in the Bali backwaters. I had nothing to lose . . . except, hopefully, a few kilos . . . and possibly my pride.

Now, although most tennis buffs would undoubtedly be thrilled at the chance to be hitting balls to a tennis professional, for an absolute beginner like me it was actually an utterly terrifying prospect. I was worried about missing the ball altogether and looking like an uncoordinated idiot. Greg might have dealt with beginners before, but not having ever touched a racquet, even as a child, I feared I might be the most uncoordinated of all.

I had my first lesson on a hazy tropical afternoon. Early afternoon. Not even mad dogs and Englishmen would brave a game of tennis at that time of day, but there we were, on the court, bearing the brunt of the intense midday heat. Even as we stood on the side of the court, scarcely moving, it felt as though every drop of energy was being drained away, as if it was being extracted intravenously—but then as a wash of opaque clouds came over and sheltered us from the sun's intensity, we figured it was worth a try.

'Let's start with a warm-up,' Greg said. 'I'll just send a few balls over to you and we'll have a bit of a hit together. Relax and enjoy it.'

Relax! Enjoy! Standing in front of a pro with a tennis racquet was scarier than standing up and giving a speech in front of two hundred people. I'd do that instead any day of the week.

An arm around my shoulder and a pat on the back as he walked me around to my side of the court did little to encourage me. When he positioned himself over on the other side of the court again, right at the net, and started firing balls at me, I felt a little like a startled rabbit staring straight into a shooter's light. The balls came hard and fast (anxiety obviously intensifies one's perception considerably), and I was sure my feet weren't going to follow my body or my arms were going to end up in a tangled mess.

Okay, one ball back went over the net, and then another. The next went over, and so did the one after that. My feet were moving and my hands began swaying in a somewhat rhythmic fashion. Maybe I wasn't looking so uncoordinated after all, I thought. Next, we worked on the grip, then the stance, and established the contact zone—the correct hitting position for the racquet at the side but also just in front of the body. We rehearsed the whole movement through the contact zone in slow motion, ending up in a theoretical finishing position. Very suave. More like a ballet arabesque than a tennis move. By this time I had the whole picture clearly imprinted in my brain, a still shot of each stage flashing before my mind's eye in perfect sequence. No worries. If that was all there was to tennis, I would be laughing.

I may have been dripping with sweat, feeling utterly mentally and physically challenged, but I was already hooked. There was no going back from that point.

The next step, said Greg, was to have a go at 'real' tennis with the ladies' tennis clinic. Now, I don't know about you, but for me the thought of ladies' tennis automatically conjured up some pretty uncomfortable stereotypes. Up until this time I had studiously avoided some of the regular expat women's activities, such as morning teas, fundraising events, shopping expeditions . . . and tennis. I had decided that these activities were for the very rich and the very bored. Because I am the sort of person who likes to give off the aura of always being busy and productive, the time and expense involved in social tennis and the hit and giggle image of women prancing lightly around the court, lollipopping balls over the net between sips of tea and snatches of local gossip—were very off-putting.

But now I wanted to learn, and I wanted to be able to practise with other people, so I tried hard to put my fears and doubts aside when I arrived at the courts for my first clinic.

On arrival, the first thing I noticed was that the women were all already present. And not only were they there before the official starting time, but they were on the courts, busily warming up. I, on the other hand, had arrived in a mad flurry, and had even forgotten to bring a tennis racquet. Very embarrassing.

I had turned up with Rita, the friend I had stayed with in Australia when Kallen was born, and her children, as well as Kallen. Rita and the boys were visiting us in Bali, and I wanted to make the most of the opportunity to be with her. 'Come along for a hit of tennis,' I had told her, 'and the boys can have a bit of a hit nearby.'

Obviously all the other women had structured their lives more appropriately and had made suitable arrangements for their children. The courts were noticeably child free. When there was a scream from the sidelines halfway through an important point of instruction, I was sure everyone else was looking at me thinking how inexcusable it was to have a child present during a serious tennis session, and I mousily crept around the back to have a stern word with the little Master.

Another thing I soon noticed was how smartly everyone else was dressed. I felt very out of place in my old scruffy t-shirt with mismatched shorts and oversized general purpose sport shoes. They may have been white, but they were not at all tennisy. Perhaps I would need to go out and splurge on something a little more appropriate. Although it was Bali, tennis was obviously tennis, it seemed.

This quick visual assessment of the other ladies and the situation made me think the game was going to be as snobby as I feared it would be, but as the time wore on I realised that I was being the judgmental one. The group was actually made up of lovely people who were enjoying playing the sport. There was a mix of Indonesians and foreigners—all obviously reasonably well off—but all from very different backgrounds.

As soon as I joined in and got on with practising, my focus was drawn back to the game itself and not the circumstances. I was once again entranced by the possibilities, driven by the potential that had been unleashed within me. We warmed up with practice shots, we rehearsed our forehand and backhand swings, we ran through some drills. Many of these ladies, I quickly discovered, were actually quite good, strong players, and took the game seriously.

Then we played an interesting game called 'King'. In this game the 'king' occupies one end of the court, while the 'peasants' line up at the other end and take turns to try to overcome the king. In order to become king, a peasant must successfully play a baseline shot, an overhead shot, and a volley—getting the king out each time. The king continues to reign for as long as none of the peasants are able to overcome her.

A very interesting revolutionary concept. I wasn't sure if anyone else was thinking about it, but the game reflected pretty much what had been going on politically in the country. It brought me back to reality in a flash. In the game I was always the poor peasant unable to better my position, still very much a beginner. And I was getting the slightest taste of what it felt like to be unable to rise above your allocated status. For so many people in the world beyond the tennis-court fence, this was a daily reality. It was a pertinent reminder of the circumstances of the country I had chosen to live in, and what was happening around me.

For so many, life is not easy. It is not a game.

I had fallen in love with tennis, but would always think, after that, how lucky I am to be able to escape in this way, to have the freedom I have always known.

Chapter 16

Health, Wealth and Holy Water

There is something spiritually cleansing, supremely relaxing, and wickedly indulgent about a massage. I think I could survive any stress, any strain, if at the end of it I could be treated to even the simplest of massages. Massage certainly played a part in transforming our lives in Bali. Seriously. I know it helped to heal the effects of stress, and helped us to achieve and maintain the balance we needed.

We enjoyed massages as often as we could—after all, they were only a fraction of the price of massages back in Australia. And Bali had to be the ultimate place to enjoy a massage. With a vast range of exotic tropical ingredients to spice up the spa experience, the most luxurious environments of natural wood, clay and stone, and the most caring and genuinely warm attendants to assist you, there was definitely no better place to spoil ourselves.

Balinese massages, we discovered, are unique cultural experiences in themselves. Massage has long been used as a form of promoting health and healing, and traditional forms of massage show how intimately the Balinese understand the body's needs. Babies are still usually massaged from an early age, as are pregnant ladies and children and adults with any number of aches or ailments.

Traditional *balian* healers will often use forms of massage as a means of specialised spiritual therapy.

Often hand ground by mortar and pestle, the traditional Indonesian herbal concoctions that form the basis of most traditional massage treatments are a sensual feast. Local plants are used to create invigorating mixtures that cannot be found anywhere else in the world: pungent cloves, spicy chilies, piquant peppers, strong Bali coffee, papaya and zesty coconut are all crushed and combined to make unusual blends.

I must admit, as much as I love a massage, I often try to save it up for a special occasion, when I can justify the pure indulgence of visiting one of the gorgeous spa centres. Imagine: walking over lily pond gardens on rough-hewn stepping stones to your own little private thatched hut; listening to the sound of a waterfall spilling into the pond and merging with soft Balinese flute music; breathing in the heady scent of the spicy essential oils fused with scattered frangipani flowers; looking out onto a hideaway garden heavy with dripping vines and colourful buds. It really is heaven. In some places they even use fresh spring water as a special 'holy water' blessing for a truly spiritual experience.

True, I'm still not sure how I feel about being totally coated from head to toe in a yoghurt mixture made yellow with turmeric—a little like a basted chicken ready for the roasting perhaps—but my skin does feel softer and more supple afterwards. It's all part of the package. Usually the total spa experience winds up with a nice hot bath with flower petals, and then sipping some herbal tea in the sarong or cotton jacket and slippers provided, tucked away in some calming lounge in a small corner of the complex.

But many visitors to Bali come across the other variety of massage first: the common beach massage. That was the way I had my massages for a long time, too. Just as familiar as the special Kuta greeting of 'You want to buy watch?', you only need to step on the sand of any of the tourist beaches here in Bali and you'll immediately be asked, 'You want massage?' Even if you say no, the massage salesperson will inevitably descend on you anyway and start kneading your shoulders. The problem is that once someone has started to locate the fatigued muscles and work on them, asking them to stop can be one of the hardest tests of self-control. But although the masseur usually seems quite competent in that introductory sales phase, you will often find that as soon as the real massage begins the effort reduces somewhat.

Massage ladies at the beaches work in co-op groups, and sometimes you'll have two or three working on you at the same time, according to whatever the unwritten union rules might be. They're quite happy, once the massage has started, to merely stroke your skin casually and chit chat the time away. It's a great social occasion for these ladies—they're often laughing wildly at some joke or other, quite distracted from the job at hand. Any notion you might have had of getting a serious rub down and some quiet relaxation is quickly destroyed. It is an essential visit-to-Bali tourist experience, but I soon found the experience more irritating than anything else.

Anyway, the beach massages were permanently crossed off the list of pleasant and positive experiences after a particularly unpleasant incident . . .

After working for up to six days a week for months on end, trying to win back the business we had lost and extend our opportunities even further, we decided we'd well and truly earnt a long weekend away with the children. And where did we go when we needed a holiday? To an even simpler, smaller hut on an even more isolated beach, of course!

We took off by boat to stay on an island near Lombok, and found the perfect spot. A small bamboo bungalow on the edge of crystal blue waters—a hammock on the balcony for sleeping the days away. Beautiful snorkelling, no cars—only *cidomo* (horses and carriages)—and perfect conditions for kite surfing! While Andrew indulged in scooting across the clear waters, the children and I delighted in exploring under them—and I managed to slip in just a massage or two.

I was swinging on the hammock one day, alternately reading patches of a good novel and looking out to where the kids were playing on the sand as well as past them to where Andrew was surfing over the water, when out of the corner of my eye, I noticed an old Balinese man standing near our hut. There appeared to be something strange about the way he was dressed, and as I turned to look more carefully I saw he was actually wearing an over-the-shoulder signboard that said, 'I am Ewan. I give good massage for 30 years.' The man was carrying a stick, edging his way slowly along the path. He was blind.

I'm a sucker for anyone who looks like they could do with some help, and I saw this as a great win-win situation, so I asked him to give me a one-hour massage. It was a pretty good massage at the beginning, actually. Blind people seem to have a good sense of touch. He was able to locate and appropriately manipulate all the right muscles in all the right ways, and it felt so good to have the tense sections worked over by an expert, obviously with years of authentic traditional Balinese healing experience.

After a little while, though, the massage became anything but relaxing. The first thing that struck me as unpleasant was the way the grey beach sand started to find its way into the massage oil and onto my back. Being sandpapered rather than smoothed over was a completely different sensation. Then the man worked his way down from my tight shoulders, to the mid section of my back, to my butt—and he kept going! The first time he brushed over my crotch, I thought I'd imagined it—or perhaps that he had just lost his way because he was blind. The second time, I sat up abruptly, thanked him for the massage, and paid him off. This was an eerie déjà vu feeling—memories of Mr India.

He looked bewildered, and groped around in midair for the money. I tried to hold the money in the right position for him, being extra careful not to make skin contact, and I noticed that his fingers were very grubby: his fingernails packed with dirt, and his hands generally rough and calloused. Sweat was running down his arms. Gross. I was feeling much more uptight now than when he started.

As it turned out, I found myself in our doctor's surgery in Sydney not long after, with a nasty skin problem on my back. Her husband is a tropical diseases specialist, so between the two of them I was confident my strange infirmity would be identified. She recognised the peculiar ailment immediately, though, as a staph infection. I wondered if I had heard correctly. A what? A staph infection? Was that all it was—a common infection? I think we were both disappointed with the ordinariness of the diagnosis. I wondered how I could possibly have gotten an infection like that on my back. The image of the dirty fingernails suddenly flashed back into my mind. Then I remembered as clearly as anything. The massage by the old man with dirty fingernails and a dirty mind. Disgusting.

I was glad at this time that I had happened to be able to see my doctor in Sydney, where I could be fairly confident in the diagnosis. With a whole range of colourful diseases in Bali—and a dubious medical system—my nasty little infection might have become a whole lot nastier.

Fortunately, apart from the odd doctor's visit for the odd tropical ailment, we had rarely needed medical assistance since we had arrived in Bali. There is no denying that these regions harbour some unique tropical diseases. But somehow, we ended up being healthier in many ways than we had been for years.

Living without a winter must have its advantages. It meant we were able to escape the brunt of that awful city flu that seems to grow more and more aggressive each year. In virtually every year of my Sydney life I had been struck down by more than one nasty cold, which would turn into a heavy chest cough, and then cause me to lose my voice and/or be confined to bed for several days' recovery period. It was a real winter drag. In Bali's endless summer, though, we'd only get regular email reminders of the nature of the beast from friends who had become victims of the current year's virulent flu.

What we did get, mostly, was annoying little discomforts. For the first few years, I was reaching the end of my tether with infected mosquito bites. Zoe's legs were always covered from top to bottom in festering globules of pus, which made her constantly itchy and miserable. We tried the strongest repellents possible (although I admit I used them erratically, and also with caution, because I was concerned about the effect on her skin). We even had special long-sleeved and -legged mosquito outfits made for her out of light cotton. But her blood must have been sweet. They just wouldn't leave her alone.

There were also the strange rashes. Kallen occasionally broke out in a painful full body rash—often after a period of heavy exertion and excessive sweating. Sometimes, though, there was no apparent cause. These rashes just came and went mysteriously.

The other thing the children constantly suffered from was dehydration or heat exhaustion, simply from running around in the hot sun and heavy humid air and not drinking enough. There were times when the kids collapsed at the end of the day, after wearing themselves out. They would complain of headaches, get a slight temperature, and need to lie down—sometimes even throwing up. Fortunately, with constant rehydration and a good night's sleep, they were usually fine by the next day.

But then, out of the blue, the household was struck down with more exotic tropical maladies. As is always the case, when it rains it pours. We were hit by a veritable plague of disasters and diseases in the dry season of the fourth year, just when we thought we had managed to successfully reclaim the paradise we had worked so hard to hang on to. The 'plague' was a series of particularly nasty and mysterious illnesses and misadventures. We thought we were going to have to put the house in quarantine.

On the first day of the plague, Mia walked in from the doctor's and was heading towards her room to get some rest.

'Well?' I asked expectantly. 'What did the doctor say?'

'The doctor said I have typhoid, Ibu.'

'The doctor said *what*!'

'Typhoid. He gave me three packets of pills to take and told me to lie down.'

'Told you to *lie down*? You should be on a stretcher and on your way to hospital if you have typhoid, for goodness sake! What are those medicines, anyway?'

'I don't know, Ibu. There's blue pills, red pills and white pills.' She held the packet out to me gingerly, obviously embarrassed that she didn't really know what was going on. But that is standard in Indonesia. You don't ask questions, you are just expected to trust the 'experts'.

'Yes. I can see that,' I said, looking at the pills. 'Let me check it all out for you on the internet . . . You should go ahead and lie down anyway, you poor thing . . .'

Grateful to be living in the age of ready access to information from anywhere in the world, we were fast becoming self-taught experts in all sorts of things. It didn't take too long to find the diagnostic checklist for typhoid, and go through it:

Nausea: Yes
High temperature: Yes
Itchy red patches on the skin: Yes
Lethargy: Yes

As I read about how infectious the disease is for people living together, I started getting nervous. The website said that you can fairly easily confirm the presence or absence of the disease through a simple blood test. Why the hell hadn't the doctor told her to get a blood test, I wondered. Silly question, I immediately reprimanded myself. Nothing is that obvious in Bali.

The next step, we decided, was to send Mia off to the lab for a blood test ourselves. You don't need a doctor's referral for pathology tests here, and all medications are available over the counter from the local chemist stores, so it's pretty easy to self-treat most illnesses. The blood test came back negative, which doesn't always mean much, but we were somewhat relieved. Next, we checked out the tablets, and told her that maybe if the nausea was not so strong any more she could at least cut out the anti-nausea tablets (the other pills were more directly related to treating the disease). The red blotchy spots immediately disappeared. Aha, probably an allergic reaction to the nausea pill. Mia then went to see another doctor, and our suspicions about the allergy were confirmed—but the doctor couldn't tell us what the problem actually was.

So what exactly did she have?

A few days later Kallen was as sick as a dog: fever, lethargy, throwing up incessantly. It lasted for a good twenty-four hours. Two days after that, it was Zoe's turn.

Their different temperaments were amplified in their illness. Kallen became much more subdued than usual, lying ever so still on his deathbed, barely able to open his eyes. The only time he spoke was to say, 'Will you please pass me the bucket?' when he was about to throw up.

Zoe, on the other hand, was even more outspoken and fiery than usual. 'Mum, I need the white straw with the green cup, and the water has to have ice in it, and the towel needs to go underneath it, and if I don't have it now I am not going to be happy!' If she was going to be deathly ill, she was going to do it at a high volume.

So. The mystery was solved. It was a virus. One of those things that strikes without warning, and disappears just as abruptly.

Two days later another strange illness hit the household. Ketut No.2 arrived for work looking very weak and washed out and saying she was not feeling well, then told us she had discovered she was passing blood with her stools. It was her turn to be shipped straight off to pathology for tests and then home again for some rest. This time it was confirmed as dysentery. Luckily, she was the only one affected.

The following week an emergency message came home from Zoe's school informing us that there were two suspected cases of tuberculosis among the students, and management was considering closing the school down. Our children happened to have coughs at the time, and I guess we did what all expat parents from the school would have done. We panicked. We heard soon after, though, that the two cases were, in fact, diagnosed as pneumonia (in Singapore). A father of one of the children, a friend of ours, told us about the harrowing ordeal afterwards. 'I never thought I'd be happy to hear my child has pneumonia!' he said.

No sooner had we got our household back on track again health-wise, than a different form of disaster struck. This time it was Ketut No.1's turn. After spending a weekend with his parents, he returned to our house the next Monday morning limping badly.

'What happened, Ketut?'

Ketut was looking very sheepish, and he was slow to answer. 'I had an accident on my motorbike.'

'On your new motorbike?!'

'Yes.' He looked at his feet as he shifted them from side to side.

'How did it happen?'

'I was picking up the motorbike from the seller's house, and I collided with another motorbike on the way to my parents' house.'

The poor thing. Such bad luck. Ketut had been diligently saving up for a razzle dazzle 'real' motorbike (most people ride small moped-style motorbikes in Bali) for over a year. He was really keen on Harley Davidsons—which were way out of his price range—but this was going to be the next best thing.

'What happened . . .? What happened . . .?' The household gathered together excitedly for a full rundown on the accident and the aftermath. The repairs, he told us, would cost him a couple of months' salary, and he was pretty battered around himself. The war wounds were shown off half ashamedly, half proudly. Ketut told us how he had spent some time in a local hospital in Denpasar, getting cleaned and sewn up. He was very lucky it wasn't much more serious, as those places are notorious for being unclean, overcrowded and understaffed.

A year or so before, a friend's husband had been involved in a serious motorcycle accident in Bali, and on arriving at the local hospital she was appalled by the conditions; shattered bleeding bodies lining the hallways, many of them crying out in pain, assistance likely to be a dim prospect for quite some time. (You even have to get someone to line up and pre-pay for any drugs you will need.) My friend was able to get assistance over the telephone from a specialist in Australia through her insurance company, and as soon as her husband's condition was stabilised he was flown out by private jet to Singapore for priority emergency treatment. Cost: a mere AUS$60,000. She gave her husband an ultimatum that if he ever wanted to take up motorcycling in Bali again he'd have to get life insurance and spend a night in the emergency ward of a local hospital as she had had to.

Fair enough!

'So where's the motorbike now, Ketut?'

'It's being fixed at the *bengkel*.'

'When will you bring it here so we can see it?'

'Maybe next weekend.'

Such a shame . . . but I had told Ketut many times how dangerous I thought motorcycles were. At least my point had been proven without too much pain.

Later that week the point was driven home even more firmly. A motorbike ran into the back of our car while Ketut was driving it. The car was barely scratched, but the bike couldn't be ridden any more and looked like a write-off. The bike rider was limping, in floods of tears. Another three days later Ketut had just parked the car when Andrew opened the door and knocked a motorbike rider over. Again, not too much damage, but it was enough to shake Ketut completely.

First thing the next morning, three members of Ketut's family were on our doorstep. Apparently he had rung them to tell them about his misfortune, and they were worried he was under a bad curse. Ibu (Ketut's mother) was wailing inconsolably. She had actually been misinformed about Ketut's condition, and thought that he was close to death after all his 'accidents'. The family had arranged for a special ceremony for him with the local shaman or *balian* witchdoctor.

When Ketut returned to us after the ceremony, the following weekend, he was without the brand-new motorbike that we had been expecting to see.

'Where is your bike, Ketut?'

'I think I will sell the bike. It brings bad luck.'

'Oh, I'm so sorry it's turned out this way, Ketut.'

'It is the will of the gods, Ibu.'

It was uncanny, but the series of maladies and misadventures did seem to cease at that point, and we resumed some sort of normalcy. Not being at all superstitious, it still pays—I figure—to hedge your bets, to ensure you are at peace with all.

Despite the weird and wonderful misfortunes we had to face during that time, we were generally healthier and better off in Bali. We were definitely less stressed and more able to fight off whatever attempted microbe attacks came our way. We enjoyed holistic health: fresh air, fresh food, freer minds—and those divine massages. Our lives were richer in so many ways.

Just so long as we could stay on the right side of the gods.

Chapter 17

Tropical Storms

They were due to sweep over Bali in the dead of night. It was Balinese New Year's Eve, and the evil spirits were being summoned to the island with wild street parades.

We were irresistibly drawn to the streets along with the whole Balinese population. All were transfixed by the huge papier-mâché monsters with sharp fangs and bulging eyes that were being jerked along down the thoroughfares by dozens of men. The sky was black, but the *oga-oga* monsters were lit up with strings of coloured lights—eyes flashing, mouths a snarling red, large hairy arms and legs brought to life with studs of light.

Some of them were fashioned in the traditional Hindu evil monster style, others were more modern versions of the concept: punk rocker monsters with green skin, pink spiked hair and nose rings; purple goblins and witch monsters; scary clowns and comics. Flaming torches were flashed around teasingly, firecrackers exploded randomly, and drums banged noisily. There was as much colour and commotion as possible, to ensure the small island could not escape the spirits' attention as they roamed the skies around the world.

Kallen was now almost three—old enough to have a basic concept of good and evil, and to be overawed by the monstrous effigies.

'They are coming this way, Mummy!' he squeaked from behind my legs, eyes growing wider by the second.

To a little fellow, these characters would be bigger than Ben Hur. I must admit, they did look pretty scary—particularly as they were spun furiously and heaved to and fro, cleverly animated by the crazy movements.

'It's okay, darling. They won't get us. They're just going to pass us by.'

Right at that moment a man wearing a painted wooden mask—bearing the same ghoulish features as the effigies, and with long, rough hair fiendishly sprawling out from the edges—came up from behind, shrieking at us threateningly. All the Balinese kids were thrown into fits of laughter, but Kallen was thrown completely off guard.

He was quite a sensitive New-Age little guy—generally gentle and affectionate—and scared of high speeds, fireworks, new environments . . . and men in strange costumes. He screamed in terror.

'This one is going to eat us, Mummy!'

I picked him up to hold him close to me, and his body was stiff with fear.

'I'll look after you, don't worry.' I motioned to Andrew and Zoe, and we moved over to a wall on the side of the road where we could watch the parade from a safe distance. Kallen continued to clutch at me tightly, hiding his head as much as possible, but he couldn't help but curiously peek at the movements from his relatively safe haven.

We followed the parade, still at a safe distance, as it moved to the beach, where the effigies would be burned. Everyone crowded around to witness the spectacle of the monsters on fire. This part of the ritual represented how evil could be overcome.

The children stared at the roaring blaze in a stunned silence. Our son then slowly started dancing, expressing some of the contagious spectacle himself, inspired by the fearless passion. We dared not stop him or interrupt him. He was in his own little world, oblivious to his environment. This newly confident form of self-expression was fascinating and beautiful to watch.

The idea of scaring kids is so strange to us. We usually try to protect our children from anything we think they can't cope with. But I began to wonder that night if sometimes we try to protect them too much. I wondered if sometimes we become too sensitive to emotional issues as adults because we simply haven't had the opportunities to develop psychologically. Perhaps we haven't learnt to deal with the good, the bad and the ugly, so we are unprepared for life's realities as adults.

By the early hours of the morning, everyone had retreated indoors and all was deathly still and quiet on the streets. Everyone would be required to be silent and remain inside their houses for the rest of that night and the whole of the next day—in order to show the evil spirits that had been attracted to the island that there were no inhabitants and they could therefore move on and leave the island alone—and everyone would be in meditation and prayer for the New Year.

No work, no leisure activities, no eating—it is supposed to be a day of complete devotion. All regular events grind to a complete halt on the Balinese New Year's Day: the shops are shut, all business ceases, schools are closed . . . even the airport doesn't function. The whole of Bali simply turns into a ghost town for twenty-four hours. Special task forces of village police in black and white sarongs patrol the streets checking that the strict religious rules are adhered to. There can be no electricity or fire used, even through the dark night.

In previous years we had remained in the house during this time. It was actually very beneficial to take some time out and to be forced to be still and quiet. This year, though, we had decided to do what many expats do: to sit out the Nyepi New Year in a hotel. We soon discovered this sort of forced rest was definitely attractive. Guests were permitted to move around the grounds freely and lighting and electricity were used in the rooms (apparently the evil spirits were not interested in us silly tourists), but the grounds stayed dark. We swam, we caught up on TV, we relaxed. When the children were asleep, Andrew and I sat together on the balcony of our room looking over the vast hotel lagoon—by this time not much more than a large dark shadow—eating the fine chocolates provided, and reflecting on life. It became our own meditation session.

This was actually our second New Year's Eve for the calendar year. The first had been spent on Sydney Harbour, while home for our annual Christmas visit. At that time we had joined the harbourfront crowds at Milsons Point for a close-up view of the dazzling fireworks. It was busy and exciting as always, a big-city, bright-lights adventure, but in the end we forgot to take time out to reflect on the past year and the one ahead.

While we were sitting on the hotel balcony feeling awestruck by the brilliant star-studded sky, contemplating life and the universe, it occurred to me that we hadn't even made any New Year's resolutions that night in Sydney. The enforced silence of the Balinese New Year's Eve was now giving us the opportunity.

'Let's make some New Year's resolutions,' I suggested.

'But it's already March!'

'Never too late. And this is our New Year now. We're living in Bali, so we need to do as the Balinese do,' I insisted.

'Well, what are yours then?'

The options were open, but I had to take time to stop and ponder the possibilities. Now that I'd initiated this process, I simply couldn't think of any. I realised that I was actually pretty happy with the way everything was going in our lives.

Why not have a year without resolutions, we thought, except perhaps to continue making the most of what we have? There was silence for a while as we thought about all we had shared together, about the years of incredible satisfaction we had known since coming to Bali . . . then our thoughts moved onto the future.

'Where do you think we'll be in five years' time?' Andrew asked.

We had been together for twenty years by this time. There had been stresses in the past, that we had left behind in the city, but there had been stresses in breaking away from the lives we once had, too. We had learnt to deal with the general uncertainties of living and working in a new culture, and with the specific pressures of political crisis and tropical disease. I knew we had both now become comfortable in the life we had found together—even with the uncertainties. I couldn't imagine being anywhere else or doing anything else. I couldn't imagine being happier with anyone else. In five years' time, I felt, I wanted to be right where we already were. I couldn't believe it could get much better than this.

Reaching out to catch each other's hands simultaneously, both of us relaxed into the warmth of the moment.

'Remember how you reacted when I first told you about my idea of coming here?' I said.

Andrew turned to look me in the eye and smiled.

'Uh huh. And I would react the same way again. It was a huge risk.' Once, this may have been a contentious issue between us, but now we were synchronised.

'What do we want for our kids?' I asked, now feeling that bottomless pit of parental pride you get when your kids are asleep and looking absolutely angelic.

Thinking about what we had risked, and what we had gained by taking that risk, I knew that the children had a great life. Enjoying the fresh outdoors, lots of people who cared for them, a different culture to learn from and broaden their perspective, our own close contact with them.

Then I experienced that streak of fear that comes when everything feels too perfect. When you watch your children sleeping, delicate faces oh so innocently silhouetted on the pillow. I wondered about what could happen next.

I expressed my fear, not wanting to lend weight to it by verbalising it, but needing some reassurance. This time it was Andrew who told me not to be concerned about the future. Not to worry.

Climbing out of my seat, I nestled into his, and rested my head on his warm chest, feeling it slowly rise and fall. My thoughts turned to how much we'd both changed and grown. I started to think back to our early years, when we were so immersed in the faith we had grown up with that it became a consuming passion. We were once driven by a desire to share our particular form of belief, but a really giving spirituality had somehow eluded me. As the years went by we both became less attached to the specifics of that faith, not needing to hang on to particular creeds or doctrines, but holding instead to the strong principles of love and trust. From this grew a compassionate acceptance of others, which then deepened through our experiences of other cultures. Being in Bali had transformed and strengthened our personal faith.

We sat in companionable silence for a while. I could hear the water fountains splashing in the lagoon below, the wind rustling in the trees.

'Remember when we were younger, and we wanted to take on the world?' I asked Andrew.

No doubt a similar picture was conjured up in each of our minds as we then smiled at each other. After twenty years together, I knew we had achieved what we had wanted to achieve. That we had taken on the world, in our own way. The shared sense of mutual achievement meant a lot to each of us.

So relaxed, so at peace in the moment, we both drifted off into a meditative sleep. I came to with a jolt not long after, though, suddenly fearful again that the living dream would come to an end. A memory had leapt into my mind. When we had been out on the street earlier that night, a firework had slipped out of someone's hands not more than a few metres from where we were standing. It spun around crazily, totally out of control, making giddy circles around startled bystanders, sending screaming sparks out in all directions.

It had been a freaky, uncertain moment, horrified expressions instantaneously captured by the flashes of bright light. No-one seemed to be hurt, but apparently plenty of burns cases were admitted to hospital in other incidents around the island that night, victims of the wild pyromania.

I had heard lots of bombs going off in the lead-up to the parade, too. I knew they were merely homemade bangers made from bamboo and I'm not sure what else, designed to highlight the sense of fun and festivity—but they triggered stark memories of the bloody bombings I had known in other places and at other times in my earlier travelling years. The memories left me with a slightly sickly fear.

We heard later that neighbouring villages had also clashed that night right where we had been standing. The wild excitement had obviously reached a feverish pitch and become uncontrollable. It all made me think about the random events that can strike anywhere, about the semi-controlled chaos constantly lurking somewhere below the surface.

I was conscious that anything could happen at any time. Somehow, our current state of bliss just seemed too good to be true.

There is a tale of a young prince and princess who live in paradise and have everything anyone could want. Prince Rama is set to inherit the Kingdom of Kosala, and has won the hand of Princess Sita in an archery contest. Both are beautiful and utterly in love.

One day the couple's happiness is threatened by a jealous half-brother whose mother supports his bid for the kingdom. Rama and Sita are sent into exile in the forest where they are threatened by demons, seduced, and finally—when all else fails—Sita is kidnapped by a demon king who has changed himself into a golden deer. Rama raises an army and, aided by the monkey king, he is able to successfully rescue Sita from the demon's palace.

Sita is devastated that she has had to live with the demon king, and fearing that she can no longer be Rama's wife according to the sacred laws, she attempts to kill herself on a funeral pyre. Because the god of fire will not accept her, however, her innocence is proven, and Rama takes her back. They both move into the palace at Kosala, where Rama takes up his rightful place as king when his half-brother finally concedes defeat. They are once again in paradise, this time having proven their love.

But the saga does not end happily there, as one might hope. Sita is not accepted by the people of the kingdom, and is once more banished to the forest. In despair, she asks to be swallowed by her mother, the earth, and becomes the goddess of the furrow . . . and when Rama discovers his loss he chooses to return to the heavens as the god Wisnu.

The scenes of this tragic story unfolded before us on the edge of a high cliff, in the grounds of one of Bali's most sacred temples. We were continuing the cultural exploration inspired by the Balinese New Year celebrations. Kallen, in particular, was fascinated to know more, now that his fear of demons was abating.

The sun was slowly sinking behind the temple, about to be buried by the intricately carved monument. The ocean was swelling and falling way below, brushed with the purples and pinks of the dying sun.

The dancers created a beautiful, haunting re-enactment of the story. We were at once mesmerised by their dramatic expressions and movements, and gasping at the power and tragedy of the story. Sita remained composed throughout. Rama was the strong and confident hero. The deer was a light, prancing spirit with bells tinkling on her ankles, so deceptive in her carefree manner. (These days many of these characters are played by women, where traditionally they would have all been played by men.) The demon god Rahwana was a fearful beast, who ranted and raved and raged around, and the lively monkey king Hanoman climbed trees in the area and sat with the audience. Hanoman and Rahwana tussled with each other over the embers of a coal fire, kicking the coals and trampling on them, scaring the audience with the fiery sparks (which would be considered a definite fire hazard back in Australia!). A priest had blessed the fire, and the dancers were in a trance, so the Balinese performers would have considered there was no danger.

Around the perimeter of the dancers' sacred space was a circle of *kecak* chanters, a group of boys and men each in checkered sarongs with no shirt, no shoes, a red hibiscus behind their ears, and white paint marking their foreheads. They were sitting cross-legged in tight rows. Together they formed a writhing mass, simultaneously raising their arms with quivering hands, then lowering them to the ground, all the time chanting the 'ke-cha ke-cha ke-cha' sounds while in a mystic trance.

For the dancers and chanters this would not have been a mere performance. Sure, there was a handful of tourists there, and this performance was scheduled for sunset each night rather than at the time of a temple festival—but the Balinese take their religion very seriously, and any re-enactment of a Hindu story is an opportunity for the dancers to show their allegiance to the gods.

We could return to see this story unfold time and time again, and never tire of it. It would come to life each and every time. The setting couldn't be more spectacular, the costumes more colourful, the movement more magical. But this time the tragedy hit me harder, reminding me that paradise can be fleeting, according to the will of the gods; that even in paradise there are struggles between life and death, between good and evil.

'How to protect yourself in the case of a bomb threat.'

The newspaper headlines in Indonesia can often be so reassuring. There it was, on the front page of the *Jakarta Post*, a step-by-step description of how to respond if you happen to come across a bomb.

After a short time of relative peace, the political tensions in Jakarta were back in the headlines, and the country was on edge. The attempted shift to democracy was a much slower and harder ride than perhaps the people of Indonesia had anticipated. The country's ongoing political saga was not over yet.

After thirty years with one president, the people suddenly started changing leaders as fast as the fashions. When Soeharto was thrown out in 1998, Vice President Habibi took over. When Habibi lost the elections, Abdurrahman Wahid came in. Later, when he was indicted by the government, it was Megawati's turn. Three new presidents in the space of as many years. But who could possibly be the best candidate to run a country in such turmoil? You would have to be superhuman to be able to negotiate the huge social, political and economic problems. And you would have to be a moral saint to be able to stand up to the institutionalised corruption of the system.

The optimism of the people was unstoppable during the first free elections; it was a great time of celebrating the country's freedom of speech, of public expression. From the time of independence, elections had always been rigged, with Soeharto conveniently banning opposition parties, jailing their leaders, disenfranchising voters, or paying for votes. Only a few cents per person could easily buy votes for many years.

Elections in Indonesia had also traditionally been very controlled, with each party being allocated one day prior to the elections in which to show party support. This tradition carried through to the first free elections. Because the main parties each have very distinct colours, we learned to check the colours we were wearing very carefully before venturing out of the house on campaign days. One day it would be all green, the next all yellow, the next red. Party supporters would go beserk with the coloured paint, cloth and flags—houses would be painted the appropriate colour in support of the favourite party; jumbo flags the size of football fields would be erected above the villages; cars and motor-cycles would be strewn with coloured ribbons. The best way to survive, it seemed, would be to try to blend in as best as possible by wearing the colour of the day.

Pre-election fervour was at an all-time high when the groups of supporters formed massive motorcades, cruising every possible street around Denpasar and then down south into our area, showing off their undying enthusiasm for their favourite party. We would be sitting in our beach hut, imagining we were far away from civilisation, when the thrumming bass sound from almost a kilometre away would slowly become audible and gradually build up into a deafening roar.

Whenever we ventured out onto the roads on these days, we would see truckloads of people wearing coloured t-shirts and waving flags; motorcycles loaded up with as many people as possible—all wearing coloured t-shirts; cars with their windows and sometimes doors wide open—people waving flags and hanging out everywhere . . . all tooting their horns and shouting their war cries. It was an explosion of colour and sound. As the moving fiesta faded off into the distance, all would grow quiet again—until the same group followed the same route but a few hours later. And each party had their turn. It was quite some show.

The majority of the population in Bali was staunchly pro-Megawati Sukarnoputri. She was the leader of the Partai Demokrasi Indonesia (PDI), and the daughter of the country's founding president, Sukarno, who was half-Balinese. She was also the favourite throughout the rest of Indonesia, because of her father's ongoing popularity. That meant PDI party day was the biggest and noisiest of all. The town was painted red, and the party's symbol—an angry, raging bull's face—appeared every-where. Nothing was going to stand in their way.

Although Megawati's party had a strong majority nationwide, somehow something did stand in their way on election day, and with some clever political manoeuvring Gus Dur managed to slip in ahead as president. Well, the Balinese were not at all impressed. In fact, they were downright furious. The first free elections, and they knew they had been tricked out of their rightful president. Suddenly, as if the island had been preparing for this eventuality, crowds of angry protesters ran amok.

We were happily working away in our office when things got out of control, and the first we knew of what was going on was when we received a phone call from our friend Peter, whose daughter Michaela was now going to the same school as Zoe. It was the middle of the day, an unusual time to call, and I instantly had the feeling something was wrong.

'There are problems on the streets. We may not be able to get the kids home. I'm going up to see if I can get them home now, but there's a possibility they might have to stay the night at the school.'

'Surely it'll calm down soon, and we can bring them home at the normal finishing time?' I suspected this was an overreaction. There was a reasonable number of people on the expat scene who continually expected and feared the worst, but I believed this drama was most likely nothing more than a brief resurgence of pre-election fervour. Nothing to worry about, I was confident.

'No, Gaia. This is really serious. I'm going to see if I can get the kids out.'

He sounded very worried, and I started to think that perhaps I should show some parental concern.

'Okay, great thanks. Perhaps you could ring me when you get to the school so I know what's happening,' I said.

A good hour later Peter rang to let us know what was going on. 'Well, I did manage to get through to the school, but it was very difficult. A lot of the streets are blocked with cut down trees and burning tyres, and there are groups of people brandishing sticks and knives, wandering around looking for trouble. I think it might be best if I bring the kids to my house as fast as I can in case it gets worse.'

The situation did not sound good at all. 'Thanks so much for helping out. I'll come to your house and meet you there.'

As has probably become apparent, I'm not usually much of a worrier, but at that moment I started worrying. I jumped into the car and headed out onto the streets, determined to face any trouble head on. My daughter was in danger, and I was going to rescue her. There would be no stopping me.

Luckily, the route to Peter's house was mainly via back streets, but when I did get near the main highway through the south of Bali I began to see the extent of the damage. A lot of trees along the side of the road had been hacked down—mainly beautiful coconut trees, and they lay in huge piles like giant bundles of chopsticks. The tar on the roads had been melted and scorched where piles of tyres lay burning. Several shops, department stores and banks I passed had their front windows smashed in, and there were bits and pieces of glass, wood and metal strewn around. Apparently lots of people also thought this would be a good opportunity to air general grievances against specific organisations. Hotel entrances were blocked off, one taxi company had all its windows smashed, some of the consulates were damaged . . . it was really quite a bizarre combination of riots.

I was able to get to Zoe and get her home reasonably quickly, considering the havoc, but many people I know got badly stranded and were quite shaken up by the experience. I knew of some people who simply had to abandon their cars and walk their children home—not arriving back to their houses until after dark. The unpredictability of the situation was as frightening as anything else.

'Why is there a big mess on the roads, Mummy?' Zoe asked when we were settled back into our hideaway.

How do you explain the intricacies of a political discontent born from years and years of subservience, the frustrations that need to be released?

'Some people are unhappy with the way the government is being run. They feel like nobody's listening to what they want. The lady they wanted in as president—as the big boss of the country—didn't get the job, and they're complaining about it.'

'But that's not very clever to make a big mess everywhere. And they shouldn't kill the trees, Mum. We need the trees to breathe, you know. And what does it help, anyway, if they're just destroying things? Why can't they talk about it like adults should?'

So simple, and yet so complex.

'Were you worried about it, darling?' I was concerned about how she might have been feeling, driving through such disturbing scenes.

'A little bit, Mummy. But you always look after me.'

Still so young. Carefree in so many ways, but also the weight of the world resting on her fragile shoulders. The responsibility of bringing up children can feel so heavy sometimes, especially when it's hard to know how best to protect your child in the face of such an unpredictable future.

Fortunately—or perhaps strategically—Megawati was placed in the position of vice president the very next day, so the demonstrations were immediately transformed into celebrations. Now there were drunken crowds of supporters cruising the streets again (that is, wherever the streets had been cleared), and the angry mood had switched to festive.

But there was a general sense of unease on the island from then on. It had been scary to think about how the mob mentality had been so malleable.

The bomb article went on to give us practical information on how to deal with what was becoming a daily reality around the country.

Protect yourself in the case of a bomb threat by:
1. Staying away from large gatherings
2. Watching for any suspicious packages
3. Alerting the bomb squad if you do come across a strange package
4. Screaming . . . (not really!)

During this time I heard the bomb squad had defused a large box of lacy underwear in Denpasar. Apparently a lady had dropped the box at a friend's house, but the friend was not home, only the daughter—who was immediately suspicious of the strange lady, the box, and the possible contents. That was when the bomb squad was called in.

Bali did face serious bomb threats, though, when militant groups suddenly announced they were going to destroy all Soeharto's assets—which included about half of Bali's hotels. We live right next door to one of the best known of Soeharto's hotels, and up until that time had planned to jump the wall and take refuge there as an emergency contingency plan. Now we were thinking that perhaps we should move further away from the hotel. Nothing ever did eventuate, but it is one thing reading about bomb threats in other parts of the country and another having them on your own doorstep.

The closest Andrew and I had ever come to actual bombings was when we spent some time in El Salvador in the early nineties. The whole country had been in civil war for eleven years, and at that time there was no end in sight. We travelled across the border by bus, and it was the strangest, eeriest feeling to know the country was at war, and at any time the bus could be shot at or a bomb could go off.

We did make it to our destination safely—an orphanage where we were going to work for a while—but I'll never forget the shock of seeing for the first time a country controlled by the army. The army trucks, soldiers, machine guns, military check points. While we stayed in the orphanage, which was on a hill overlooking the San Salvador valley, we went to sleep each night to the sound of bombs going off in the distance, echoing around the valley. Sadly, you soon get used to the background sound of bombs exploding— rather like becoming numb to the sound of traffic when you live on a busy road, or to waves crashing on the shore when you live by the sea. Those sorts of sounds can become a regular part of the sensory landscape.

There was a definite difference one night, though, when we were brought to life at three in the morning by the distinct rattling boom of a bomb exploding just around the corner from where we were staying—not more than fifty metres away. Suddenly, we were wide awake, sitting up in bed, straining our ears to trying to give the shock some sort of context.

Do we jump out of bed and get dressed? . . . Do we hide under the bed? . . . Do we leave the room immediately? . . . Do we scream for help? . . . After sitting still for a long time, clinging on to each other for some sort of comfort, occasionally discussing the dilemma in hushed tones, we eventually lay down again, and some time just before dawn fell into a deep sleep with disturbing dreams. We found out when we finally emerged later that morning that someone had blown up the election office of one of the many political parties. No need to worry. This was normal for San Salvador.

I had been the one interested in going to El Salvador, hoping to find a way to help the people in their struggle. Andrew had the same interest in helping people, but just wasn't so sure about having to do it in a war zone. He had eventually agreed when he knew the surf was good there. Although he had enjoyed remarkably uncrowded waves on his weekends off—once it was just him and the president's son (plus several heavily armed bodyguards)—this was pushing the limit of his tolerance. And it was starting to freak me out, too. Having never lived with that sort of fear and tragedy on a daily basis, it was definitely a relief when it was time to leave the country.

But this time around, with the threat of violence in Bali, we were not prepared to simply walk away.

Although Bali had generally remained a relatively idyllic island almost cut off from the rest of the world, there were also often storms on the horizon. Every time Indonesia went through a new stage of transition, we felt the impact to some extent. There had been years of local, national and regional dips and troughs caused by a number of different factors. Each dip had shown how fragile paradise can be—especially so far as our living in Indonesia was concerned.

We could literally see the storms coming early in our stay when the sunsets on the west coast turned a fiery red. We could look out our bedroom window late in the afternoon, and catch the eerie glow of the sun deflected by smoke particles, way off in the distance. As soon as the international community had a whiff of the problem—a smoke haze from forest fires created by illegal loggers in Kalimantan—there was outrage and concern.

The haze spread right across the archipelago—as well as south to Western Australia and north to Thailand—but it managed to stop just short of Bali. It didn't actually pollute Bali's clear skies, but as we were soon to learn, anything that affects any part of Indonesia has serious repercussions for tourism in Bali. Programs were cancelled and tourist numbers went right down for quite some time. We only discovered later that this sort of disaster was nothing compared to what was to come . . .

After the overthrow of Soeharto, separatist movements were active and there were signs of religious intolerance all over the country. The nation was made up of a wide range of cultures and religions and everyone was keen to now express their views and air the grievances that the oppressive dictatorship had once kept in check. In Sumatra, the Malluccas and Irian Jaya, in Lombok, East Java and East Timor. Hardly any region was left unaffected.

On top of the internal turmoil, there was soon international tension as the eyes of the world focused on the progress of the reform movement. Ties with Australia became strained, particularly when Australia became directly involved in assisting the East Timorese towards independence. There was also a huge ongoing kerfuffle over the issue of asylum seekers—refugees who were passing through Indonesia in huge overcrowded old boats on their way to Australia—with Australia blaming the existence of this 'people smuggling industry' on the laxity of the Indonesian government.

There was a time when Australians were so unpopular in Indonesia that many Indonesians made comments to us about the inappropriateness of Australia's stance. Taxi drivers, shopkeepers and business associates all put in their two cents' worth, quite often telling us to our face how much they hated Australians. We tried to avoid revealing our nationality where possible. It was so strange to know what it is like to be a target of prejudice—a good 'standing-in-someone-else's-shoes' experience, I guess.

From environmental destruction to violent uprisings, we were to witness the full range of possible disasters. Often these were seen from a distance, as if the storms were in the same region but passing by on a far ridge, threatening to swing by our own little patch but skidding past instead. Sometimes, though, we were in the middle of the storm, and we felt the impact of the fury on our island.

Try to imagine the changing moods of a storm: the foreboding heaviness of black clouds looming, the strange green-grey colours of the sky signalling a darkening mood, the occasional claps of thunder that suddenly scare you and shake you to your bones, the flashes of lightning that put everything in stark contrast, the deafening roar of wind and rain. That's what living in a dramatically changing country can be like.

Although the sun still shone on our paradise and we were able to make the most of our tranquil beachside existence, there were often threatening clouds on the horizon. So much in the background had been unpredictable for so long.

So many times since we'd been in Bali, and in so many ways, Indonesia had been a black smudge of conflict on the world map. We had often felt the pressure to simply give up and go home. But we had survived the turmoil before, and we had become determined to hang on.

Chapter 18

A Bad Omen

There was quite a sizeable graveyard in the coconut field out the back of our house. It was not a public graveyard, but a private cemetery for all the animals that had the misfortune to pass through our household. GC No.1, the rabbit, the chickens and the fish were all buried there.

In the end I was right to worry about GC No.2 mixing with the local dogs on the beach. One day he contracted a dreadful virus—distemper, so the vet said—and he was dead within forty-eight hours. I just don't know about the justice of it all. There were scores upon scores of street dogs roaming around freely—particularly on the beach in front of our house, searching for some fish from the cafes—and although some of them had awful-looking skin diseases, they otherwise seemed to survive reasonably happily and healthily. But our GC, the dog we had become attached to and had tried to protect and look after, was the one to suffer in the end.

Shooing away the local cows to find a suitable burial patch, we placed him carefully in a freshly dug pit. After the corpse was covered over with a mound of moist, dark soil, some frangipani leaves and flowers were laid on the grave.

No sooner had we all returned to the house after the burial, than Andrew made an announcement.

'We need another guard dog. Who knows what might happen

next? We need to be protected. Let's just go straight out and get a new puppy. It will help the children not to feel so sad, and help me to feel more secure.'

I was reeling at the suggestion. As much as I loved GC No.2—after all, I was the one up till midnight syringing water into his mouth to stop him dehydrating, out of bed again at five in the morning to check his condition and find he was dead—he was more than a handful. Having a guard dog just sounded like damned hard work to me.

'But we couldn't handle GC,' I replied in exasperation. 'I don't think I could face trying to train another dog again.'

'We won't get a Bali beach dog this time. We'll try to find a more controllable breed.' Andrew tried to be reassuring, but I was not convinced.

Too late. The kids had caught on to the idea like wildfire.

'Please, Mum, can't we get a new puppy? Please. The house is too quiet without GC . . . C'mon, Mum . . . pleeeaase . . .'

'Well, we could just go and have a look, then. Let's wait a little before we make a decision about buying. We'll just see what sorts of dogs are around. Okay?'

'Yay! Okay, Mum, we'll just look.'

I should have known better. Minutes later, we were in the car heading towards Denpasar. Andrew was on the mobile phone checking with all his friends about the best breed to get and the best place to go.

When we had first arrived in Bali, there was not a pet shop in sight. The best you could do was go to the bird markets and see what other animals were also available. But now there were pet shops galore. You could get yourself a nice dalmatian, dachshund or poodle for several hundred to thousands of dollars—or some people smuggled their own pets in from outside (the strict rabies regulations make it difficult and expensive to get dogs in through the proper channels).

I suggested trying the bird markets first, just to get an idea of what was around. A mistake. We fell for the local sales tricks, hook, line, and sinker. All of us were oohing and aahing at the gorgeous little bundles of fluff we saw by the side of the road even as we drove up to find a parking spot. As soon as we stepped out of the car, a beautiful little black puppy was thrust in front of us. We almost bought him then and there, but restrained ourselves enough to check the animals and prices on the other side of the road.

We stopped at what we thought was a relatively healthy-looking batch of puppies. They were the local Balinese breed—Kintamani dogs from the mountain region, with lovely long fur and faces a little like border collies. We hoped this would be a decent step up from the Balinese beach mutts.

'How much for the puppies?' we asked.

'Which one do you like?' the sales lady replied.

One of them jumped up to the side of the cage and wagged his tail enthusiastically at us. As soon as the owner of the puppies saw us paying attention to him she put him in our hands. He started jumping around in delight, licking us.

'How much is this one?'

She gave us a price, and we responded in mock horror—as is the regular custom when you're bargaining. After bantering backwards and forwards for a while, we finally got her down to about half of the original price she had been asking.

Andrew and I looked again into the cage, just to check we really had chosen the right one, and saw a great big fluffy white puppy smiling up at us. We discussed the choice between the two, considering which way to go.

'Why not take two?' The lady said shrewdly—and the white puppy was immediately also with us.

'Oh no. Definitely not,' I said. 'One dog is a lot of work, two is crazy.'

'Oh, but one puppy will be lonely by itself. They need company,' Zoe chipped in.

True, I thought. Maybe GC No.2 had wanted a friend. Maybe he'd wanted to escape all the time because he had been lonely.

'Just take two and I give you good price.'

'Let's take two,' agreed Andrew unhelpfully.

'Yes, yes . . . please, pleeease . . .' It was hopeless trying to make sensible decisions and decent negotiations with kids around.

'Maybe—it would be nice for them to have company . . .'

We were by now stroking and holding both puppies, and had fallen in love with both. I offered a price for the two.

'Oh,' she said, 'but the white one is more expensive.'

'Really?' I said, wary of her sales tricks. 'What is the difference?'

'He is fatter.'

Hmmph! I was not convinced that argument should hold any water. The negotiations went on, and I finally offered a price for the two that I thought she would not accept, but to my surprise she agreed.

Trying to move fast from that point on, before she could change her mind, the next thing we knew the money was in her hands and we were walking away with two puppies. Somehow in the rush of paying, though, we realised that she had switched the white puppy, and the one we were carrying away with us was smaller and scrawnier-looking. But—you know what happens—you only need to be holding the soft little bundles and you fall in love with them. And this one looked like he could do with some extra loving care. We took the new scrawnier white one anyway.

All excited about our new pets, we rushed straight to a supplies shop in the centre of the market and came away with a bundle of dog biscuits, shampoos, collars and other canine goodies. Then we made our way back to the car, past the hundreds of cages of birds, fluffy white rabbits, guinea pigs, monkeys, squirrels . . . they had just about everything for sale there.

Exhausted from a busy morning of negotiating and meandering around overcrowded stalls in the steamy heat, we found a little food barrow to sit down at and rest. Four weary butts squatted on four small plastic stools. The two fluffy puppies jumped from lap to lap. We ordered some sticky *es campur* treats—shaved ice with fluorescent pink and green cubes of agar jelly, red food colouring and sweetened condensed milk drizzled luxuriously over the top. They helped to cool us down just a little.

I took in the scene around us more completely: the crammed in stalls all competing for space and attention, the resident stall-holders either excitedly discussing purchases and prices or casually contemplating the scene themselves, waiting their turn. No matter what goes on in the world at large, no matter what the external political realities, life had to continue on a day-to-day basis. Everyday realities would prevail over the larger uncertainties.

I considered my family as they slushed their way through the local icy treat, and thought about the way we were switching from one level to another, from one reality to the next. Like the puppies, the kids were flexible enough to make the most of each new situation. They seemed to flit easily enough between scenarios. So adaptable. I then looked at Andrew. Were we adaptable enough, was our conviction strong enough—our relationship solid enough, I wondered?

One of the puppies fell out of Kallen's lap, tumbling onto the ground and rolling away towards the stalls. It stood up, disoriented, and then trotted away from us. A few stallkeepers were taken aback, a few knocked off balance. There was hardly the space for even a small bundle of black fluff to manoeuvre. We all jumped up to the rescue, knocking the plastic seats in all directions like pins in a bowling alley. There was some mild annoyance, which quickly switched to mild amusement at our chaotic antics. After a bit of a fluster and some chasing of fluff through the narrow market alleys, the black puppy was back in our arms, where—we hoped—he would begin to feel he belonged.

It struck again. That feeling that I couldn't necessarily control what was going on around me. That anything could happen at any time.

When we got them home, we found they were both gorgeous puppies with lovely temperaments. We got attached too quickly. Only a few weeks (and several expensive vet bills) later, they died of exactly the same disease that GC had had. They would have already had the disease when we bought them. They were buried in the large graveyard in the open field, alongside both GC and the others.

We just could not seem to keep our pets.

When our two new puppies died, the 'mysteries of life and death stories' had to be told again, this time to Kallen, who was now old enough to be asking the string of 'Why?' questions. But this time there was a difference. Our little ceremony in the back paddock helped to give the event some meaning.

'*Salamat jalan*,' Ketut said as we put the final frangipanis on the grave—'happy journey'. It is the Balinese way.

It helped to cement the idea that perhaps death is not the end, perhaps there is more. I told the kids that we were being watched over and protected. I think they were learning to grow up with less fear and more of a sense of purpose. I was definitely continually learning the lesson of trust. This lesson comes over and over in life when you open yourself up to new possibilities. When you are prepared to follow your dreams and convictions, even through uncertain times.

The deaths were, however, a bad omen.

Perhaps I was being paranoid, perhaps my fears were justified—but when Kallen became sick the day after the puppies died, I went into a bit of a panic. The symptoms were the same: a temperature, lethargy, a rash, a loss of appetite, an inability to keep food down. We checked it out that he could not have caught distemper from the puppies, but still had no idea what it was. I was very concerned.

By pure coincidence, we were heading back to Australia that night, so I crossed my fingers, hoping that we would be able to make it in time to find out what was going on.

We got to Sydney without any problems. In fact it was the easiest plane flight I have ever had with the children—Kallen simply slept the whole way. Once we were in Australia, the symptoms came and went just often enough for me to imagine that maybe he was okay. One minute he was looking as though life was slowly seeping out of him, the next he was running around full of energy. Just like the puppies. I kept seeing flashing images of their small weak bodies as they took their last desperate gasps for air before dying. Interspersed with these were the long ingrained images of my father, as he took his last breaths. I had been there at his side with the rest of my family through those last days. Death burns an impression into the mind that is impossible to erase.

When the symptoms had continued long enough for me to think that maybe this was more than a passing virus, I took Kallen to see a doctor. We were staying with my mother and stepfather on their farm, though, a good six hours' train ride from Sydney and so I wondered if the local doctors would be used to looking for the strange tropical ailments we were exposed to. I felt it would be nice to have some reassurance that it was just a virus, anyway.

The first doctor I went to prescribed antibiotics.

'There is probably a secondary infection,' he explained, 'from the viruses you say your son has already had.'

But the symptoms only got worse.

The second doctor took him off the antibiotics, thinking that maybe the rash was an allergic reaction.

'It's a virus,' she said, 'and there's really nothing much you can do about it. I am sure the symptoms will eventually clear. This is the sort of thing I see every day; children come in here with these symptoms all the time. Just let me know if the symptoms get worse.'

The symptoms did get worse. I decided to return to the city to get some tests done by our regular family doctor. I made an emergency call on the mobile phone from the train to let the clinic know we were on our way as I was really concerned about Kallen by this stage. He had hardly stirred the whole train trip.

'He's a good little boy, isn't he?' one kindly old lady had commented, having noticed that he had barely moved or made a sound.

'Yes, he is,' I replied weakly, unwilling to take the conversation further, concerned that if I started to talk about his illness I might break down.

Andrew picked us up from the train station (he had been travelling with work while we had been staying with my mother), and was horrified to see Kallen looking so unwell. He drove us straight to the clinic. The doctor had wall-to-wall bookings, but she was concerned enough to slip Kallen in between her other appointments. She wanted to make an assessment to see if he needed to be admitted straight to hospital.

Just as we rushed into the doctor's surgery, Kallen sat up and looked around as if he'd just woken up from a refreshing sleep and was ready to bounce out of bed and greet a new day. I explained to him that we were visiting the doctor to see if she could help to make him better.

'Can I have the jelly beans?' he asked enthusiastically.

'I'm sure if the doctor has them she'll be happy to give some to you.' I was so relieved to be having a relatively normal conversation with him.

'That will make me better, Mummy.'

'I hope so . . .'

He got up and ran around the waiting room like a wound up toy. When the doctor called us into her consulting room, I was feeling like a paranoid mother. Kallen was a picture of health and vitality.

'What exactly is the problem?' If she was thinking that we were overly anxious parents, she didn't show it. She was brisk and matter of fact, as always, and she listened to our concerns carefully.

'Right,' she said after my rundown of the symptoms. 'I'm going to arrange for a series of tests. Urine tests and stool tests, to check that there's no amoeba or other bugs in the system, and blood tests to look for the other tropical ailments.'

She listed the things she wanted the lab to look for in the blood test: typhoid, malaria, dengue fever, hepatitis A, hepatitis B, Japanese B encephalitis . . . It was a long and scary-looking list.

'We'll need different types of cultures and different tubes for the various tests,' she explained.

I wasn't sure if I was feeling relieved that everything was being checked and we'd soon know what was really going on, or if the whole procedure was simply making me more anxious about the possibilities.

Down the hall at pathology, we were told to see Mandy, who had the most experience and the best manner with children. The whole family crowded into the small clinic where the blood sample would be taken. Kallen was still the picture of good health, and I imagined Mandy must have been wondering what the big panic was.

Kallen watched the needle going in, and slowly the corners of his mouth started to drop and the tears began to well up in his eyes. His expression was clearly saying, 'How could anyone possibly do this to me?'

He whimpered pathetically, tragically, but never really cried. The nurse moved the needle around, desperately trying to extract more blood from his skinny little arm. When asked about the blood test by a friend later, all Kallen could say was, 'The lady hurt me. She just wanted to hurt me.'

'You are such a brave boy,' Mandy said afterwards.

'Yes,' I laughed, relieved it was over. 'He's tough like his mum.' I cuddled him, proud of the way he had handled it, still happy that he'd come to life again.

At that very second, there was a loud buzzing in my ears. The world started to close in on me. All the sounds in the room became muffled, and my vision narrowed and blurred. I desperately tried to continue the conversation, now recognising that I was on my way to passing out. Making a dive for the floor just as I was starting to lose contact with reality completely, suddenly the medical focus in the clinic was on me, rather than Kallen. I think the stress and worry had caught up with me.

Although I am usually pretty calm, this incident had touched a nerve and revealed the deeper fear I must have had about whether we were doing the right thing for the children. Perhaps the tension and uncertainty of living in a country in transition was catching up. I was thoroughly embarrassed to be so weak and unable to be the all-protecting strong parent. It showed me that I was not so tough after all. It reminded me that I would have to be willing to admit to my uncertainties and fears and be open about sharing them with others.

When Kallen's test results came back, we returned to the doctor's office. A few days had passed for the cultures to grow, and I had recovered from the disorientation and embarrassment of passing out in the pathology clinic. Our son had been fighting fit, and I was quite sure that whatever it was had passed, and all the worry had been for nothing.

'Dengue fever,' the doctor said, characteristically calmly. 'I thought so.'

Dengue fever! I started fretting in earnest. From what I had heard, dengue fever could kill children. It was the one mosquito-borne disease that was a problem in Bali, the one we had always feared while living on the island. I had heard that once the disease is in your system, it keeps coming back. It is known as 'bone-breaking disease' because of its terrible symptoms and debilitating effects.

I tried to act as calmly as the doctor, thinking of all the questions I should be asking while I had the chance. 'Will the symptoms return? . . . Are there any long-term effects? . . . Should he be taking any medication? . . .'

The doctor managed to allay my worst fears with the information that there are four strains of dengue, and apparently Kallen had one of the milder strains. And no, she said, it does not return.

Okay, so it didn't look like the disease was life threatening this time around. We could thank the gods for that. But still, it had been a sobering scare—to say the least. What would happen if there was a next time? And, even if it wasn't dengue, what else could he get that might threaten his health? It certainly made us think seriously. Would we be prepared to give up our patch of paradise? Of course, we thought, we would leave tomorrow if needed for the sake of our children. But so often the lines are grey . . . and our patch of paradise had already become so much a part of our lives . . .

It was at this time, in the first year of the new millennium, that we experienced the toughest test on our relationship.

We had already survived so many potentially stressful changes together: having children, moving countries, building a new home, changing careers, starting an international business from scratch, living with the country's political tensions . . . We had survived the major traumas, and had adapted to the minor annoying inconveniences of our newfound home: the cultural adjustments, the illnesses, the bureaucratic inefficiencies. We had thought that by this stage we could just sit back and relax and enjoy all the benefits. Not so. The scare Kallen's illness gave us triggered off a whole lot of concerns that each of us had obviously pushed to the backs of our minds.

Of course there had been plenty of times over the past years when stress became directed inwards in each of us, and our suppressed worries would flare out, causing us to blame each other for problems. There would be times when I would wonder whether I had done the right thing by uprooting the whole family. I would sometimes feel the responsibility for anything that went wrong. It was, after all, originally my dream, my wild idea. Usually, once we were able to regain our common vision, however, we were able to get back on track. We were able to resolve those issues as they arose and prevent them from leading to a deeper resentment. The lifestyle we had come to enjoy in Bali had helped to cushion the impact of the stress, too. It absorbed a great deal of the pressure, any negative feelings quickly evaporating.

But this time it was different. Our energies became more intensely focused inwards. Being back in Australia under stressful circumstances stripped us of the protection we'd enjoyed all these years. It felt like we were back to square one—rushing to fit in appointments with clients, trying to squash a year's worth of business and personal affairs into a few weeks, arguing over who would get the computer next, who would do the cleaning and cooking, who was responsible for looking after the children, whether the children were being adequately cared for.

We got sucked into the resentment cycle once again, accusing, attacking and defending, rather than negotiating difficult situations sensibly.

'You haven't changed, have you?' I accused Andrew when I felt that I had ended up taking more than a fair share of the responsibility for looking after the household. 'All these years away, all these changes in our lives and here we are again, back to square one.'

'You're the one who hasn't changed,' Andrew threw back at me, then taking the conflict to another deeper level, 'You took us to Bali, and now you're not taking responsibility for looking after the children. What's keeping a house clean compared to our children's health? We can't continue to live in Bali if you're going to be so irresponsible. I always insist the children have mosquito cream or mosquito-proof clothes on, and you are just not supporting me in this. It's so typical of your careless attitude. You have these wild ideas, and then I'm expected to follow through on them.'

'And I'm tired of you barking the commands and then going off and doing your own thing. We made this change together, you've got to be committed to making it work, too . . .' I knew that I hadn't been as vigilant as I should have been, and felt guilty about that. But I did think the responsibility should have gone both ways.

'I'm still trying to get over all the years of following you and your dreams. When are you going to change? When are you going to start to become more responsible?' Andrew continued.

'I have changed! I'm not asking you to move again. I'm happy where we are. I thought you were, too . . .' I was hurt. I really felt we had achieved so much together. It was demoralising to think that perhaps it hadn't counted after all.

'I do like where we're living and what we're doing, but you have put us in a position of risk. I wish you'd admit it and put more effort into taking the right precautions.'

'Forget it. I can never do anything that meets with your standards. My best efforts are never good enough for you . . .'

We dwelt on our own dissatisfactions for a while, and as we were both simmering I remembered where we had come from all those years ago, before I had been motivated to make the change. I eventually began to see that I was upset because I felt that Andrew was not acknowledging a change in me—the same way that I was not really acknowledging a change in him. We both needed to feel supported in the progress we had made. We both needed to cling closer at this time, not drive each other apart. And I needed to be the one to take the initiative in apologising this time around.

Apologising was really hard. I was so used to thinking of myself as always being the one in the right. My strength and determination usually got me through. But I knew that the most important lesson through this time was going to be humility. The art of admitting weakness and allowing for a different perspective.

In the end we were strengthened by the ordeal. This time had brought to the surface some of the lingering fears that were still obviously haunting us, deep down. I knew we could never escape the fears of tropical risks. They were real. But we could learn to deal with the way we coped with that fear, and the way we communicated it to each other. We had to accept that there were going to be risks involved, and support each other in dealing with them.

Once I started to open up again and allowed myself to become more accepting of those differences that had threatened to drive us apart, I realised that of course we had both grown and changed. Most of our experiences through our years in Bali had been wonderful. It was just that every so often we had let ourselves get dragged down by the potentially negative rather than focusing on the positive. The strain of fear had simply brought out the worst.

Through the experience I realised, too, that it was going to be important for us both to continue to maintain a spiritual balance, an outward focus that would help us to keep learning and growing. We learnt to be mindful that finding a positive environment is simply not enough. The inner state must be challenged at the same time. The soul needs to be constantly refreshed and transformed.

'We must,' I reflected to Andrew, when we were back in Bali and finally starting to feel in control again, 'continue to make New Year's resolutions, continue to strive and pray for more—to make sure we stay on track. We must never be overly confident about where we are and what we have.'

'You're right,' he admitted. 'It's so important that we never take what we have for granted. We should make sure we always take one day at a time, one week at a time, one year at a time.'

For even in paradise, the environment could not be controlled. One is always at the whim of the spirits.

Back in Bali, with the perspective of rubber time, without the stress-magnifying distortions of life in fast motion, everything started to look good again. There was once more a growing sense of relaxed contentment. But, ironically, it would be the big black international disaster looming on the horizon that would finally and truly break our own storm, and bring the brightest, clearest rainbow to our world. The havoc that was to come would have a dramatic impact all around the world, and more than ever before we would be forced to cling on to the core values that had been shaping our lives.

Chapter 19

Trouble in the Global Village

When a butterfly flaps its wings in the Amazon jungle, the weather patterns thousands of miles away in the tropics can be affected. True. The world is connected.

On 11 September 2001, when nineteen men took to the air in the United States and crashed hijacked planes into the great symbols of western power and globalisation, the whole world was turned upside down, and paradise everywhere was threatened.

Asia had its own unique tropical storms, and by this stage we'd well and truly experienced some of the worst of them. But the storm we heard rumbling in the distance on September 11 showed us that our tropical existence was not immune to the fallout from trouble in the global village.

It's funny how we all remember where we were at significant times, when world-shattering news pierces our regular daily existence and throws us into a hyper-aware state, a reminder that there are greater forces at work. I can remember seeing the Apollo 11 landing on the moon on our black and white TV when I was very young, catching news about the space shuttle disaster late at night at a friend's house, hearing of Princess Diana's death on my car radio while driving through an outer Sydney suburb.

On this occasion, we were awoken early the morning after by

Andrew's surfing friend Cam calling to break the news. Only semi-conscious when he rang, I saw Andrew looking totally perplexed—uncertain of whether this was a bad April Fool's joke or the awful truth.

'Tell him we're still in bed and he can call you back later,' I said.

I was in no mood for being awoken by an early-morning surf report.

Andrew was caught completely off guard. After his friend's description of the tragedy, Andrew asked the habitual question: 'So how is the surf, anyway?' It was only when he got off the phone and described to me what had happened that the magnitude of this disaster dawned on us both.

Not ten years before, we had been together in a Mexican bar, on the edge of a lonely desert, and had been stunned by the CNN report of American forces at work in another scorched patch of earth in the Middle East. Sleeping in hammocks at night to keep away from deadly scorpions, the stinging reality of the Gulf War seemed both familiar and distant. We had travelled on nearly empty planes and buses through North and South America during that time, feeling from different perspectives the anxious fear of a nation at war. CNN had remained our one 'guiding star' along every step of the way, consistently reporting on the mayhem and devastation in dramatic, full-frontal images.

But here in Bali, we still had no TV of our own, so on this particular morning we woke ourselves up as quickly as we could, threw on some clothes, then ducked around to the hotel next door to watch CNN do it all over again. People all around the world were watching the same images over and over with us: the second plane angling in to meet the second tower while the first tower blazed beside it; people running away from the huge, apocalyptic billows of dust that rose as both high-rise buildings collapsed to street level; crowds of dust-choked New York City refugees being evacuated on buses.

Those images will be etched in our minds forever. More unreal than any Spielberg movie, the breadth of such masterminded drama was greater than anything our generation had witnessed before. And the impact was much deeper.

Parents had trouble explaining to their children what had happened and why, businesses were brought to their knees. Even airlines that usually operate on a more strictly business-as-usual basis were getting close and personal—on one post-event plane the pilot was heard announcing, 'Remember, we are all like one big family while we are in the air.'

It was the first time in our lives that the threat of another world war felt very real, and the possible implications were absolutely frightening. Were we going to be drawn into a long, extended battle? Would our day-to-day lives ever be quite the same again? Perhaps the scariest implication was that the world was suddenly being neatly divided into two sections: Muslims, and others. We happened to be living in the largest Muslim country in the world. That could only spell trouble.

An international awareness campaign had to be quickly implemented to educate people about the fact that, just as in any religion, there are moderate Muslims as well as extremist Muslims. The majority of Muslims are actually peace-loving moderates, but the extremists easily grab the attention of the press and gain wider exposure. There are Muslim groups in Indonesia that can be as militant as anywhere else. There are those who seem to enjoy calling for holy jihad wars, but fortunately they don't have the same access to advanced weaponry as their counterparts in the Middle East. At one stage, there were days, weeks, and months on end where the front page of the local and international papers continued to show hoards of angry demonstrators on the streets of Jakarta, shouting and screaming and generally causing havoc—ready to die for a cause.

These groups would often travel into Jakarta from outlying village *kampungs,* brandishing knives tied onto bamboo poles to prove their point. They were suicide fighters, claiming that they would risk their lives for whatever cause they were supporting at the time as a show of solidarity. As soon as the attacks on Afghanistan were announced, there was a groundswell from these groups demanding justice, pledging to travel to Afghanistan themselves to fight alongside the Taliban and to cause problems for the government if they didn't immediately oppose all retaliatory action from the United States. More demonstrations, threats and violent actions followed. In fact, at one stage there was such a rash of demonstrations that the streets were choked with different groups all criss-crossing their way across Jakarta.

The police there must often have been acting as human-traffic police, directing one demonstration this way, another that way. When looking at or reading the news, we sometimes had to spend some time assessing what particular cause was being represented. There were so many.

There was definitely a humorous side to these demonstrations, though. Many of the street protests in Jakarta were actually comprised of paid demonstrators. Whole villages of people were involved—usually poor people looking for some quick income, or others who were apparently totally unaware of what was going on, merely following the village chief's orders (who would have been benefiting significantly from the arrangement). All these people were provided with placards, lunch, and a nice little sum of money—and bussed into the capital. Often they had no idea what they were demonstrating against or why. They were merely there to swell the numbers, giving the organisers a greater chance of gaining international air time. Sad for the serious demonstrators, with real issues to be resolved. But that is, of course, how politics in Indonesia have run for decades. When he was in power President Soeharto had paid for many of his votes.

The impact of this political crisis on our own business and livelihood was immediate. With a general fear of travel and very real security risks, plans to hold conferences in Bali were quickly snuffed out. The training budgets of many of our major regular clients around Asia were slashed in the wake of the huge economic downturn that followed the events of September 11, affecting industries in all different sectors. Our business had boomed consistently for the past few years, and now suddenly we had all work cancelled for the foreseeable future.

The calendar was blank. The world was under threat of war.

Strangely, the three months following the attacks turned out to be the best three months of our lives. The sunny side to the disaster for us personally was that we suddenly had a hugely demanding workload lifted off our shoulders. We were able to make the most of the quiet after the storm.

Although shaken by the implications of the disaster, it was also another reminder of the importance of regaining priorities, of making the most of what we have. No deadlines, no restrictions. Our time became our own. It grew into a time of healing and renewal. There had been slumps before in the business, and they had been stressful. There had been times when we had wondered if the business would ever come back. But this was different. The company was secure.

This would be a temporary trough, we knew, but we had no idea how long it would continue or how deep it would be. It actually provided us with some much needed time out that we had not been able to take since starting out on our venture. There are still always maintenance tasks that have to be kept up when you run a company, no matter how slow business might be, but these were much more easily dealt with and much less consuming during this lull.

For the first time in a while I had time to write, which usually had to take a back seat. I always find it so calming, so therapeutic, to be able to bury myself in my thoughts for hours on end, to be challenged to transfer them to paper. I went for long walks on the beach, breathing in the spicy tropical air, contemplating life. Andrew had more time for reading, for gathering new ideas . . . and more time for kite surfing. He went out each day, almost without fail, and inevitably came back physically exhausted, glowing and enthused with creative energy.

We went away for weekends: to the mountains, to rivers, to clifftop retreats. We took time off to be with our children. We took the time to socialise, to be with friends. And we took time to be together, outside of the office, as husband and wife. It was just what we needed. Our friends started to comment that we were the most relaxed we had ever looked and our relationship was certainly much more intimate than it had ever been. Contemplating our future and the state of the world, we felt stronger than ever in our abilities to cope with whatever would come our way. Our personal storm had broken, and Andrew and I had moved on to a new level of trust and commitment—and enjoyment—in our relationship.

I saw gangs of thugs surrounding our house one night, shadows under the oily moonless sky. They were carrying fire sticks and demanding we come out and show ourselves for who we really were, as strangers who didn't belong. Andrew and I grabbed the kids out of their beds and huddled in the darkest corner of the room with them, petrified that we would be discovered and hauled out into the open.

Moments later I was confused to find myself back in bed, sweaty and shaken. I checked on Andrew, and found he was fast asleep beside me. It had only been a dream, probably triggered by the sounds of a loud party of locals at the cafes in front of our house. But dreams can feel so real.

I had fallen asleep that night reading about the slaughter of Indonesian communists in 1965. After an attempted coup was thwarted, Soeharto had organised a counter coup and an anti-communism purge swept through the country—mainly through Java and Bali. Groups of government supporters travelled from village to village, from house to house, pulling out anyone sus-pected of communism. This was the first time the concept of 'sweeping' was introduced to the Indonesian vocabulary (they spell it 'swiping'!). Hundreds of thousands of people were killed or imprisoned, many others went into hiding—some estimates say at least 500,000 people were murdered at this time. The terror had woven its way into my subconscious.

That era had apparently not ended, though. Some still believed that if the unsavoury elements could be purged from the country, traditional religious values and political purity would prevail. Every so often we'd read in the paper about groups of conservative Muslims who had embarked on their own moral missions. They would attack nightclubs frequented by foreign-ers, outraged by the blatant disregard for Islamic moral rules. Sometimes they would enter hotels. They would check out the names of foreigners registered to stay there in order to purge the area of unwanted foreign influences.

During the attacks on Afghanistan, there were constant embassy warnings for foreigners to leave the country. The US Ambassador announced that Indonesia was the most dangerous country for foreigners outside of Afghanistan. Those who chose to remain in the country were told to stay indoors. All foreign businesses shut down for a few days until the political situation could be properly assessed.

Many extremist Muslim groups had threatened to step up their sweeping campaigns as part of their contribution to the jihad cause. The Balinese were livid. They couldn't stand the thought of their tourism industry being held to ransom yet again. The governor of Bali held a press conference to assure foreigners that Bali would remain safe.

'The only sweeping that might go on around here,' he emphatically stated, 'is the daily sweeping of houses and yards!'

Articles in the local papers showed Balinese men in their traditional tribal warfare outfits claiming that they would fight to protect Bali.

I rang our friend Made Sudarno of Gianyar—the chief Balinese artistic and cultural adviser for many of our programs—to let him know how bleak everything was looking for future programs. I can remember being taken by surprise by his response. Our usually bright and cheery, if somewhat impish friend, was burdened with concerns about our safety.

'Gaia, don't you worry. We won't let anything happen to you. You just let me know if anyone causes you trouble, okay? Is anyone causing you trouble down there?'

'No, everything's fine, thanks, Made. We're being well looked after down here.'

'Well, if you ever have even the slightest problem, you just ring me up straightaway, okay? If there's ever any problem, I'll just ring the *kul-kul* bell and the whole village will meet me, and we'll bring our knives and all come down to help you. We'll kill anyone who causes problems for you, okay? Don't you worry, we'll just kill them. We'll look after you.'

'Hey—thanks so much, Made. No need to kill anyone, everything's fine.' I tried to calm him, knowing that he was serious in his promise. 'But I know where to turn if I need help!'

Many groups were certainly planning to do their best to fight against violence, all around the world. The problem is that I think we all got a bit confused about who the real perpetrators of violence were. When two parties fight neither is necessarily innocent or justified in proving their point. The US claimed it had been present in the Middle East merely to help with security and curb violence. The terrorists who attacked the World Trade Centre did so because they said they were opposed to the violence caused by the presence of US troops in the Middle East. The Taliban claimed that the US were the terrorists after they started bombing Afghanistan. The US said that they were trying to deal with the violent actions of terrorists by starting an offensive against Afghanistan.

The Indonesian anti-US protesters that were threatening to 'sweep' foreigners—drive them from the country, take them as hostages, or even kill them—said they were opposing the violent actions of the US. Soon after came the anti-sweeping groups that said they would defend foreigners by force if necessary in order to deal with the violence. There are layers and layers of irony in the cycle of violence.

Back in our little household, Ketut No.1 gave an interesting perspective on the root of all evil and a sure-fire way to end this cycle of violence. His theory was based around the fact that while the Muslims eat beef but not pork (which they consider unclean), the Balinese Hindus eat pork but not beef (the Hindus believe cows are sacred). Those who eat beef, Ketut claimed, are prone to violence and irrational behaviour. If only everyone could eat pork instead, he said, the world would be at peace.

If only life were that simple!

Who can blame anyone for wanting to shut down fast food chains? I must say I didn't mind seeing footage of cans of Coca Cola being emptied onto the streets, and McDonald's and KFC stores being taped up and sealed from the outside during the TV coverage of the anti-US protests in Jakarta.

I had to laugh, though, when I read about the Bogor University Student Front Against United States Terrorism (BUSFAUST—or some other equally lengthy and absurd acronym), who threatened the local KFC and McDonald's stores in Bogor by telling them they had to pay two million rupiah each (about AUS$500) or else their establishments would be vandalised. They ended up managing to collect 200,000 rupiah (about AUS$50) from each in the end.

The opposition sometimes went from the sublime to the ridiculous, but still, the apparently unstoppable forces of corporate imperialism were being challenged. Did you know that the two most recognised symbols in the world are the Coca Cola logo and those large golden arches? The Christian cross only comes in at third place—I'm not sure where the other major religious symbols sit. An interesting reflection of our priorities in life.

At about the same time as the anti-globalism and anti-US protests were going on around the country and around the world, we observed gangs of workers constantly at work on a building site at one of the main entrances to our village. Judging by the dimensions of the property, the position, and the sheer speed at which the building was taking shape, I knew it was something significant. First guess was that it was an important government or religious building.

'Hey, any idea what's going up here?' I asked Yulia as she passed by in her car one day. 'It's unusual to see so much activity on a building site!'

Yulia always seemed to be in touch with the local goings-on in the area. 'Uh huh,' she said. 'It's going to be a new McDonald's store.'

'What?' I was devastated. Up until that point, our village had consisted of fishermen and their fishing boats, the barbeque fish cafes and art shops, and traditional fruit and veggie markets—with only a few modern hotels discreetly hidden under the foliage of coconut palms as a reminder of our presence in the 21st century. Sure, we were totally surrounded by tourist suburbs and a four-lane freeway skimmed past the village perimeter—but somehow until now we had escaped the full effects of consumer tourism.

McDonald's had arrived in Bali only about six years before, and now already this was to be store number eight in a small patch of about a twenty kilometre radius. KFC, Baskin Robbins, and Dunkin Donuts had also made appearances in the same area during that time. Huge monolithic trendy stores of all types had popped up everywhere—many with famous international brand names—and our part of Bali was starting to resemble an American chain store mall rather than the unique hippy shopping haven it had been not so long before.

Yulia turned to her daughter and her daughter's friend in the back of the car. 'Let's make a pact right now. We're not going to start having McDonald's every day after school, are we!' It was a statement, not a question. The two thoroughly westernised Indonesian nine-year-olds with perfect American accents groaned in unison.

'But, Mum . . . !' Yulia's daughter protested.

I took advantage of Yulia's support and threw the same statement to my own daughter. Now there were three groans—all in American accented harmony. (The American influence from a large number of American expats had been so strong that my children now had much more of a twang than a drawl, and our Aussie relatives and friends were horrified at this apparent disloyalty whenever we returned to Australia!)

'Just for a special treat then, Mum. Like every Friday because it's the end of the week.'

Grrrrrr . . . Sometimes you just have to grit you teeth and bear it.

As it turned out, we were probably some of the first customers in our new neighbourhood McDonald's. We were driving out of our street the night it officially opened, when we were rudely confronted by a huge golden 'M'.

'Aaaarghh!' I immediately exclaimed. 'They've invaded our territory completely! Now we can't even drive out of our street without being reminded that they're lurking here somewhere, waiting to lure us into their evil den!'

The children were sitting in the back seat of the car, staring at me as if I had a serious problem. Then an idea occurred to our daughter . . .

'Hey, can we have McDonald's for dinner tonight, Mum?'

'Are you kidding?! We are *not* having McDonald's. No way are we giving in to that . . .'

I stopped mid-sentence, and in that split second I let the idea register. I thought about how late it was getting, about how we were heading out for a Balinese dinner with some friends a good half-hour away. I considered how the kids would complain about the spicy food (the Balinese have no concept of preparing a meal without a significant amount of chili in it), how late the meal would come, about how they would probably fall asleep in the middle of the meal anyway.

Just as we reached the McDonald's turnoff, I made a spontaneous decision and swerved suddenly into the side road.

'Hey . . . what's going on . . . where are we going . . . ?!' There were exclamations coming from all corners of the car.

'I've decided you kids are going to have McDonald's for dinner.'

'Yeah!' The kids were happy.

'What!' said Andrew, horrified. 'I thought you were going to boycott the place!'

'I was, but how can you beat it for convenience and speed? We'll be able to get the kids something we know they'll like now, and have them asleep before we get to our dinner, so we can relax and enjoy it . . . It'll be much easier, really.'

'You're such a hypocrite,' he said, with a satisfied smile. With all my high ideals, he loves catching me out whenever he can and reminding me I'm human after all!

'I know, I can't believe it. So much for taking a strong stance. No wonder the world's being overtaken by fast food chains.'

We were in and out of the drive-through section in no time, and on a road of no return. It was another major encroachment upon our carefully cloistered existence, I could already tell. The long tentacles of global consumerism were reaching everywhere, into every corner of the world—including our patch of paradise.

At this stage, internationally, there was a significant number of people prepared to fight back, to attempt to protect themselves from the apparently inevitable future. A complex global scenario was unfolding.

The police stopped us at the traffic lights just as we were leaving the airport. Not very considerate, I thought, pouncing on people who might have just entered the country for the first time. I was particularly concerned about Andrew's elderly mother, who was very active and healthy for her seventy-six years, but still likely to become anxious in potentially threatening situations in a foreign country—especially a country that had received a lot of news coverage lately for its violent demonstrations.

Of course we were quite used to being stopped by the police ourselves. It is a fact of life here. You have to make sure you obey the unfathomable and ever-changing road rules and that your papers are all thoroughly in order, or be prepared to pay. The police actually make so little in their regular monthly salary that they rely on these 'gifts' as extra pocket money to boost their income.

A recent survey has shown that the most corrupt institution in Indonesia is the police force, followed by the legal and immigration systems. I have, throughout my years in Bali, had to deal with all three institutions several times over. Each time I have taken many different stances and tried many different tactics: pleading, demanding, sympathising. And I must admit that over time you end up feeling it's just easier to pay the money than prolong the agony.

The day Andrew's mum arrived, though, things were looking very unsettled around the country and so we were even keener than usual to pay up and be on our way.

Andrew was driving at the time, and he had stopped a few centimetres over the white line at the intersection. We had been caught out for this same traffic infringement before. I didn't recall it being such a major crime in Australia—if at all—but in Bali it is considered a serious offence. More serious than going through a red light (of course we'd now realised it would have been better to run the red light than try to stop at the last minute and end up over the line!).

The policeman came to Andrew's window and asked to see his driver's licence, then briskly whisked it away from him and marched it over to one of those famous little police boxes that are placed strategically along the main streets. I could see that Andrew's mum was already starting to get flustered, so I told Andrew to park the car at the side of the road while I dealt with the situation—before she decided to turn around and go back to the airport.

Inside the box I was encouraged to sit down, and the policeman began the laborious process of filling out what looked like bogus forms. I stood, to indicate I was in a hurry, but bowed my head in humility and spoke in my sweetest, most humble voice:

'Pak, I'm sorry my husband went over the famous white line. Please can I just pay and leave?'

This was not the usual protocol! I had broken an unwritten rule. But this man wanted to continue with his prepared script, and continue he would.

'Do you realise that it's an offence to go over that line?'

'Yes, I know. I've been in trouble for that before. Mind you I think it's a ridiculous rule—you wouldn't have to pay a fine for going over a white line in my country. For speeding, yes. For parking in a non-parking area, yes. But not for going over a little white line. Definitely not.' It was going to be hard for me to maintain my humble demeanour.

'Do you understand that you will have to pay a fine, or you will have to go to court?'

'Yes, I understand. I've got my money ready. How much do you want?' Under control again. I had to remind myself to just play the game.

'The fee is Rp50,000.'

'Don't be ridiculous! I only ever pay Rp20,000 maximum for an offence such as that!'

'It's 50,000.'

Come on, stay cool, I told myself. Change of tack. 'Look, I've got 20,000 right here. Please just take it. My elderly mother is in the car—she's seventy-six years old, you know, and she's travelled for six hours on the aeroplane all by herself all the way from Australia because she wants to see her grandchildren and come to beautiful Indonesia. We went to so much trouble to convince her that Bali is safe, that there is nothing to fear in Bali. All she sees on her television in Australia is fighting and trouble in Indonesia. We had to convince her to come here by promising it would be safe, and then the first thing she sees as soon as she exits the airport is police in uniform! The car was stopped by armed police! She's scared, and I'm worried about her. I just want to get back in the car and take her home. Please take the 20,000.'

I actually tried to lighten up the situation by this stage, using the amusing sing-song speaking style that Indonesians use when they're dealing with a difficult situation, and got the police officer smiling.

'Okay,' he simply said. 'Have a good day!'

I was out of that box in record time, I swear—and with the bribe money bargained down to a reasonable rate. I had a feeling that the faster negotiations had something to do with a changing awareness of how Indonesia was now being viewed by outsiders, and an increasing national pride. It would take time for the reformation to really take root—the corruption was so ingrained at all levels—but we were starting to see, in many ways, a growing consciousness of international perceptions. We could only hope that it would at least be a positive starting point for the slow process of change.

Fortunately, my mother-in-law remained pretty oblivious to the outside political tensions throughout her stay. That's the beauty of Bali. Apart from those odd occasions when the anger boiled over, we could usually tuck ourselves away and be protected from what was going on in the rest of the country and the rest of the world. Even after a local disaster, things quickly regained their calm and composed state, and we could easily get lulled into believing once again that we were on an idyllic island, a long way away from the concerns of the rest of the world. As long as we kept our eyes off the horizon . . .

Living without a television certainly meant that we were able to isolate ourselves from the big picture, which was both good and bad. We didn't feel like we needed to know every detail of Tom and Nicole's marriage breakdown or Oprah Winfrey's weight-loss program, but it did become a problem when areas of the world erupted into a war and we had no idea what was going on.

There had been a time in our lives when we had been thoroughly up to date with the latest news and current affairs. Andrew and I both grew up in households where news and current affairs programs were considered acceptable TV viewing. Then when we went on to become teachers, we prided ourselves on having up-to-date information and being contemporary in our approach. That meant checking the major news and current affairs stories, reading a wide range of newspapers and magazines, going to all the latest movies—often not for pure enjoyment—always with a notebook and pen in hand, jotting down relevant statistics, quotes and stories. But you can't keep up that sort of heavy vigilance over time. Your mind becomes saturated, and you start to become numb to all the data.

That was definitely one of the motivating factors for the escape to Bali in the first place. Being on an island and being cut off from the rest of the world for a while. Having a clear mind, being able to follow interests and become focused on ourselves and our family, not feeling that heavy sense of responsibility for the world.

Going cold turkey with the media initially gave us some great breathing space, but we knew that at some point we were going to have to re-enter the 'real' world. This truth was brought home to us when someone rang from Australia one day to check if we were still alive, and we were not at all sure what they were talking about.

'Is everything okay over there?'

'Hi! Great to hear from you! Yes thanks, everything's fine. We're just finishing breakfast, then we're off to the beach for the day. What have you all been up to?'

'Do you realise there's a riot going on in Indonesia? Aren't you worried about it?'

'Oh, right, is there? Better check the news then. Thanks very much for letting us know about it. So how are your kids going?'

'Don't you know how serious this could be . . . ? Don't you think it's time you moved back to Australia?'

'Everything looks fine from where we are.' (As it does when you've got no idea what's going on around you.)

Eventually we regained a sense of balance, by subscribing to the national English language newspaper as well as the *Economist* and *Time* magazines (not that any of these arrives on time—so we are still, essentially, always behind in our news!). We also put more effort into reading good books that we had picked up from various international airports. Occasionally we checked international news websites and our neighbours' TVs. Otherwise, we still had that feeling of peace and serenity that comes with not being overloaded with too many facts and figures.

I never missed being immersed in everyone else's affairs, but we did learn that maintaining some sense of what's going on out there was a responsibility to ourselves, our children, and the world at large. The island we chose to live on was in a fragile state, the country seemed to be falling apart, and it felt as though the world could spiral out of control at any time—so it was good to at least feel somewhat prepared and know in some sense how to respond.

We continued to enjoy our mostly sunny paradise, but recognised we would always need to check the horizon to remind ourselves that the sun does not always shine. Not always, and not in every corner of the globe.

Chapter 20

Paradise is a State of Mind

We had come to Bali in search of a different way of life. For inspiration, for time and space to create different experiences and opportunities than we might otherwise have had. We found what we were looking for. Living in Bali was never quite what we expected, always full of surprises, but to us it remained an idyllic retreat. It gave us the framework for making the changes in our lives we had needed to make.

Plenty of others have also come to know and love the island in the same way—we were by no means the first or last to want to believe in Bali as a paradise. Many people have come to Bali in search of something, whether it's for a different cultural experience, a relaxing break, a good time, the chance to make a big buck quick, or spiritual enlightenment. Some people leave empty handed, some are enticed to stay, as we have been. Like Ali Baba's cave, Bali has become the soul searchers' sometimes elusive treasure trove.

Even the rich and infamous are drawn irresistibly to the lure of the exotic, to the promise of a deeper, richer, spiritual experience. Mick Jagger and Jerry Hall got married here, wrapped in the traditional garb. David Bowie escaped here and spent some time in a mountain retreat. Elle MacPherson spoiled herself with lavish Javanese body treatments.

Although we continued to appreciate what all these people had been looking for in Bali, the full impact of our amazing find struck us afresh when we recently hosted a Hollywood blockbuster actor on the island. This actor had been enticed here by the promise of an idyllic getaway at the other end of the earth. I won't reveal who he was, in respect of his need for privacy, but suffice to say we already felt we knew him well from numerous films and countless tabloid articles. He was researching a film he was planning to write, taking time out in the middle of a busy working schedule. We were called in by an associate to help him organise a program. Although we had no real idea of what this was going to involve, we were intrigued.

Andrew and I were invited to meet this actor and his girlfriend over dinner at his place—an enormous luxurious villa, about the size of a small hotel, but completely private. It was right on the beach, with leafy tropical gardens creeping around the edges of the grand main residence. There would have been at least twenty staff running around catering to their every need.

Dinner was fairly informal, an authentic Balinese meal eaten on the leather lounges—but the full entourage of Balinese dancers and musicians presenting the after-dinner entertainment (numbering at least thirty) was quite elaborate.

'So how can we help you?' we asked after dinner, when the large open lounge area had been vacated by the artistic troupe.

'We've got a month in Bali, and I want to prepare for a new movie I'm planning to write. I'll need some help with doing the research for that. We also need to have some time for regeneration. We want to do some yoga, meditation, tennis, surfing . . .'

'Sounds pretty straightforward. Do you want to have a look around the island first, so we can give you an idea of what's here?' Andrew asked. It was quite off the track of what we usually did, but sounded like fun.

'Sure, great idea. Give us a few days to wind down and settle in, and then let's do a tour. I'll give you a call.'

The call came a few days later, as arranged. 'Hey. Are you free today for that tour?'

Andrew had answered the phone. 'No problem,' he said, looking regretfully at the pile of papers he was planning to get through, but knowing it was probably more important to accommodate the VIP. 'That's fine.'

When we arrived at the villa—a good forty minutes away—we piled into their comfortable hire car and took off. We covered some of the green-paddied countryside and combed the palm-fringed coast.

While we travelled, we found out more about their quest. The couple had just arrived from Fiji, where they had stayed on a private island for a few weeks. They had already fallen in love with this part of the world, and had become even more fascinated by the cultural explosion they had discovered in Bali. They were even considering buying some land in Bali, and were looking at setting up a more permanent retreat or a base for making the movie. At every corner we turned, with every pocket of the island that was revealed, they were thoroughly enchanted. It occurred to me that they could have bought a whole regency at a whim—could probably have bought up half the island.

Famous as he was, this guy was a regular lout at heart, hanging out the window and hooting at the locals. Or perhaps he was just starting to unwind, enjoying being in a place where he was just another white tourist. He had grown some sideburns and wore dark glasses wherever he went, but I was quite sure none of the locals would have known who he was. They are not quite as media savvy as the minority of the world's population with the majority of wealth.

Although most people do have TVs here, the programming is pretty limited to Indonesian and Mexican soap operas and Indian Bollywood movies (I have no idea why). There had only been one movie theatre in Denpasar for a number of years, and again there the choice could be very limited. A new theatre was recently built not far from our home, but it was designed more to capture the tourist market—and was double the price. They even installed a slick American-style 'Planet Hollywood' restaurant right next to the new cinema.

We had actually been asked to assist with the Planet Hollywood launch—to help coordinate Sylvester's, Demi's, Bruce's and whoever else's arrival and the launch program itself—but we passed on that one. Too many egos to accommodate in too unpredictable an environment. We were well and truly at the stage where we were prepared to walk away from the contracts that we didn't feel comfortable with. All the glitz and glamour didn't mean much to us by then. It was more important to us that anyone who came to Bali should have the opportunity to experience something of the community spirit. That there should be a two-way cultural exchange, rather than a one-way cultural plunder. At this stage we were enjoying dealing with the famous individual who had come to Bali with a humble searching spirit.

After finishing our VIP tour of the island, we returned to the villa and our new friend decided he was ready to start on his health reform program. He and his girlfriend had, he said, been so busy working that they had unwittingly gained weight and lost the level of fitness they would have liked. They also wanted to regain some balance in their lives, some sort of equilibrium between their physical and mental selves.

They both launched into a serious tennis, yoga, meditation and diet program. The actor also wanted to include in his program something he hadn't done for a while—surfing.

'Well,' we told him confidently, 'you've come to just the right people.'

'So how long is it since you went surfing last?' Andrew asked casually.

'Oh, probably about twenty years,' he responded, just as casually.

Andrew's jaw dropped a few centimetres. He was going to have to take responsibility for a virtual novice. The surf around Bali is world renowned for having some of the most treacherous reefs and gnarly waves. It is not the place to learn to surf. We could only imagine how dramatic the headlines would be if anything happened to this VIP.

Calling up a few surfing mates for backup support, Andrew arranged a surfing safari to a private surf spot on the southern peninsula. We met at our house (a decidedly humble abode compared to the movie star's villa), and all clambered aboard a traditional *jukung* sailing boat on the beach in front of our house.

The scenery from this perspective, from out on the water, was spectacular. Small sandy white inlets set among jutting rocks. High cliff overhangs, tufts of greenery spilling down the cliff edges from the top. But the weather was looking ominous. Big black clouds were accumulating overhead, the water was getting choppy. We cautioned our friend about the dangerous conditions, but he was determined. Great, we were thinking, something happens to this guy and our names are going to be splashed all over the tabloid papers. We couldn't talk him out of it.

As soon as our movie-star friend was in the water, paddling for waves, he started to appreciate the fact that he might have been a little out of his depth—literally. He wouldn't give up without a good fight, though. He went for one wave, narrowly missed catching it and was almost thrown head over heels in the process. Undeterred, he went for another, this time skidding down the wave recklessly on his backside. I was seriously concerned about his safety, but luckily the surfing session came to an abrupt end.

Actually, I shouldn't say luckily, because I think it was a case of leaping out of the frying pan and into the fire. A huge thunderstorm descended on us that cracked open the heavens and threatened to blow us to oblivion with driving rain. The skies can often be a saturated grey during the wet season in Bali, ominous and foreboding, heavy with rain. We do not usually get the full monsoonal typhoons here, but we do get the tail ends of cyclones coming up from Australia. They can certainly pack quite a punch.

As the full force of the storm hit, we all scrambled back into the boat, under the flimsy blue tarpaulin strung across the top, and headed for home as fast as the straining engine could take us.

The small boat, overloaded with soggy surfers, battled against the waves. We were getting seasick with the heaving of the little craft against the rising swell, hanging on to the side of the boat and hoping somehow we could hold it together. Soon drenched through to the bone, I could hear jaws grinding and teeth chattering.

I had been out in big swells in these small boats before. I had even been all the way across the straits to Java on a hellish stomach-churning fourteen-hour ride in a slightly bigger fishing boat. And I learnt one thing: these boats are not safe. In fact many lives are lost in the treacherous Balinese waters—most unreported casualties. But I was praying hard—I think we all were, in our own languages and to our own gods—and the prayers were heard. Before long our home beach was in sight, and we moved into the calmer more protected waters of the bay. A few hundred metres out from the beach, someone started to laugh at the absurdity of it all, and we all gave in to the lighter mood. Soon we were killing ourselves laughing, wiping away the tears of euphoric relief.

Our friend and his girlfriend climbed ashore, sopping wet and exhausted from the ordeal, but there was a keen fire in his eyes. We had more experiences together after that one, but I think that this incident was a turning point for him.

'Thank you so much for all you've done for us,' he said when it was time to say our farewells. 'We've had an adventurous and spiritual experience of the island that we probably would not otherwise have had. I feel ready to face the world again.'

I don't know if he found exactly what he came for. But I do know that something on the island touched his spirit. I could see the change just in a month.

Bali really is a place of healing and transformation for so many people.

Life has a funny way of turning everything inside out and upside down. It's easy to marvel now at how the puzzle pieces eventually slot themselves into place.

We have come the full circle, in some ways. We are carefree teenagers again, unconcerned about possible financial restrictions, about what others think. We are following our passions. Enjoying the simple pleasures in life. Staying true, as much as possible, to our beliefs and ideals. And yet we are also further ahead (in terms of contemporary success measures) than we ever imagined we'd be.

Andrew and I now work with some of the world's top companies, training the highest level of executives and running large programs. We still live on the site of our original simple-living dream, but we are daily transported into the world of hi-tech business, either literally by travelling to work with corporate clients, or electronically, through cyberspace. A quick plane trip to Singapore or Hong Kong, and the bamboo-hut setting is replaced by luxury office space. We are but a short email or conference call away from 'civilisation'.

Through all the changes we have clung on to the belief that the simple pleasures in life are always the most profound. The more contrast we have found in life, the more sensitive we have become to experiencing those simple pleasures. Cutting back and reprioritising has in fact enabled us to experience more, has opened us up to a whole new world of possibilities. We always hope to see and feel the contrasts in life; they remind us that simple living needs to be a personal choice that benefits those who have more than enough, not an imposed state of discomfort endured by those who simply don't have enough.

Ultimately for us, the elements of luxury and prestige our new life has brought are unexpected surprises; they are not the major prize. They are more the icing on the cake, something which can be enjoyed but can just as easily be done without. They are insignificant to us in the scheme of things. The real satisfaction comes from being able to share the benefits of our life with others, hopefully making our small contribution to greater equity in our community and our region. We try to take the principles that we believe make life worthwhile—such as positive relationships and a healthy attitude and outlook—and use these to bring the best to those we live and work with.

Because Bali has been such a place of healing for us, we feel so fortunate that we are now able to share the healing with others. Opportunities have opened up for us to be able to get back to the aid work that we have always believed is so important, in ways we hadn't anticipated. Whereas we could not have continued the voluntary development work, such as that we did in India, on a long-term basis, we now have the infrastructure and resources to contribute to development work in other ways. Not only are we able to support small projects in our own Balinese community, but we

282

have also been able to find ways to support other areas in crisis. On a personal level, we have had the opportunity to support local people in need as well as refugees and those affected by the crises all over Indonesia. We have found so many possible ways to contribute—through providing food, clothing and other required items, and through encouraging schools to educate about wider community needs and be a focal point for supporting other children.

On a professional level, we have been able to facilitate meetings of the leadership teams of development agencies, to assist with the development of curriculum resources, and to commit a proportion of our company profit to aid work. By also making a point of increasing the awareness of local needs and issues to client visitors to the island, it is our hope that people who come here for conferences end up both profiting from the cultural experience and giving something back to the island. We are able to share what we have learnt ourselves from this rich culture and we are able to give because of the financial abundance we now receive from our corporate work.

It is truly amazing how the way ahead becomes clear when you continue following your convictions, when you hang on to the values you really believe in. It was only through taking that initial risk and persevering with those ideals that we have been able to benefit from the opportunities, to give and receive in the ways we now experience.

We continue to enjoy each day because, I am now convinced, paradise is an attitude.

I came across an interesting letter in a Bali expat newspaper the other day. It said it all:

Dear Iris

I came to Bali to find a better lifestyle. I had a very stressful, busy life in my home country, and was hoping that moving to the tropics would make a difference. However, I am now sitting in my new house, looking out at my tropical garden, but I am feeling as lonely and depressed as ever. This place just isn't what everyone says it is supposed to be.

What can I do?

S.T.

Plenty of people have come to settle in Bali short or long term, trying to find something that might have eluded them thus far. But everyone's experience here is completely different. For us and many others, Bali has been the perfect place for renewal. But not everyone's idea of paradise is the same. Bali just isn't a paradise for everyone.

Some people have raved about their own patch of paradise—or their idea of paradise, completely unaffected by the charms of what Andrew and I think is an idyllic location in Bali. We have friends who came to Bali from Samoa, and have been pining to return to the less developed island ever since. Another friend cannot forget Hawaii, where everything is more developed and seems to be less complicated to them. Others can't stand the tropical humid environment or the Asian culture, and would rather be in some mountain cabin in the snow or on a farm in Europe if they had their one wish. Then there are those who are not prepared to put up with the underlying social and political tensions in Indonesia.

Sometimes, though, it's not the place itself but the attitude and expectations that make all the difference.

The columnist who responded to the above letter was very perceptive in her answer. Rather than advising that the writer should try to find another location that would suit better, she suggested that perhaps the writer needed to look inside him or herself for the cause of the unhappiness.

'You may end up taking your unhappiness with you wherever you go,' the columnist replied, 'unless you are prepared to search for its real source.'

I have discovered that many people come here expecting that life will be picture postcard perfect, and end up feeling disappointed and dissatisfied. Those who have closed minds and high expectations will invariably be unhappy. Complaining about the heat, the mosquitoes, the pollution, the corruption, the tropical ailments, the political problems, the jealousy from locals, the hassling, the crime, the lack of good western-style facilities . . . it is difficult to enjoy your stay here when your focus is on these.

A positive experience comes largely from an appreciation of the place and the people. You will not find much here if you remain inwardly focused. It is only those who come with an open mind and an accepting spirit who can reap the treasures of a tropical, community-oriented lifestyle.

Perhaps paradise is not a place, but a process. It is all about learning to adapt to and grow through change.

Paradise Bali certainly ain't what it used to be. Bali is but a shadow of what it was many years ago, when it was an untouched oasis.

Our own patch of paradise has continued to shrink, slowly but surely. Political pressures from the outside have cast a shadow of unpredictability over the country, and little by little the uncontrollable forces of modernisation and development have encroached on our ideal. Our patch continued to get smaller as the patronage of the shops and cafes at the front of our house increased. As the piles of refuse from those businesses grew higher. As the smoke from the barbeques reached their long tendrils into our family compound. As the barking of the ever increasing number of stray dogs got louder. As we grappled with more complex political and moral issues.

It's enough to make anyone cry to look at the way things are now and compare today's scene with photos of the pristine, white, completely untouched Kuta Beach of the 1930s—'the most beautiful beach anywhere in the world' according to travellers Robert and Louise Koke, who were the first westerners to surf its waves and who built the first bungalow-style hotel there in 1936.

The sheer overdevelopment of the tourist pockets of the island and the exponentially increasing pollution are depressing. There are now problems with the water table being poisoned, with water pollution in the oceans, with inappropriate sewage disposal, and valuable flora and fauna are facing extinction. Even the smallest of changes brought about by modernity have had disastrous effects. There are often mountains of plastic rubbish simply neatly swept to the side of the road. Worse still, when these piles are actually cleaned up and disposed of, plastics and other toxic materials are often burned so that the smoke—which is apparently 350 times more toxic than inhaling cigarette smoke as a passive smoker—is inhaled by all the passing villagers (and tourists).

Socially, many Balinese people continue to be dispossessed of their land in order to make way for the sprawling tourist developments. Then there are the problems associated with the sleazier sex industry and drug abuse on the island. These often come hand in hand with heavy tourism in Asia, where attractive women and mind-altering substances are made cheap and available.

There are brothels and gambling dens. There are karaoke bars where you can choose from rows of numbered and heavily made-up girls posing behind glass. There are nightclubs where the drugs come with the drinks. There are full-moon beach parties where hordes of beautiful young people go tripping and dancing through till dawn. These places are worlds away from the beautiful traditional culture that still dominates the island. They have not maimed the culture, but they have marred it.

I have already talked about the visa issues, the frustrations with the power going out, cultural differences, sicknesses, political problems . . . But in the end these can pale into insignificance. They do not characterise Bali.

As difficult as the negative experiences can be, they do not define the main part of our experience here. We do not deny them, we have not ignored these problems. We have merely contributed in whatever ways we can to assist with improving these conditions, and have accepted as 'different' or 'inevitable' that which we cannot change or which cannot be changed.

In these ways, Bali is the same as any other place on earth. Paradise, wherever it is, is not perfect. Over the long term, the attraction is to the challenge, the wisdom that comes from altered perspectives.

Even as our patch of paradise grows ever smaller, our appreciation for what we can experience and what we have here continues to grow. That has shown me that paradise really is just a state of mind.

We live in an eternal beach summer, we live and work closely together as a husband and wife, we are not completely separated from our children when we work, we have a supportive community living and working with us that we care about, we have the opportunity to reach out to and give to the world beyond. We no longer have a drive to change the world, but our world has definitely changed us, and allowed us to feel free to make whatever small changes we can in whatever ways we can.

To us, that is the dream come true.

'Mum, it's time for us to go to the beach before dinner.'

Zoe had interrupted my thoughts. I was trying to find that final evocative sentence, the perfect way to wrap up the long emotional journey I had been struggling to write about. She brought me back to the present.

'Yes, darling. I've just got some writing I want to finish off. You go ahead and I'll catch you up.'

But my child would not give up that easily. She was certainly her mother's daughter.

'No, Mum. Close down the computer and come to the beach now. I know if I leave you'll never come, you'll just keep writing and writing and you'll forget all about it. Dad and Kallen have gone ahead, and I've come back to get you.'

'Don't worry about it. I'll go tomorrow night.'

I was already feeling like the errant child.

'We have a deal that we always go to the beach. 'Even if it's only for ten minutes,' you always tell me. We've made a pact.'

Zoe was so strong, so sure of herself. She had already learnt so much responsibility.

I looked at her. She was the spitting image of me when I was her age, except for Andrew's blue eyes and long, thick lashes. The stern look of a mother chastising her child could not erase the beautiful softness and freshness of youth. I was so deeply touched by who she was and what she was becoming.

'What are you writing about anyway, Mum?'

'Oh, I'm just finishing off the book I'm writing about us living in Bali.'

'Let me see what you've written . . . : "*To us that is the dream come true.*" What on earth does that mean? This book has to be interesting, Mum, Don't write boring stuff. Just write down, "*My daughter says hurry up and come to the beach because that's why we live in Bali so we can have fun on the beach together*"—because that's what I am saying right now. Make sure you write exactly what I say, Mum. Don't change it. It has to be interesting for people to read.'

'I'll check everything with you before I finish, sweetheart. What you think is very valuable to me . . .'

Once I was looking away from the computer screen, I could see that the sky was once more awash with the bright lights of the late afternoon sun, that the water was a shimmering gold. There it was, the distinctive sunset that marked the end of each special day and gave a calming definition to our existence in Bali. I was once more conscious of the sound of the waves, of the strong, salty smell of fish in the air. Kallen and Andrew were already skipping and running together down towards the waves, surfboards tucked under their arms.

'Okay then. I'll leave the rest till later.'

How could I refuse? She had put everything back into perspective once again.

'I'm coming now.'

The Story Continues . . .

It is close to midnight, and I am just putting the final touches to the manuscript. I have a deadline to get it in to the publisher by the morning. That trip to the beach held me up a little time-wise, but I now have a renewed energy and enthusiasm.

It has been a push to get the final changes made by the deadline anyway, as the week has been an exhausting one. A couple of days ago we negotiated a big contract that will probably take our company to a higher level. We have been losing sleep thinking about how we can grow the company without risking the personal contact we have so much enjoyed, which has become an important defining character of what we offer.

Just yesterday we looked at buying a small block of land—still in the vicinity of where we live now, but tucked away in a more secluded and relatively untouched area. The need to make a decision about where we want to be based for the long term has been pushed along by the sudden appearance this week of a new sign in the street adjacent to our laneway, only metres from the huge McDonald's golden arches, a large glossy sign that says: 'Own a Slice of Paradise—Villas for Sale'. Some million-dollar villas have just been completed further up the road and will rent for up to $8,000 a night, and another luxury villa development is due to begin on the other side of our property in the next few months. We're surrounded. There's no going back now. It looks as though we will have to either be more determined to hang on to our own little patch, or claim a new one now—before it's too late!

Right now, though, I am sitting in that original thatched hut, typing away on the latest laptop and looking out at the coconut trees, which are now brushed with silver by the bright full moon. There is a platinum trail on the water in front of the cafes, leading up to their tin roofs, which also reflect the bright lunar light. The whole area, usually so alive during the day, has fallen into quiet and peaceful sleep.

My dear extended family is asleep in the main house, too: Ana, Mia, Ketut and Mustaf downstairs—and Andrew and the children upstairs. Our new puppy is tucked away out the back. The office gecko is nibbling on a leftover biscuit on the desk next to mine. Although there have been many significant changes to the physical and social landscape, the things that are most important to us have remained the same. In fact, the greatest changes that have taken place are those we have experienced within ourselves.

Tomorrow we will be up early for our regular routine. We've kept the same routine going now for all these years, no matter what obstacles have threatened to disrupt it, and whenever we go away we always know we can return to it. Buying fish from the boats at the crack of dawn, tropical fruits, dodgem cars to school, office work behind grass walls, the evening beach walk, Sundays at leisure . . . It's a great life. I still have to keep pinching myself to prove that it's all really happening.

Our paradise will no doubt continue to dramatically change shape. There will be more national and international crises. The development will not cease. But somehow, I feel hopeful now, we will always find a way to hang on to the sweet essence of contentment that has filtered into our lives. Whatever happens will be just another adventure on this always exciting journey . . .

Good luck in finding your own patch of paradise . . . wherever or whatever it is!

ABOUT THE AUTHOR

When she's not on the beach in Bali with her two young children, Gaia Grant and her husband Andrew are in high demand as international speakers and consultants to corporate executives and community groups. Their company Tirian specialises in personal and organisational development.